THE FRAGILE
PEACE
—— 1919-39 ——

THE FRAGILE PEACE

FOREWORD

To celebrate the turn of the century and the new millennium, **THE EVENTFUL CENTURY** series presents the vast panorama of the last hundred years—a century which has witnessed the transition from horse-drawn transport to space travel, and from the first telephones to the information superhighway.

THE EVENTFUL CENTURY chronicles epoch-making events like the outbreak of the two world wars, the Russian Revolution and the rise and fall of communism. But major events are only part of this glittering kaleidoscope. It also describes the everyday background—the way people lived, how they worked, what they ate and drank, how much they earned, the way they spent their leisure time, the books they read, and the crimes, scandals and unsolved mysteries that set them talking. Here are fads and crazes like the Hula-Hoop and Rubik's Cube . . . fashions like the New Look and the miniskirt . . . breakthroughs in entertainment, such as the birth of the movies . . . medical milestones such as the discovery of penicillin . . . and marvels of modern architecture and engineering.

THE FRAGILE PEACE chronicles the two dizzying decades that followed the cataclysm of the First World War. For many the 1920s and 30s were a time of liberation. In the "Roaring Twenties" hemlines rose for young Western women, the "flappers," who were revelling in new freedoms to work and play. The "talkies" transformed the movie industry and spawned a new firmament of stars, from Garbo to Astaire, Dietrich to Gable, while the radio transformed home entertainment with music, drama, news and information programs. At sea, on land and in the air, daring men and women vied with each other to set new records for speed and endurance. Yet for many people these were also decades of anxiety, haunted by the fear of unemployment, poverty and hunger. In the early 1920s Germany suffered hyperinflation; turmoil and civil war in Russia brought famine to millions. By the end of the decade the whole world was plunging into the Great Depression following the Wall Street Crash. Conditions were ripe for dictatorship, fascism and, finally, German Nazism. Mussolini blazed the trail in Italy; Hitler far exceeded him with a barbarism matched only by his mirror image, Russia's communist dictator Stalin. The stage was set once more for a gigantic clash of nations, the Second World War.

THE FRAGILE PEACE
—— 1919-39 ——

The Reader's Digest Association, Inc.
Pleasantville, New York/Montreal

THE FRAGILE PEACE
Edited and designed by Toucan Books Limited
Written by James Cochrane
Edited by Andrew Kerr-Jarrett
Designed by Bradbury and Williams
Picture research by Christine Vincent

FOR THE AMERICAN EDITION
Produced by The Reference Works
Editor-in-Chief Harold Rabinowitz
Editor Douglas Heyman
Editor Lorraine Martindale
Production Bob Antler/Antler Designworks

FOR READER'S DIGEST US
Group Editorial Director Fred DuBose
Senior Designer Judith Carmel

READER'S DIGEST ILLUSTRATED REFERENCE BOOKS
Editor-in-Chief Christopher Cavanaugh
Art Director Joan Mazzeo
Operations Manager William J. Cassidy

Copyright © 2000
The Reader's Digest Association, Inc.
Reader's Digest Road
Pleasantville, NY 10570

Copyright © 2000
The Reader's Digest Association (Canada) Ltd.
Copyright © 2000
Reader's Digest Association Far East Limited
Philippine copyright © 2000
Reader's Digest Association Far East Limited

First English Edition Copyright © 1996
The Reader's Digest Association Limited, Berkeley
Square House, Berkeley Square, London W1X 6AB

Address any comments about The Fragile Peace to:
Reader's Digest,
Editor-in-Chief, U.S. Illustrated Reference Books,
Reader's Digest Road, Pleasantville, NY 10570

To order additional copies of The Fragile Peace,
call 1-800-846-2100

You can also visit us on the World Wide Web at:
www.readersdigest.com

Printed in the United States of America
Second Printing, May 2001

Library of Congess Cataloging in Publication Data
The fragile peace, 1919–39.
  p. cm. — (The eventful 20th century)
 Includes index.
 ISBN 0-7621-0270-5
 1. World politics—1919-1932. 2. World War,
 1914-1918—Peace. 3. World War, 1939-1945
 —Causes. I. Reader's Digest Association. II.
 Series.
D723 .F73 2000
940.5'1—dc21   99-051309

FRONT COVER
From top: FDR ready to throw out the first baseball
of the season; a 1934 Hupmobile; Jesse Owens at the
1936 Olympics.

BACK COVER
From top: Shirley Temple, America's sweetheart;
poster advertising a Nazi youth festival; opening of
the Golden Gate bridge in 1937.

Page 3 (from left to right): Gandhi during the Salt
March, 1930; St. Louis Cardinal pitcher Dizzy Dean;
from a Lufthansa poster; Mussolini.

Background pictures:
Page 15: A traffic jam in New York, mid 1930s
Page 33: From *Gold Diggers of 1933*
Page 73: Anti-British demonstration in Bombay,
May 1930
Page 117: Sudeten Germans welcome the German
army into Czechoslovakia, October 1938

Contents

BETWEEN TWO WARS

POSTWAR OPTIMISM GAVE WAY TO ANXIETY AS FRAGILE DEMOCRACIES TOPPLED AND THE WORLD'S FINANCIAL SYSTEM COLLAPSED

At 11 o'clock on the morning of November 11, 1918, the guns on the Western Front fell silent. Two days before, the German kaiser had fled to Holland and a German republic had been proclaimed. As its first act the new social democratic government of Germany was obliged to accept an armistice on the most humiliating terms.

At last, the hideous nightmare of the Great War was over. In the course of the war at least 8.5 million soldiers had lost their lives— France alone had lost 1.3 million dead out of a population of 41.5 million. Millions of young men had been permanently disabled

NEW LIMBS With tens of thousands maimed, making artificial limbs was a busy industry in Berlin in 1919. Below: German tanks being broken up outside Berlin. Iron and steel were desperately needed for reconstruction.

in mind or body. A Europe which might have supposed itself, just a few years before, to have reached a peak of humane civilization had discovered how far war could brutalize sentiments. It had learnt what its great achievements in science and technology could do in the way of high-explosive shells, machine guns, gas attacks, aerial bombardment of civilians and unrestricted submarine warfare; how the popular press could stir up primeval hatreds, spread lies and dehumanize opponents. Among the casualties of Flanders, Gallipoli, Verdun and the Somme lay much of the 19th century's optimism concerning the essential upward progress of

SAD PILGRIMAGE A Scottish woman places flowers on a war grave near Poperinghe in the Ypres sector of the former Western Front. This is just one of 130 cemeteries in the area.

the human species and many of its old habits of deference toward traditional authority.

The war of 1914-18 had truly been the First World War, although it was not called that at the time. Scarcely any country had not been involved in it or affected by it. As well as Europeans, men from Australia, New Zealand, the United States, Canada, India, Africa, China and Japan had been engaged. Its battles had been fought in Europe, in the Middle East, in Africa and on all the oceans of the world. Only a few years earlier, at the start of the century, the Russian Empire of the Romanovs, the Austro-Hungarian Empire of the Habsburgs and the German Empire of the Hohenzollerns had seemed unassailable. Yet by the end of the war, all three had collapsed, while the centuries-old Ottoman Empire was teetering on the brink—the last sultan would hang on until 1922. Within the British Empire, the ties of the self-governing dominions to the mother country had been weakened rather than strengthened by their experience of the conflict; Canada, Australia, New Zealand and South Africa would sign the peace treaties as independent nations. In all Europe's overseas empires the great bluff of white supremacy and of the strength and integrity of white institutions, which had allowed a handful of Europeans to govern, patronize or exploit the other

THE CHANGING MAP OF EUROPE

At first glance, the map of Europe established by the Treaty of Versailles in 1919 looks much like the one we are familiar with today. It would have looked very strange, however, to people in 1914. It shows a Germany stripped of territory east and west; Austria and Hungary have been reduced to separate countries of modest size, with huge swathes of territory transferred to Poland, Romania, Czechoslovakia and the Kingdom of Serbs, Croats and Slovenes (often known as Yugoslavia, "Land of the Southern Slavs," though not officially renamed that until 1929).

Poland itself has new territory taken from its old masters, Russia, Germany and Austria. There are two entirely new countries: the republic of Czechoslovakia, created from the old Habsburg provinces of Bohemia, Moravia and Ruthenia; and Yugoslavia, an uncomfortable enlargement of Serbia, mixing peoples formerly ruled by Austria-Hungary and Turkey. Romania, on the victors' side in the 1914-18 war, has been greatly enlarged by the acquisition of a large chunk of Hungary. The map also shows a detail that would become significant in the run-up to the Second World War: Polish territory extended to the sea at Danzig (Gdansk), dividing East Prussia from the rest of Germany—the "Danzig corridor."

By 1945 the map would look different again. The post-Second World War settlement saw Estonia, Latvia and Lithuania swallowed up by the U.S.S.R. while Poland was pushed westward—the victorious Russians held its eastern provinces but granted it territory taken from Germany. By 1948 a line—known as the "Iron Curtain" from a phrase made famous by Churchill—would be drawn across Europe, dividing the countries occupied by the Soviet Union from those of the West.

By 1997 the map had changed again. In some respects the ghost of the pre-First World War map had returned as old countries re-emerged from the collapse of the 1919 settlements. In particular, Czechoslovakia had split into the Czech Republic and Slovakia, and Yugoslavia had dissolved into the elements from which it was formed. In other respects Europe had returned to the map of 1920, with the Baltic states re-established as independent countries. The line of the Iron Curtain had grown faint, though leaving a still noticeable cultural and economic gap between Eastern and Western Europe. At the same time, there was a new line across the map of Europe, dividing those countries that were members of the European Union from those that were not.

BEFORE AND AFTER In Europe as it emerged from the postwar treaties (below) scarcely any frontier remained unchanged from the prewar map (left). Even the British Isles were affected. After a treaty between the Irish and the British in 1921, Ireland was partitioned between North and South.

PEACE TREATY President Wilson went to Versailles with 14 points for peace. This 1919 advertisement shows him holding a 15th—an endorsement for Rizla.

nations of the world, had to a large extent been called by the spectacle of Europe's murderous quarrel with itself. Nationalist sentiments were stirring into powerful life.

Versailles and the future

In January 1919 the conference summoned to design the terms of peace—enshrined in due course in the treaties of Versailles, Saint-Germain, Neuilly, Sèvres and Trianon—met in Paris. The realities faced by the participants were grim. Within Europe, victors as well as vanquished had been brought low. France had lost not only vital manpower but also farms, mines, factories and industrial machinery. Belgium, one of the war's battlefields, was in ruins. In much of central and eastern Europe large parts of the population faced starvation. In the cities of the former German and Austro-Hungarian empires there was fighting in the streets as extremists from both right and left challenged new liberal democratic governments. In Russia, where the Bolsheviks had seized power in 1917, famine and disease were aggravated by political terror and continuing civil war. As if all this were not enough, a worldwide epidemic of influenza had broken out as the war was ending; at least 21 million people died of it in the world as a whole.

The three statesmen who dominated the conference were Georges Clemenceau, prime minister of France, David Lloyd George, prime minister of Great Britain, and U.S. President Woodrow Wilson. American

soldiers had been engaged only in the final 15 months of the war, but their arrival had been decisive; moreover, the European powers were now dependent on the United States for finance and supplies. President Wilson could bring powerful pressure to bear, and he was determined to use it to design a new Europe on the highest principles of justice and self-determination, to, in his words, "make the world safe for democracy."

There were two basic items on the agenda. One was to decide the terms to be imposed on the vanquished. The other was to redraw the map of Europe; this was to be pieced together from the fragments scattered by the collapse of the former empires and thereby meet the national aspirations of Poles, Czechs, Slovaks, Romanians and the peoples of the Balkans. In deciding what terms to impose, many on the victorious side felt strongly that the countries that had started the war should pay for it. Germany, in particular, should be decisively weakened, both militarily and industrially, so that it could never again be a threat to its neighbors.

Lloyd George was personally inclined to be merciful; he saw that British interests called for a peaceful and prosperous Germany to trade with. But public opinion was inflamed, and the French, to whom the war had been so costly, were not inclined to compromise. In the end, the measures taken were, indeed, punitive. German indemnities were set at such a huge figure (roughly $33 billion) that they never could be, and never were, paid. Parts of German territory were occupied, pending payment; Germany's merchant fleet and much of its railway rolling stock were seized. Its pride, its army, was severely reduced in numbers and its armaments limited. Alsace-Lorraine, seized by Germany from the French in 1870-1, was returned to France. Other territory was transferred to Poland, and the German overseas colonies were divided among the Allies.

Austria, the heartland of the great Habsburg Empire which had ruled areas of central and eastern Europe for centuries, was reduced to a republic of 6 million people and forbidden to unite with Germany. New lines would also be drawn on the map of the former Ottoman Empire. The wartime exploits of Arab nationalists with their British allies, Lawrence of Arabia and General Edmund

DICTATORSHIP OF THE POET

D'ANNUNZIO AND FRIENDS The poet-hero (right) with some of his officers after the seizure of Fiume.

On September 23, 1919, the Italian Gabriele D'Annunzio embarked on an extraordinary adventure. He and 2,600 followers, clad in cloaks, armed with daggers and with eagle feathers in their hats, flew into the Dalmatian port of Fiume (now Rijeka in Croatia). He then ruled it as a dictator for three years until, in 1921, an embarrassed Italian government had the unpopular task of driving him out and handing the port over to Yugoslavia.

D'Annunzio (1863-1938) was already a well-known poet, novelist and dramatist when Italy had joined in the war in 1915. Although in his fifties, he plunged himself into the fighting, becoming an aviator and losing an eye. Although Italy was on the victorious side, it gained much less from the Versailles settlement than it had expected. This, combined with severe economic disruption caused by the war, provoked much popular resentment. D'Annunzio's raid was meant to right one of these "wrongs," since Fiume was among the territorial gains the Italians had been hoping for.

Later, D'Annunzio became an enthusiastic Fascist, and when Mussolini came to power was rewarded with the title Prince of Montenevoso. Ernest Hemingway described him as "that old, bald-headed, perhaps a little insane but thoroughly sincere, divinely brave swashbuckler, Gabriele D'Annunzio." It was in his dictatorship of Fiume that the stiff-armed Roman salute was officially used for the first time in modern history.

DICTATOR TO DICTATOR Mussolini had been in power for more than a decade when Hitler became chancellor. However, by the time of this visit of *Il Duce* to the Führer in September 1937, Hitler was the dominant partner. Here, the two dictators, visiting an art exhibition, are dwarfed by sculptures on a monumental scale.

Allenby, would lead to the creation, or the re-creation, of Iraq, Syria, Transjordan, Palestine, Lebanon and, before long, Saudi Arabia.

To keep the peace among the nations, new and old, Woodrow Wilson pushed for a League of Nations, a body that would resolve future conflicts by means other than war. This was duly established in Geneva in neutral Switzerland in 1920. Like much else about the Versailles settlement, however, it had, at best, mixed success. When its assembly met for the first time the United States was absent; an isolationist U.S. Congress had declined to join. Bolshevik Russia also refused membership, and Germany was deemed unfit for it until 1926. In an organization set up to solve world problems peacefully, many of the key players were absent.

A troubled world

During the 1920s, Europe began to rebuild its homes and industries. Although there were some severe setbacks—notably Germany's catastrophic hyperinflation in 1922-3—the years before 1929 saw an overall rise in prosperity. But the troubles of the world had not ended with the cessation of hostilities in 1918.

EMBLEM OF TERROR A badge of the Soviet secret police. The organization had several name changes, but each one cast a shadow of fear.

Russia emerged from a terrible civil war to discover what it meant to live under the "dictatorship of the proletariat." Though the country enjoyed a brief respite under Lenin's New Economic Plan, before the 1920s were over it had fallen into the hands of a ruthless dictator, Joseph Stalin. In the 1930s it endured famine, terror on an unprecedented scale and the enslavement of a large percentage of its population.

The brutalizing experience of war and the example of Soviet Russia led to a widespread brutalization of political methods. Italy, disillusioned by the few gains it had made from the sacrifices of war, welcomed the dictator Mussolini and the new doctrine of Fascism. Its achievements, in inspiring and energizing the Italian people and in increasing national efficiency, were real enough, but its methods of suppressing dissent were blatantly cruel. The appeal of nationalism was strong, but its nature was inevitably militaristic and aggressive, as Mussolini demonstrated when he invaded Abyssinia (Ethiopia) in 1935.

Fascism appealed to the young Adolf Hitler, who saw how his own version of it, National Socialism, could lead him to fulfill what he believed to be his destiny: to cleanse Germany of "impure elements" and restore it to its old pride and power. The country's miseries promised to assist his cause.

In China, the dynasty at the head of the world's oldest empire had collapsed before the Great War. Now nominally a republic, the huge country was in a state of chaos, torn apart by wars between nationalists, communists and local warlords, while the United States, Japan and the European powers continued to enjoy privileged trading conditions in its great coastal cities. Weakened by division, China was easy prey to the ruthless territorial ambitions of nationalist Japan.

In India, Britain started to introduce elements of power-sharing that would lead to internal self-government by the late 1930s, but for many Western-educated Indians this was too little too late. One of them, Mohandas Gandhi, began a campaign of civil disobedience, aimed at bringing an end to British rule. Similar movements began in other parts of the overseas empires of the European powers.

Britain and France, although they had won the war, had been badly damaged economically by it. Their attempts at improving the conditions of working men were insufficient to appease social and industrial discontent, which flared up from time to time in violent demonstrations and strikes.

Ireland became a Free State within the British Empire in 1921, and was at once

ART FOR WAR'S SAKE A poster by the Spanish painter Miró calls for support for the republicans in the Spanish Civil War.

plunged into civil war between those who accepted their country's new status, with six of its counties still linked to Great Britain, and those who would settle for nothing less than a totally united Irish Republic.

Democracy versus dictatorship

To a troubled world, the United States shone like a beacon of hope, an example of the prosperity that democratic institutions and an unfettered free market could bring. Already prosperous by 1900, the United States had prospered still more during the war. Its population included far more millionaires than the whole of Europe combined. But more impressive even than that, the great majority of its citizens seemed to enjoy a standard of comfort and spending power far greater than anything known in the rest of the world at that time or at any earlier period in history. The United States might have chosen political isolation, but its economic might was overwhelming, while its social and cultural influence on the world, through its films and popular music, was no less imposing.

Then came the Wall Street Crash of October 1929 that tilted the political balance between East and West. The Depression spread around the world in the early 1930s, leaving millions unemployed and destitute,

CELEBRATING FREEDOM On the streets of Dublin, children cheer the setting up of the Irish Free State in 1921, acknowledging the crucial support of Irish-Americans by waving the Stars and Stripes.

and it seemed to many that capitalism and democracy had failed. When the Soviet Union boasted of full employment and ever-rising living standards, only a few commentators in the West noted that its citizens were compelled to work or starve and that millions of them were dying in labor camps. Many more preferred to believe what would become known as the Great Lie: that Stalin was leading his people into a workers' paradise that could serve as a model for people everywhere. In the underdeveloped parts of the world, the prestige of Russian communism was greatly enhanced.

In Germany, the National Socialists expressed their contempt for democracy and their hostility toward big business. The Depression enormously increased their popular support and finally helped to bring Adolf Hitler to power in 1933.

In 1936 a new European war broke out when the Spanish General Franco invaded his own country to overthrow its republican government. The dictatorships of Germany and Italy sent both manpower and material aid to Franco; the dictatorship of Soviet Russia, through the Communist International, organized support for the Republic, which in due course it would cynically betray. The governments of the democracies stood aside—though numbers of their individual

citizens joined in on one side or the other. Democratic politicians declined to intervene in a terrible civil war that was in many ways a rehearsal for the world war to come.

Jazz and anxiety

The mood of the 1920s was set by experience of the Great War. Millions of young men had been uprooted from the farms and towns in which they might otherwise have spent the rest of their lives; they found their acquaintance with the varieties of life greatly enlarged as a result. Inevitably, they returned to their homes questioning old assumptions. Confidence in the established authorities of Church and State, which had condoned and prolonged the conflict, was greatly diminished. There was a widespread feeling that if the colossal effort invested in the arts of war were now invested in the peace, there could be a great and palpable improvement in the condition of ordinary humanity—in "homes fit for heroes," in decent wages and in a reduction of the grosser inequalities of society.

Among artists and intellectuals, the urge to "make things new," which had been stimulated at the beginning of the century, revived with a fresh vigor after the war; in art, architecture, poetry, music, it was another age of the avant-garde.

Women, employed in huge numbers during the war because of a shortage of civilian male workers, resented attempts to return them to restricted prewar lives. Experience of life outside the home had emancipated them. In most of the industrialized countries of the world—though not France—they now enjoyed the vote. Young women enjoyed a new ease in their relations with the opposite sex and the world at large; they symbolized it by a dramatic change in their outward appearance—with short skirts, flimsy clothing, cropped hair and slim, boyish figures.

Among the more prosperous classes, the young devoted themselves to the frantic pursuit of pleasure—to parties, movies, drinking, dancing, music. It was as if they were celebrating the fact that, after so much death, they were still alive, as if they dare not stop to contemplate the horror of what had gone before. To these young people America was the inspiration: American movies, American manners, American prosperity. Above all, it was American music that gave the beat to a decade that people, even at the time, began to call the Jazz Age.

The Jazz Age ended in 1929. But despite the Depression, living standards of those fortunate enough to escape its effects went on rising. The 1930s, especially in the United States and Britain, saw the continuing growth of a consumer society. Radio broadcasting along with movies and spectator sports produced an age of mass entertainment providing distraction for even the poorest. The

continued on page 14

HIGH SOCIETY With her short skirt, cloche hat and snappy roadster, this wealthy Washington debutante epitomizes the spirit of the Jazz Age, captured in fiction by F. Scott Fitzgerald.

FAILED REVOLUTIONS

IN THE CITIES OF THE DEFEATED NATIONS, REVOLUTIONARIES FOUGHT TO OVERTHROW THE POSTWAR GOVERNMENTS AND WERE RUTHLESSLY SUPPRESSED

A s 1919 dawned, the countries that had been defeated in the Great War were in a state of social and economic breakdown, and it seemed for a while as if the pattern of violent revolution that had taken place in Russia would be repeated elsewhere. In Berlin, Munich, Vienna and Budapest there were communist attempts to seize power, all of them ruthlessly suppressed.

In Germany the provisional government, dominated by Social Democrats, represented a return to social order and discipline and was supported, if reluctantly, by the Army High Command, by liberals and moderate conservatives, by the country's business interests and by the majority of the German people. But it did not satisfy the extremists, either the communists on the one hand or the reactionaries and royalists on the other. It was at this time that

the Freikorps, volunteer forces manned by discharged soldiers and students, were formed to combat Bolshevism. At this time, too, the German Workers' Party, soon to become the National Socialist German Workers' Party, was formed.

THE FIRING LINE Rolls of newspaper make a barricade for Spartacist supporters in Berlin. Right: "Vote Spartacus," exhorts a poster, showing capitalists fleeing before the mighty fist of the workers' revolution.

REVOLUTION IN HUNGARY The government of Count Karolyi (right) was overthrown by the Moscow-trained communist Béla Kun (far right, on the right), but his Soviet republic was short-lived.

Soon after the outbreak of war in 1914 the Marxists Rosa Luxemburg and Karl Liebknecht had formed the Spartacus League, named after a gladiator who led a slave revolt against the Romans in the 1st century AD. Both had spent the war years in exile or in prison. Released in November 1918 they began agitating for elected workers' and soldiers' councils to seize power in opposition to the moderate Social Democrats. In December they formed the German Communist Party. This they tried to keep free of Bolshevik influence, since Luxemburg was highly critical of Lenin. She disliked his dictatorial methods and his use of terror, and she had disagreed with him about the need for a tightly organized party structure. She argued that the workers would bring about the revolution in a spontaneous uprising against their conditions.

These idealistic views may well explain the failure of the Spartacists. In January 1919 they were involved in heavy street fighting with

TENACIOUS FIGHTER Rosa Luxemburg first became involved in revolutionary politics when she was in high school in what was then Russian-ruled Poland.

the police and the Freikorps. Luxemburg and Liebknecht themselves were captured and then brutally murdered by the Freikorps on January 15. Liebknecht's body was thrown into the lake in the Tiergarten; Luxemburg's floated to the surface of the Landwehr Canal six months later.

Hungary, meanwhile, had lost much of its territory under the postwar peace treaties—in particular the province of Transylvania, which had been given to Romania. When the Hungarians failed to recover it in the spring of 1919, the liberal government of Mihaly Karolyi, an aristocrat who had handed over his own estates to the peasants, collapsed. The communist Béla Kun, trained in Russia and a friend of Lenin, saw his opportunity and proclaimed a Soviet-style republic. The Western Powers, alarmed at this advance of Bolshevism, blockaded the country and threatened armed intervention. The Romanians invaded Hungary and occupied Budapest.

Béla Kun fled, and in November 1919 Admiral Miklos Horthy, a former officer in a now nonexistent Austro-Hungarian navy, assumed power as virtual dictator, ruthlessly weeding out communists but also suppressing liberal democracy. Hungarian parliamentary democracy had lasted some five months, and was not to be revived for another 70 years. Béla Kun continued his career as an activist for the Third International but was liquidated in one of Stalin's purges in the late 1930s.

ZIEGFELD GIRLS A bathing suit lunch in a New York restaurant in 1925—staged as a publicity stunt by Florenz Ziegfeld, the king of American show business.

mood of the 1930s was different, however. Guilt about the condition of the unemployed politicized many young men and women. By the middle of the decade the more thoughtful were anxiously watching the storm clouds gathering over the world, living in the shadow of a probable war to come.

Nonetheless, the reaction of most people to this "Age of Anxiety" could be summed up in two words: escapism and appeasement. The rhythms of jazz gave way to the soothing tones of the crooner. Films, rather than engaging the problems of the day, became more glamorous and sentimental. People sought refuge in safe politics and conservative morals. A minority might urge radical solutions, whether of the left or right; other minorities, among them the discredited British politician Winston Churchill, might call for rearmament against the dictatorships. But the majority of people in the democracies preferred to listen to those politicians who called for peace at any price.

Peace or nationalism?

On the international scene, the body set up to resolve crises, Woodrow Wilson's brainchild, the League of Nations, proved to be largely impotent, not least because of the

LOVE IN THE 1930s

The Hungarian-born writer Arthur Koestler was a communist in the Berlin of the early 1930s, the first years of Nazi rule. In his memoirs he recalls a story about a friend he calls Ehrendorf:

"During the carnival season of 1932, Ehrendorf went to a dance and picked up a tall, pretty blonde. She wore a large swastika brooch on her breast, was about nineteen or twenty, gay, uninhibited and brimful of healthy animal spirits—in short, the ideal Hitler-Mädchen of the Brave New World. After the dance, Ehrendorf persuaded her to go back with him to his flat, where she met his advances more than halfway. Then, at the climactic moment, the girl raised herself on one elbow, stretched out the other arm in the Roman salute, and breathed in a dying voice a fervent 'Heil Hitler.' Poor Ehrendorf nearly had a stroke. When he had recovered, the blonde sweetie explained to him that she and a bunch of her girlfriends had taken a solemn vow, pledging themselves 'to remember the Führer every time at the most sacred moment in a woman's life.'"

absence of the United States itself. From the start, questions about what would happen if its mechanisms failed or were ignored had received no proper answer; a French proposal that it should have a strong military force of its own had been rejected. It had attempted, with little success, to reduce the level of armaments and arms trading. However, it did have a solid record in controlling such matters as slavery, child labor and the international opium trade, as well as improving worldwide standards in public health.

In 1928 the Briand-Kellogg Pact, signed by 61 states, reaffirmed the League's basic principles, renouncing war as a national policy. But with the new decade its impotence was increasingly apparent, as it did nothing to prevent the rearmament of Nazi Germany, Japan's invasion of China, Mussolini's invasion of Abyssinia, or the intervention of fascist and communist governments in the civil war in Spain. Member states simply walked out before going to war. The British writer G.K. Chesterton had put his finger on a key problem in 1923: "A League of Nations means a League of Nationalists." By the end of the 1930s, it seemed as if half the world was marching under the banners of militant nationalism, and the other half, like the ostrich, had buried its head in the sand.

ALL THAT JAZZ Otto Dix's painting captures the bittersweet atmosphere of 1920s Berlin. From 1927, Dix was professor of art at Dresden until the Nazis dismissed him in 1933.

In the Twenties

THE WORLD SEEMED TO HAVE THE CHOICE OF TWO ALTERNATIVES IN THE TWENTIES: DEMOCRACY AND TRIUMPHANT AMERICAN-STYLE CAPITALISM ON THE ONE HAND; THE NEW SOCIAL ORDER PROMISED BY RUSSIAN COMMUNISM ON THE OTHER. WHEN CAPITALISM STUMBLED, DEMOCRACY LOOKED FEEBLE AND COMMUNISM TURNED TO NAKED TYRANNY. THE CALLS OF FASCIST DICTATORS FOR ORDER, DISCIPLINE AND DECISIVE ACTION HAD A STRONG APPEAL FOR MANY PEOPLE.

FROM MOSCOW TO BERLIN

WHILE RUSSIA UNDERWENT CIVIL WAR, FAMINE AND TERROR, POSTWAR MISERY IN GERMANY PROMOTED THE RISE OF NATIONAL SOCIALISM

With the treaty of Brest-Litovsk, signed in March 1918, Bolshevik Russia ended its war with Germany. It surrendered a large amount of territory to the Germans, but for Lenin and the Bolsheviks it was a price worth paying: they had won the freedom to pursue their program of revolutionary change. They set about handing over factories to the workers and landed estates to the peasants. Property was confiscated from the bourgeoisie. Banks were shut down and all foreign debt repudiated. The result was almost complete economic breakdown.

A great exodus began, not only of aristocrats and wealthy capitalists, but also of a large part of the educated middle class. The tsar and his family were brought to the small town of Ekaterinburg (Yekaterinburg) in the Urals and imprisoned there.

The Western Allies, horrified at the prospect that Germany might have to fight a war on one front only, dispatched troops to Russia. Their aim was not so much to suppress the revolution as to keep Russia in the war by supporting anti-Bolshevik elements. A savage civil war ensued that pitted Red Russians, the Bolsheviks, against White Russians – an ill-assorted coalition of monarchists, liberals, moderate socialists, officers of the old regime and simple peasants and soldiers loyal to their religion and their tsar.

In this somewhat confused situation, 60,000 Czech troops also became embroiled. They had been part of the Austrian army fighting on the Russian front, but anxious to see their nation's freedom from Vienna, they happily threw in their lot with Austria's enemies. Austria's enemies were the Allies, and the Allies' allies were the anti-Bolsheviks— so the Czechs clashed with the Bolsheviks. Troops from their legion arrived in Ekaterinburg a week too late to save the tsar, who had been murdered there with his wife and children on the night of July 16/17, 1918.

Civil war

The war was fought in a spirit of passionate mutual hatred. All over Russia, when a town was taken by the Reds, "counter-revolutionary elements" were dragged from hiding and executed. Days or weeks later, the same town might be captured by White forces, who would reply in kind.

The White forces were powerful and the result of the war was by no means a foregone conclusion. With Allied support the White Russian Admiral Kolchak formed an Eastern Front in Siberia and in early 1919 advanced almost to the Volga. Another tsarist officer, General Denikin, led the White forces from the south. In October 1919 the Whites reached the suburbs of Petrograd (St. Petersburg) before being beaten back. A Cossack officer, Baron von Wrangel, held out, meanwhile, in the Crimea.

CIVIL WAR IN RUSSIA A Bolshevik poster (left) suggests that Western capitalists control the White generals. Below: Red Army soldiers celebrate the defeat of Baron von Wrangel (right), the White commander in the south.

ARCHITECT OF VICTORY Trotsky (center) inspecting Red Army soldiers. He proved himself a military genius during the civil war, but afterwards Stalin would outmaneuver him and finally have him killed.

rank, among them the cavalry leader, General Budenny. Above all, the Russian peasants, having been told that they were the owners of the land, had no wish to see it restored to the former landlords by a White victory.

The Bolsheviks in power

Ever since the Revolution of October 1917 conditions in the country had been desperate. In the days of revolutionary idealism it had been believed that workers, given control of their factories, would gladly produce goods for their fellow citizens. Likewise, peasants would keep only the food they needed for themselves and give their surpluses to the towns. When neither of these happened, the Bolsheviks resorted to force. Workers who failed to meet their production targets were denounced as saboteurs. Troops were sent into the country to seize food supplies from

By the end of 1919, the tide had turned in the Bolsheviks' favor. Kolchak was driven back to Irkutsk in southern Siberia in February 1920. A British expeditionary force at Archangel withdrew later the same month. Wrangel was forced to withdraw from Russia in November, closing an escape route for emigrés via the Crimea. By 1921 the Bolsheviks were in command of most of a country ruined by war and revolution.

There were several reasons for the Reds' victory. They had fought with one purpose, while the Whites were united only in their opposition to Bolshevism. Many of the White officers were extreme reactionaries, guilty of atrocities that matched anything committed by the Reds. Then, with the end of the Great War, the Western Allies lost interest in keeping Russia on their side; their support for the Whites began to drop away.

The Red Army, meanwhile, was superbly organized by Leon Trotsky, the revolutionary intellectual who, with no previous military experience, turned out to have some of the gifts of a Napoleon. As in the French Revolutionary wars, talents emerged from the lower ranks of the army and were promoted to high

LENIN: THE MARXIST WHO CHANGED HISTORY

Lenin was the name Vladimir Ilich Ulyanov adopted while in political exile. He was born in 1870 to middle-class parents. He was a brilliant school student, but in his teens he was drawn into the revolutionary movement, especially after 1887 when his older brother was hanged—he had been a member of a terrorist group that planned to assassinate the tsar. By 1889 he had read Marx's *Das Kapital* and become a Marxist.

He graduated as a lawyer in 1891, but was henceforth a dedicated revolutionary, spending much of his time in prison or in exile in Siberia or abroad. By 1903 he was a leading member of the Russian Social Democratic Workers' Party. At its Second Congress that year, held in London, the party split over his contention that a disciplined revolutionary party was needed that would have nothing to do with bourgeois socialism. From then on he was the leader of the faction known as the Bolsheviks ("the majority group").

Lenin spent the war years in exile, despairing of revolution in his own country. After the first Russian Revolution in March 1917, however, the German authorities, recognizing the force of his personality, smuggled him across Germany in a sealed train in the hope that he would foment a second revolution that would take Russia out of the war. The plan worked: the Bolsheviks seized power in October and later signed a peace treaty with Germany. From 1917 until 1922, Lenin was in control of Russia's communist government. He was incapacitated by a stroke in 1922 and died in January 1924.

MAKER OF THE REVOLUTION Lenin addresses a crowd in May 1920 during the civil war; Trotsky (below) looks on. Later, Stalin would have Trotsky's image removed from Russian copies of this photograph.

the peasants which, disastrously, included the seed corn for future harvests. Untold millions died in the famine that resulted.

In 1921 Lenin took action. The country was on the verge of starvation while industrial production had virtually ground to a halt. He introduced a New Economic Plan, which permitted a return to something like normal business activity. Peasants were allowed to sell their surpluses on the open market and goods reappeared for sale in the shops. The NEP was a remarkable success, despite the resentment that it provoked at the fortunes made by "Nepmen," the new entrepreneurs.

The rise of Stalin

A year later Lenin suffered a stroke and had to retire from active life. After his death in January 1924 the former capital, Petrograd, was renamed Leningrad in his honor, and his tomb in Moscow—where the Bolsheviks had transferred the capital in 1918—became a national shrine.

Since 1922, three men had controlled the country: Stalin, Kamenev and Zinoviev. Of the three, Kamenev and Zinoviev had

TERROR AND FAMINE Officially opposed to organized religion, the Bolsheviks killed thousands of priests (right). Below: Starving villagers are victims of civil war and government seizures of food stores.

more distinguished records than Stalin. Kamenev had been one of Lenin's closest associates since 1908; Zinoviev was, among other things, head of the Comintern, the Communist International. Stalin's rise had been steady but not, at first, spectacular. His first post was that of Commissar for Nationalities, responsible for incorporating into the new state the almost 200 non-Russian nationalities of the old tsarist empire, including Uzbeks, Tajiks, Kirghiz and his own people, the Georgians. In 1922 he became Secretary-General of the Communist Party. Trotsky, meanwhile, had been sidelined. He was distrusted by Lenin as a nonconformist and former Menshevik— a rival faction in the pre-1917 revolutionary

UNEQUAL AMBITIONS Stalin relaxes with fellow Bolshevik leaders Rykov, Zinoviev and Bukharin in 1924. The latter three would perish in Stalin's Great Purge of the 1930s.

movement. Trotsky was also the loser in an ideological battle in which he argued for continuing world revolution.

For different reasons, Lenin had distrusted Stalin and had warned that "Comrade Stalin, having become Secretary-General, has concentrated enormous power in his hands; and I am not sure that he will always know how to use that power with sufficient caution." In 1923 Stalin brought into being the Union of Soviet Socialist Republics. Each republic had its own Communist Party, all ultimately under the control of Moscow. As Secretary-General, Stalin had immense influence over party appointments and a major say in party policy. He used both these advantages with immense skill and utter cynicism in his rise to the top—Lenin had been right in his fears.

At the Party Congress in December 1925 Kamenev and Zinoviev challenged Stalin: "We are against one-man rule, against the creation of a Leader," Kamenev shouted. But the delegates had been handpicked by Stalin's henchmen, and when a vote was taken, the two men were defeated by 559 votes to 65. By the end of 1928 Kamenev and Zinoviev had been eased out and Stalin had reached the pinnacle of supreme power. Although in name he was still no more than Secretary-General, to all intents and purposes he ruled the Soviet Union as its dictator.

The new republic

Germany's postwar history was scarcely less turbulent than Russia's. In February 1919, an elected National Assembly met in Weimar to draw up a constitution. Under constant threat

1919

1919 Weimar constitution in Germany

1921 New Economic Plan in Russia

1922 Lenin suffers a stroke

1923 Hyperinflation in Germany

1924 Death of Lenin

1925 Locarno Pact

from both left and right-wing extremists, all trying to detonate their particular brands of revolution, the government, a coalition of the center and moderate left, was obliged to use armed force to restore order. Then it set out on a program of national reconstruction, which included some of the most advanced social welfare legislation in the world. To do this, however, it had to rely on massive borrowings, mainly from the United States, and to allow a steady devaluation of the German mark, which fell from a pre-1914 level of 4.20 marks to the dollar to more than 7,000 by the end of 1922.

Under the Versailles Treaty, signed on June 28, 1919, Germany had to pay reparations to the Allies. In agreeing to

this, the Germans had in effect signed a blank check, for the figure could not be agreed on at the time. In April 1921 their liability was at last fixed at the colossal figure of 132 billion gold marks (about $33 billion). The first payment, made possible only by a loan raised in London, was handed over in August. Thereafter payments were made in goods and raw materials. At the beginning of 1923 the German government informed the Allies that it could no longer make any payments at all. The French and Belgians responded by occupying the important industrial zone of the Ruhr, where the German workers, acting on government instructions, simply shut down the mines and factories. The government started to pour

RUNAWAY CURRENCY The German State Railways and other organizations started issuing their own vouchers, such as this one (left) for 10 billion marks. Only free issues of bread and soup kept children like these from starvation.

" SUITS FOR BUTTER— BARTER TAKES THE PLACE OF MONEY

Strange stories were emerging from Germany in 1922-3. "SAUSAGE FEE FOR DOCTOR," ran a headline in Britain's *Daily Mail* on November 27, 1922. As German hyperinflation spiralled on, the paper's Berlin correspondent reported some extraordinary barter transactions taking place:

"'Barter,' or when the direct exchange of goods is impossible, the payment of professional services in kind is a growing practice in different parts of Germany.

"In various agricultural districts clergymen, doctors and lawyers insist on payment in sausages, butter, potatoes, or—when they perform services for a baker— in bread. In Pomerania a schedule of medical fees just issued contains the following:

"For a night-time visit, involving a journey of more than seven miles: 30 pounds of butter, a ham weighing 20 pounds, or 1,000 pounds of potatoes.

"For an ordinary daytime visit: 19 pounds of butter, 7 pounds of sausages, or 300 pounds of potatoes.

"For a serious operation such as for appendicitis: one pig.

"The school authorities of Weimar now charge farmers 100 pounds of rye per term per child; the electrical company at Auma demands for an hour's supply 10 eggs, 3 pounds of flour, or 25 pounds of potatoes; travelling tailors declare they are ready to furnish serviceable suits to farmers for from 60 to 80 pounds of butter per suit."

"The so-called 'rye bank,' which was founded recently by the Prime Minister of the Free State of Oldenburg, is doing so well as to have numerous imitators. 'Rye bonds,' each worth 250 pounds of rye, have been issued bearing interest to the value per annum of 5 pounds of rye, and redeemable on or after April 1, 1927, at the then prevailing price of rye. Farmers and townspeople alike are eagerly buying these rye bonds, which offer a guarantee against losses on savings due to the mark depreciation."

out paper currency to pay for essential supplies, and by the end of 1923 the German mark was worthless, having fallen from 20,000 to the dollar in January 1923 to 630 billion to the dollar in November.

Hyperinflation turned everyday life into a nightmare. Wages had to be revised daily, then twice daily, and could not keep up with prices; in the end people resorted to barter. By the evening of a typical day during the period when inflation was at its height, a loaf of bread cost what a house had that very morning. Foreign visitors with a handful of

continued on page 22

1933 Hitler takes power in Germany

MUSSOLINI: THE GREAT SHOWMAN

A FORMER MARXIST, MUSSOLINI CREATED A POTENT MIXTURE OF NATIONALISM AND SOCIALISM AT A TIME WHEN DEMOCRACY SEEMED TO BE FAILING

Italy was in a volatile mood. It had gained little territory from the First World War, while suffering even more economic hardship than the other victors. Since it had started to industrialize at the end of the 19th century, thousands of workers had crowded into the cities of its industrial heartland, the northwest. They formed a new proletariat that was discontented and attracted to radical socialism and communism. The middle classes were enraged as postwar inflation destroyed their savings. Government followed government in rapid succession.

Into this situation marched the former socialist Benito Mussolini and the Fascist Party he had founded in Milan in 1919. He promised the middle classes restoration of order; the workers and peasants a balancing of their interests with those of capitalists and landowners; the Italian people as a whole firm government and national glory.

The fascists wore distinctive uniforms with black shirts. Their *squadristi*, or squads of street fighters, fought off socialist and communist opponents at public meetings and marched through the towns of Italy singing party songs and shouting slogans. Mussolini was The Leader, *Il Duce*, a compelling orator.

In 1922, with the country approaching near chaos, Italian socialists organized a general strike in a bid to halt the fascist threat. In a rousing speech in Naples, Mussolini declared that if the government did not restore order, the fascists would. He called for a march on Rome and thousands of his followers took up the cry. In the event, Mussolini hesitated, considering some sort of negotiated settlement with the authorities. He was not present when fascist columns staged a spectacular march on the Eternal City on October 28, 1922, having previously seized key installations in a classic coup d'état. When, eventually, King Victor Emmanuel III summoned him

CUBS OF THE ROMAN WOLF Five- and six-year-olds on parade on a Saturday afternoon in 1939. Mussolini banned all non-fascist youth organizations, introducing "wolf cub packs" like these.

MACHO MAN Italians were more used to seeing their leader in a splendidly impressive uniform, the imperial Caesar of a New Rome, but tobogganing bare-chested in the snow also made its point.

by telegram, he travelled to Rome by train. On October 31, 1922, aged 39, he took office as Italy's youngest-ever prime minister.

Mussolini was welcomed by the Italian people. He promised an improvement in the country's economy, and the economy did indeed begin to improve. The elections that followed his appointment were corrupt, but there is no doubt that even if they had not been, he would still have enjoyed an overwhelming victory. Over the next three years he moved steadily toward a one-party state. Opponents— liberals, socialists or communists—were dealt with by the *squadristi*: beaten up, or made to suffer the humiliation of being force-fed with castor oil, or confined in island prisons—and in some cases, killed. By 1925 a complete dictatorship had been established.

The fascists took control of the press and radio, of universities and schools. All other political parties were abolished. In 1929 Mussolini signed the Lateran Treaty and Concordat with the Vatican, which recognized the 109 acres of the Vatican City as an independent sovereign state in the heart of Rome, and Catholicism as the religion of Italy. In fact, Italians were invited to join in a state religion, the worship of *Il Duce*. The slogan, "*Il Duce a sempre ragione*" ("The Duce is always right"), appeared on walls all over the country.

The majority of Italians accepted an end to their civil and political rights in return for what they believed Mussolini had given them: a new sense of national confidence. The trains ran on time; the marshlands of the south were reclaimed for agriculture; the Sicilian Mafia

GESTURE POLITICS
Mussolini was a master
of dramatic oratory;
his speeches were
delivered amid great
pomp and ceremony.

CHURCH AND STATE
In a German cartoon drawn
after the signing of the
Lateran Treaty in 1929,
Il Duce salutes Pope
Pius XI. In his left hand
Mussolini is holding an axe
and bundle of rods, an
ancient Roman symbol of
authority known as a fasces.

was crushed. To a large extent Italians worshipped Mussolini for giving them what, inspired by his brilliant oratory, they had in fact achieved for themselves. Mussolini was at heart an orator and a journalist. He understood the attraction of show and spectacle; he provided uniforms, banners, ceremonies, grand public building projects, all in the name of the Italian people. In return the people went to work with a new energy, giving Mussolini the credit for the prosperity that resulted.

Fascism was a success in the 1920s, its achievements admired by many even in the democracies despite the brutality of its methods. Mussolini might have gone on enjoying the devotion of the Italian people for many decades. In the end, however, he overstretched himself and Italy, for there was another aspect to the agenda of the New Rome: territorial expansion. In the 1930s it led him to create a new empire in Africa through the conquest of Abyssinia (Ethiopia), which did much to alienate international opinion. Even so, he might have survived and prospered. But when his ambition led him to take Italy into the Second World War on the side of Nazi Germany, he brought disaster on himself and his country.

THE BEER HALL PUTSCH

For once Hitler's timing was misjudged. In November 1923 Munich, like the rest of Germany, was experiencing great social unrest. He believed that the conditions were ripe for a coup d'état. This would lead to a march on Berlin similar to Mussolini's march on Rome the year before.

The intended revolution began on the evening of November 8 in the Bavarian capital's *Bürgerbräukeller* ("Citizens' Beer Hall"). A machine gun was set up in the doorway. Hitler fired his revolver at the ceiling and declared: "The national revolution has broken out!" General Ludendorff arrived, wearing tweed hunting clothes. Meanwhile, Ernst Röhm's stormtroopers were taking control of the Munich Military District Headquarters.

Ludendorff had expected support from Bavaria's right-wing government, but by the next morning it was clear that he was wrong. Nonetheless, the Nazis stuck to their plan for a march through the streets. They were encouraged when cheering crowds fell in beside them. At length, forced to tighten their column in a narrow street, they were confronted by a line of armed police. Scuffles broke out, with both sides using fists and rifle butts. Then the police opened fire. In minutes the putsch was over. Goering was badly wounded; the pain he suffered made him a morphine addict for the rest of his life. Ludendorff was arrested, but soon released. Hitler was captured on November 11 and confined in the Landsberg Fortress. During nine months in prison he dictated the first part of his memoirs, *Mein Kampf* (*My Struggle*), in which he described his life up until that time, his view of Germany's future and his own part in that destiny.

HITLER'S FIRST FOLLOWERS A special unit of Nazi stormtroopers ready to back the revolution that Hitler announced from a Munich beer hall.

dollars could live like princes. Savings, investments and pensions all vanished into the black hole of inflation. Finally, in 1924, the government managed to restore the currency, and wages and salaries resumed meaningful value. But by then a large portion of the middle and lower-middle class had been ruined, and would not forget or forgive the experience. People noted, too, that speculators and owners of any substantial property had not only survived the crisis but also prospered mightily. Among those who had suffered there was a mood of rage and hatred: against the government, against the speculators and—ominously—against the Jews, who were falsely accused of spearheading the speculation.

Rise of the Nazis

One person, perhaps more than any other in Europe, was alive to these currents of ill-feeling. Adolf Hitler had joined the German Workers' Party in September 1919. By 1923 it had been renamed the National Socialist Workers' Party and he was its leader. Its name signified its potent mix of right- and left-wing

BAR-ROOM BRAWL Nazi stormtroopers of the *Sturmabteilungen* (SA) battle with communists of the Red Front in a Berlin bar.

passions, borrowed in part from Mussolini's fascism. On the one hand it was nationalist, anti-Semitic, anti-communist, anti-democratic; on the other, as a socialist party, it pandered to the working class hatred of big business and promised full employment, economic planning, even nationalization.

Hitler had established himself by the extraordinary power of his oratory and the force of his personality, which had attracted not only ex-soldiers and an infuriated middle class, but also men of the officer class, including General Ludendorff and the war hero Hermann Goering. Men like these were drawn by his vision of revenge for the humiliation of 1918 and of the restoration of German military greatness.

In November 1923, calculating that the time was ripe for a right-wing revolution, Hitler attempted a putsch in Munich. It was easily dispersed by armed police, however, and Hitler was arrested. Sentenced to five years' imprisonment, he served only nine months. He emerged to find the National Socialist Party divided and in disarray. At the same time, Germany was enjoying a brief period of economic stability, making conditions unripe for revolution.

Respite and revolution

In 1924 a committee was set up under the American Charles Dawes to work out a way for Germany to pay reparations without suffering total economic and industrial collapse. Under the Dawes plan, announced in April that year, there would be a two-year moratorium; the industrial Ruhr would be returned to Germany; and the Germans would receive a foreign loan of $200 million to aid industrial reconstruction. This, it was hoped, would

JOIN THE PARTY Spectacular events, such as this *Jugendfest* (youth festival) of 1934, were used to wrap an almost mythical aura around Hitler and National Socialism.

enable them to resume payment later. It was planned that the liability would be cleared by 1987.

The plan worked well, and for five years Germany enjoyed growing prosperity, building new factories, houses, hospitals and schools. It seemed as if all might yet be well. In 1925 the Locarno Pact, guaranteeing Germany's frontiers with Belgium and France, restored the German people to international respectability. The following year Germany joined the League of Nations.

Forbidden to make speeches in many German states, Hitler spent these relatively prosperous years in Munich, rebuilding the Nazi movement, establishing his leadership and working to achieve power by legal means. He already had allegiance from the men who would share power with him in the future: Rudolf Hess, Hermann Goering, Heinrich Himmler, Alfred Rosenberg and Julius Streicher. By 1926 he had asserted his leadership over the left-leaning Gregor Strasser who had headed the party in the north since 1923. Meanwhile, the party's brownshirted private army, the SA, built up by Ernst Röhm, grew steadily in numbers.

In the autumn of 1926 Joseph Goebbels arrived in Berlin with a letter from Hitler that appointed him Nazi Gauleiter ("district leader") of Greater Berlin. At that time party membership in the capital was well under 1,000 compared with nearly 400,000 for the communists. A brilliant and cynical propagandist, Goebbels deliberately pitted his stormtroopers against the communists in street battles, knowing that this would get them public attention. He started his own newspaper, *Der Angriff* ("The Attack"), and made headline news of every SA fatality, which he labelled "martyrdom." When a young street fighter, Horst Wessel, was shot by a Communist, he made him the supreme Nazi martyr, borrowing the tune of a communist marching song and giving it words written by Wessel. The "Horst Wessel Song" became the Nazi anthem and would later become a German national hymn.

It was the Wall Street Crash of 1929 and the disastrous worldwide economic conditions that followed that brought the Nazis to power. With millions unemployed and unrest mounting, they were able to obtain massive financial support from industrialists and businessmen willing to support a party that was anti-trade unionist and anti-communist. Unemployed men, many of them former Communists, flocked to join the SA, which offered them food, clothing, a purpose in life, enemies to hate and the promise that the Nazi Party had the answer to most of their problems. Ernst Röhm built SA membership to 170,000, twice as large as the German army. He also turned it from a mob into a disciplined, efficient fighting force.

At the same time, increased financial support enabled Hitler to conduct a propaganda campaign on a nationwide scale. Voters disillusioned with the failures of their democratic government began to turn to the National Socialists. In the election of 1930 the Nazis took more than 6 million votes, becoming the second-largest party in the Reichstag. Making no bones of his contempt for democracy, Hitler continued to use the same democracy in his pursuit of power. In further elections in July 1932 the Germans gave the Nazis 230 seats in the Reichstag, making them the largest party. After complicated maneuverings among the political class, Hitler was finally offered and accepted the chancellorship in January 1933. In March of that year an enabling bill effectively abolished democracy in Germany and made him dictator.

ON THE WAY UP Hitler was still a political outsider when photographed in 1926 at a party rally in Nuremberg (above). Seven years later, President Hindenburg greeted him as German chancellor (right).

NORMALCY, BOOM AND BUST

THE RISE IN AMERICAN LIVING STANDARDS ENDED ABRUPTLY WITH THE CRASH, WHICH SPELLED ECONOMIC DISASTER FOR THE ENTIRE WORLD

President Wilson was determinedly internationalist; Congress was not. When Wilson returned to Washington after the Paris Peace Conference he sought ratification for the League of Nations, only to find that Congress had returned to its traditional isolationism; the proposal failed to win the necessary majority in the Senate. Wilson never recovered from this setback. In October 1919 he

BUSINESS IS BUSINESS Calvin Coolidge campaigned in 1924 with the message that things could only get better—so long as government did not interfere with business.

suffered a severe stroke and although he remained in office until March 1921, his grasp of affairs became uncertain. For a period, it was his wife Edith who was effectively running the U.S. government.

Americans were proud of the part that more than a million of them had played in the Great War, but the country was undergoing a postwar depression and there was a strong desire to return to the safe and prosperous prewar days. When the Republican presidential candidate Warren Harding campaigned in 1920, his slogan was: "Less government in business, more business in government." At his inaugural, after a decisive victory, he promised a return to "normalcy" and no further entanglement in European affairs. His administration introduced major tax cuts and used tariffs to protect American agriculture and manufacturing from foreign competition.

In 1921 the United States began to introduce immigration quotas. In 1920, 800,000 men, women and children had arrived from overseas; by 1924 the numbers were down to 164,000, with a preference for immigrants from northwestern Europe. Behind this lay a fear of political radicals—communists, in particular—arriving among the poor and dispossessed of Eastern Europe and an element of racism. Immigration from East Asia, with the Japanese and Chinese in mind, was banned altogether.

By 1923 the U.S. economy was booming again. The United States was a consumer society to an extent that the rest of the world could only wonder at. The towering skyscrapers thrusting upward in New York and Chicago, unlike anything elsewhere in the world, symbolized a country bursting with pride and confidence. Average wages rose far higher than in Europe, though employers went to considerable lengths to keep them under restraint, resorting to violence to resist trade union activity.

Times were good. Yet even in the middle of "the roaring Twenties" there were perils, especially the danger of creating more goods than there were buyers. Working people, collectively, did not have the spending power to purchase all the goods and services they were producing. This imbalance generated undercurrents of potential deflation which would come dramatically to the surface in the autumn of 1929. Agriculture, meanwhile, remained in a state of near depression as farmers fought a never-ending battle to repay the bank loans on which they depended.

Harding died of a heart attack in 1923, his administration tainted by charges of corruption. His successor, Calvin Coolidge, was a man of unimpeachable integrity. His 1924 campaign slogan was: "Keep cool with Coolidge." He continued his predecessor's policy of placing no restrictions on business.

The good life

The 1920s were the Prohibition years in the United States. Americans read about the gangsters who flourished—or perished—as a result, but the gangsters' violence was very localized. Apart from the minor risk of a police raid while visiting a speakeasy, most could enjoy their drinking in peace. For some, speakeasies and jazz epitomized the

CHARLESTON, CHARLESTON Young revelers dance the night away at a New York nightclub. With its roots in the dances of West Africa, the Charleston became all the rage among whites in the 1920s.

1923 French franc drops sharply in value

1924 Zinoviev letter published; Britain's first Labor government

1925 Churchill returns Britain to gold standard

1926 General Strike in Britain ; Poincaré stabilizes franc

1928 Hoover elected president

1929 Wall Street Crash

CHEERS! Illegal drinking places, or speakeasies, were occasionally closed down by police, but new ones soon took their place.

1920s—the world described by F. Scott Fitzgerald, in which crop-haired girls showed shocking amounts of leg as they danced the Charleston. In fact, the fast-living, cocktail-drinking, nightclubbing set were scarcely more representative of ordinary life than the bootleggers. The average Mr. and Mrs. America were more likely to be improving their homes, listening to music or comedy shows on the radio, going to the movies, or out driving in the family automobile.

To accommodate the automobile, now within the means of all but the poorest families, Americans were building highways. With fine roads complementing the biggest railroad network in the world, and with the telephone and radio, they were communicating as never before. Moviegoers from Maine to Albuquerque could see Hollywood's notion of American life unfolded before them, just as they read about it in magazines with coast-to-coast distribution. A uniform sense of what it meant to be American, whatever one's ethnic origin, was being created in a way that had not been possible 20 years before.

The South, meanwhile, where older people still remembered the Civil War, brooded

PROHIBITION AND GANGSTERISM

A new decade brought victory for America's prohibitionists. The state of Maine had gone "dry" as early as 1851; other states had followed suit and calls had grown for a federal ban—for the benefit, it was said, of the family, the workplace, the social fabric as a whole. Preachers, women's campaigners, even hard-headed industrialists rejoiced on January 16, 1920, when the 18th Amendment to the Constitution came into force, prohibiting the manufacture and sale of intoxicating liquor.

In fact, the victory of Prohibition was more apparent than real. Massive resources would have been needed to enforce it, and they were not made available. Alcohol was smuggled in from Canada, whose economy benefited greatly as a result; it was manufactured in illegal breweries and distilleries; it was even made at home. It is probable that among working people the consumption of alcohol fell during the Prohibition years; it is also certainly true that the "noble experiment" turned many moderate drinkers into hardened ones and that it greatly increased the level of organized crime.

The potential profits were immediately attractive to gangs such as that of "Diamond Joe" Colosimo in Chicago, which were already in the business of prostitution and illegal gambling. Joe Colosimo was shot dead in 1920. Alphonse "Al" Capone, hired from New York by Colosimo's successor, Johnny Torrio, to handle the enforcement side of the business in Chicago, became the most famous gangster of the 1920s. By mid-decade he had control of the Chicago suburb of Cicero, even appointing the mayor there. He had several hundred men at his disposal, many of them armed with Thompson submachine guns, and an estimated annual income from liquor of $60 million, of which perhaps half went to bribe politicians, judges and police. If Capone was the best-known gangster of the Prohibition era, he was not the biggest. A key figure was the Sicilian Charles "Lucky" Luciano, who, with his partners Frank Costello, Meyer Lansky and Benny "Bugsy" Siegel, dominated organized crime throughout the United States.

When the Crash came, the gangsters were convinced that Prohibition would not last much longer. As Luciano put it: "The public won't buy it no more. When they ain't got nothin' else, they gotta have a drink or there's gonna be trouble. And they're gonna want to have that drink legal." Prohibition was indeed repealed in 1933, and the gangs had to look for alternative ways of maintaining their profits. After the Crash, the banks were unable or unwilling to lend money; the gangsters, with millions of dollars in cash, went into loan-sharking. And as thousands of Americans, unemployed and broke, turned to gambling in hope of a windfall, the gangsters saw another opportunity. Soon the "numbers" (illegal street lotteries), slot machines and off-track betting on the horses had turned into another multimillion dollar business.

RUBBED OUT Beer baron "Dutch" Schultz, killed in a shoot-out with the police.

CRIME WARS Armed Chicago police and a bulletproof car.

CROSS OF HATRED   A meeting of the Ku Klux Klan in Pennsylvania in September 1922. Disguised in long white robes and hoods, Klansmen terrorized black communities with violence and murder.

over its past. Parts of it had found new wealth in oil wells, but elsewhere it was the nation's backward, agrarian, undeveloped half. The Ku Klux Klan, originally founded in the aftermath of the Civil War to oppose political rights for blacks, had been resuscitated in 1915 and grew alarmingly in the 1920s. It was nourished among poor whites by an abiding hatred of black people, still blamed for the South's defeat in the Civil War and its subsequent miseries. In 1923 the Klan claimed a million members. Lynchings of blacks merely suspected of robbery or rape were all too common.

Anti-Catholic as well as anti-black, the Klan lent its support to the 1928 Republican presidential candidate, Herbert Hoover, against the Democrat Alfred E. Smith, a Catholic and an opponent of Prohibition. Hoover won by a large majority.

Problems of the victors

For the nations across the Atlantic, the Great War had been immensely costly, and not just in lives. All the European victors were deeply in debt to the United States. The fact that they were now debtors rather than creditors meant that they had to export more than they imported. Free trade was abandoned as they erected tariff barriers to protect their own manufacturing industries.

Their collective efforts to be sellers rather than buyers made a return to prewar levels of trade difficult. At the same time, the need to repay war debts made it hard to find the capital for rebuilding peacetime industries. The British tried to solve the problem by heavy taxation and cuts in public expenditure; the French, like the Germans, continued to borrow and permitted inflation of their currency. The result was that Britain suffered a depression in 1921-2, but weathered the storm when the German mark collapsed in 1923. France, on the other hand, was hit less severely by the depression of 1921, but in 1923 saw the franc drop sharply in value. By 1926 it had fallen from a prewar value of 19 cents to just 2 cents, and it was only by imposing severe emergency measures that the conservative prime minister, Raymond Poincaré, managed to stabilize it at a quarter of its prewar value.

Determined not to pay off his country's debts by currency inflation, the British chancellor of the exchequer, Winston Churchill, returned Britain to the gold standard in 1925. This had the effect of making British goods expensive in export markets and was one of the causes of a severe and growing problem of unemployment.

France's situation was different. In the prewar era it had been much less industrialized than Britain and largely self-sufficient in food production; consequently, its exports were less than Britain's, as were its imports. But the war had forced change upon it. With its industrial and mining areas in the war zone, it had been obliged to industrialize the rest of the country and to develop its other resources. With its coalfields, for example, largely out of action, it had developed hydroelectric power. When the industrial northeast was restored after the war along with Alsace-Lorraine, this process of modernization was greatly enlarged. Despite underlying economic problems, France became a truly modern industrial country in the 1920s and a major exporter, with an industrial output in 1925 that was twice that of 1919.

A fragile prosperity

The years 1924 to 1929 saw a real growth in prosperity in Western Europe. Average income was substantially higher than before the war. There was far greater spending power and a wider range of consumer goods

A JOB FIT FOR HEROES?   Their faces covered with masks, two former army officers resort to street entertainment in postwar Britain.

THE GOOD DOCTOR A French cartoon of 1928 gives Prime Minister Poincaré the credit for healing the ailing franc.

than in 1914; the development of hire purchase, which enabled people to acquire goods before they were fully paid for, helped to create the beginnings of a consumer society. No European country as yet approached the living standards of North America, but there was a widespread optimism that for the first time in history the general mass of humanity could expect to enjoy not only the basic necessities of life, but also some of its luxuries.

But there were problems. One was the constant threat of unemployment; where the price of labor, in a free market, grew too high, it was dispensed with. Another was the uneven distribution of wealth. The major beneficiaries of the prosperity of the 1920s were the middle classes and skilled workers in the newer industries; by contrast, many working-class families continued to exist on wages that were barely above subsistence level. A third, less evident, problem was the disparity between the flow of goods being produced and the purchasing power available to pay for them; there was a danger of flooding the markets with too many goods.

With its concern for sound money and its declining share of world markets, Britain suffered particularly acutely from unemployment. To alleviate it, the government introduced a system of unemployment insurance. But it was not available to the long-term unemployed; it was strictly means-tested, and it was barely enough to meet the basic needs of an unemployed man and his family.

France again differed. Its new industrial revolution meant that for most of the 1920s there was a problem, not of unemployment, but of labor shortage. At the same time, a carefully protected peasant agriculture kept the cost of food high. This, combined with the demand for labor, made for relatively high industrial wages, which tended to make French goods uncompetitive abroad.

In all countries, the juggling act was bound to be difficult because there were three balls to keep in the air: on the one hand, wage costs had to be kept low; on the other, public spending power had to be kept high enough to keep people buying mass-produced goods; at the same time, social discontent had to be appeased. Nowhere in the democratic world did either governments or the private sector succeed in keeping these three factors in balance by the end of the 1920s.

The politics of discontent

The governments of France and Britain were unable to deliver on wartime promises of "homes fit for heroes" and a better life for working people. Ironically, defeated Germany, through massive borrowings, set out on more ambitious programs of social security and public housing than the victor countries. Disillusionment in both France and Britain led to the growth of socialist and communist parties and of trade union movements. Although conservatives such as Raymond Poincaré in France and Stanley Baldwin in Britain dominated the decade, both countries had periods of socialist government. In Britain there was a first Labor government under Ramsay MacDonald in 1924 and a second in 1929; during the decade, the Labor Party replaced the Liberals, with whom it was in coalition, as the alternative party of government. In France there were two years of socialist-liberal coalition under Edouard Herriot and Aristide Briand between 1924 and 1926, after which Poincaré returned to power. But neither in Britain nor France did these liberal-socialist governments succeed *continued on page 30*

A ROYAL WEDDING

On April 26, 1923, the Duke of York, the future King George VI, married Lady Elizabeth Bowes-Lyon, daughter of the 14th Earl of Strathmore and Kinghorne, at Westminster Abbey. Huge excitement surrounded this romantic royal event, and the new BBC had wanted to broadcast the service live. This was vetoed by the Abbey Chapter, on the grounds that the broadcast might be received "by persons in public houses with their hats on."

On the morning of the great day a crowd estimated at a million had gathered along the wedding route. The weather earlier had been cold and wet, but as Lady Elizabeth entered the Abbey at the appointed time of 11.30 am "the sun actually came out," as the groom's father, King George V, noted in his diary that night. Lady Elizabeth wore a dress "of old ivory color, and of a simple medieval style embroidered with silver thread and pearls." The groom, known in the family as Bertie, wore the uniform of a group captain in the Royal Air Force. His best man was his older brother, David (the future Edward VIII and later Duke of Windsor), dressed as colonel of the Welsh Guards.

On her way up the aisle, Lady Elizabeth, in an unrehearsed gesture, laid her bouquet on the tomb of the Unknown Warrior. Having entered the Abbey a commoner, she left it a princess. The crowd outside fell in love with the young woman who became known as "the Smiling Duchess" until, 13 years later, she became queen. Fifteen years after that, following the early death of her husband, she became the "Queen Mum."

Later on their wedding day, the couple stood on the balcony of Buckingham Palace to receive the cheers of a vast crowd. At the wedding breakfast, the cake weighed 800 pounds and stood 9 feet high. The remains of it were later sent to underprivileged children. In the late afternoon the couple drove to Waterloo Station on the way to their honeymoon, which was spent at the ancestral homes of the Duchess's family, Polesden Lacey and Glamis, and at Frogmore in Windsor Park.

FUTURE DESTINY In 1923 no one guessed that the Yorks would become king and queen.

IRELAND BREAKS FREE

IRISH LONGINGS FOR AN INDEPENDENT STATE WERE FULFILLED IN THE 1920S, BUT ONLY AT THE COST OF CIVIL WAR AND WITHOUT THE PROTESTANT-DOMINATED NORTH

In January 1919 an Irish parliament, the Dáil Eireann, unrecognized by the British government, met to choose delegates to represent Ireland at the Paris Peace Conference. The conference declined to recognize the delegates of what it called "the so-called Irish Republic."

The "Irish problem" had been the subject of feverish debate for more than a century. In the last decades of the 19th century the Liberal leader, Gladstone, had twice introduced an Irish Home Rule Bill; it had twice been defeated and the Liberal Party had split on the issue. Many British Liberals might sympathize with the desire of Irishmen to govern themselves, but the Protestant majority in the six counties of Northern Ireland were passionately opposed to becoming part of a Catholic Ireland. This was the "Ulster question" which exacerbated the Irish problem. Another Home Rule Bill finally received the royal assent as the First World War broke out, but was put on hold for the duration of the war.

In 1916 a few hundred Irish republicans rose in rebellion. The Easter Rising, conducted by idealists who insisted on paying the fares on the tramcars they commandeered for the occasion, infuriated the British, for whom it was a stab in the back in time of war. It was not popular either with the majority of Irish, thousands of whose young men had volunteered to serve in the war. When, however, the British government reacted by executing 15 of the republican leaders, Irish sentiment changed almost overnight and the popular demand for a truly independent Ireland became irresistible.

When the United Kingdom went to the polls in December 1918, the Irish took things into their own hands. Rather than going to Westminster, 73 newly elected MPs from the nationalist party, Sinn Fein, simply stayed in Dublin as the Dáil Eireann. They proclaimed an Irish Republic and elected Eamon de Valera, a survivor of the Easter Rising, as President of the Dáil, effectively head of a new Irish government. At the same time, the Irish Republican Army (IRA) emerged out of earlier militant republican organizations and soon took to the streets in armed rebellion against the British authorities. A leading figure in the violence that ensued was the finance minister in de Valera's government, Michael Collins, who also proved to be a skilled guerrilla commander.

For their part, the British authorities strengthened the numbers of the Royal Irish Constabulary by enlisting volunteer auxiliaries, mainly British ex-servicemen, who became known as the "Black and Tans" from their khaki and black uniforms. More ruthless than the regular Irish police, they came to be deeply hated. British intelligence agents also organized a network of informers in the

THE ROAD TO INDEPENDENCE A casualty lies dead in the street after the IRA bombing of the Dublin Customs House in May 1921. De Valera (left) fought against the British, then against the Irish government, then against the IRA.

BEHIND BARBED WIRE Hundreds of republican activists were interned by the British, as here in January 1921. Many would be interned again by the Irish Free State, and by their old comrade de Valera.

ranks of the republicans. When detected, these informers were summarily executed in what was from the start a savage war.

In 1920 the British government of Lloyd George introduced a Government of Ireland Bill, which provided for a partition between Northern Ireland—the six counties of Ulster—and Southern Ireland. North and South would each have its own parliament and remain part of the United Kingdom. Northern Ireland accepted the proposal and its parliament was officially opened in June 1921. Sinn Fein, however, would accept nothing less than the total independence of a united Ireland.

The violence intensified. The republicans robbed banks to finance their purchase of arms. They derailed trains, overturned armored cars and ambushed British soldiers and police. In the first seven months of 1921, 244 police and 94 soldiers were killed and many more wounded. In May that year units of the Republican Army seized the Dublin Customs House and set it on fire. The response of the British security forces was merciless. When innocent bystanders as well as republican activists were killed or wounded in reprisals by the army and police, popular fury provided new volunteers for the Republican Army. A commission set up by the British Labor Party stated: "Things are being done in the name of Britain which must make her name stink in the nostrils of the whole world."

In October 1921 the Dáil sent delegates to a conference in London, set up by the British government to try to find a peaceful settlement. After eight weeks of argument and discussion they signed a document agreeing to the establishment of an Irish Free State which excluded the six counties of Northern Ireland. It would have the same dominion status as, say, Canada, with a parliament which would swear allegiance to the British Crown. Sinn Fein was now split. Among those who accepted the treaty were the veteran Home Rule campaigner, Arthur Griffith, and Michael Collins, who believed that it was the best solution possible in the circumstances—although he was also certain that in signing the

treaty he was signing his life away. Eamon de Valera, who had not been present at the conference, denounced the treaty and resigned as President of the Dáil. In January 1922 a provisional government, recognized by London, took office in Dublin. Griffith had succeeded de Valera as President of the Dáil while, as result of a complicated constitutional overlap between the old order and the new, Collins headed the provisional government.

The Anglo-Irish war now gave way to a civil war between an official Free State army, with Collins as its commander-in-chief, and anti-treaty irregulars of the Irish Republican Army. Between them they spread terror across the entire country, dividing whole communities. The pressure of events took its toll on the 50-year-old Arthur Griffith, who died suddenly on August 12, 1922. Ten days later, Collins was ambushed and killed by the IRA—as he had foreseen, his pro-treaty stance had been his death warrant. His successors in government continued to enforce law and order with the greatest severity, including executions of captured irregulars. In December 1922, a constitution for the Irish Free State was proclaimed; by May 1923 the Free State authorities had won the civil war.

Despite the bitterness of the past, relations between Ireland and Britain remained surprisingly friendly. The Irish government paid compensation to the British for seizures of British-owned land; the British cooperated in development projects and continued to invest in the country. The IRA, however, went on with its activities, now directed against the Dublin government and the existence of a separate Protestant Ulster. When its former comrade de Valera became Taoiseach (prime minister) in 1932 the IRA continued to oppose the government. De Valera responded by interning IRA members without trial. At the same time, he worked to sever Ireland's last ties with mainland Britain. A new constitution in 1937 removed all reference to the British Crown, leaving Ireland as a republic (still claiming the six counties of the North), though it did not leave the Commonwealth until 1949.

SECURITY CHECK A British soldier on the streets of Dublin searches a vehicle for weapons or explosives in October 1920. Attacks and reprisals between the British and republicans became increasingly bloody.

in providing financial stability or in appeasing social discontent.

In the Europe of the early 1920s there was a decisive separation between the Marxist revolutionaries of the Communist International and the social democrats who were willing to work within a democratic parliamentary system and form alliances with the older liberal parties. In Britain the Conservatives made successful propaganda of the link between the Communist International and the Labor movement when the so-called Zinoviev letter, addressed to the British Communist Party and urging violent revolution, was published in 1924. Although the Comintern had links with the trade unions, and Zinoviev, its president, had sent similar letters to communist parties in other countries, the Zinoviev letter was probably a forgery. It was not in any case addressed to the British Labor Party. The fact that it was used as a smear was bitterly resented.

A crisis in British industrial relations came with the General Strike of 1926. This grew out of a miners' strike called in protest at proposals to reduce wages; sympathetic workers in other industries then joined in. The government of Stanley Baldwin sent troops to man the docks and power stations and organized volunteers to maintain basic transport and communications. The Trades Union Council called off the strike after nine days, although the miners' strike dragged on for six months. The General Strike had never come close to bringing about a revolutionary situation. Although there was some violence, it was still a strike and not an attempt to overthrow the government by violence. The TUC refused to accept financial help offered by Moscow; strikers and police played a rugby match together (which the strikers won). The necessary spark of profound class hatred was simply absent.

The boom years

Through mass production, high wages, advertising-enhanced consumerism and easy credit, the United States appeared to have solved the basic social and economic conundrums that bedevilled the countries of Europe. It was by far the world's largest creditor nation, and since it was practically self-sufficient and its economy protected by tariff barriers, the rest of the world had to pay its debts to the United States not in goods but in currency backed by gold. In the early 1920s most of the world's gold was stored in Fort Knox.

The United States spent much of its enormous financial surpluses on overseas loans, but otherwise it pursued its policy of isolation. After demobilization at the end of the First World War the U.S. army shrank to become the world's 16th largest, on a par with Yugoslavia's, though less well equipped.

The economy went on booming. Automobile ownership went from 6 million in 1919 to 27 million in 1929; output of refrigerators went from 27,000 in 1923 to over 750,000 in 1928. But the country's prosperity was unevenly distributed. Farmers, particularly in the South, had been doing badly since the postwar collapse in agricultural prices, and some long-established industries such as textiles and shipbuilding were in decline. There were pockets of extreme poverty in the deep

SPECTER OF WALL STREET The activities of New York Stock Market traders affected economies all over the world in ways that had not been possible just thirty years earlier. When Wall Street "laid an egg" in 1929, the repercussions were global.

South, in the uplands of the Alleghenies, even in New England. Americans may have been better off than any other people in the world, but in 1929, 40 percent of them had annual incomes of less than $1,500.

There was increased public spending on roads and on schools and hospitals. But in general the Republican governments were reluctant to intervene in the economic life of the country or to restrict the activities of big business. "The Business of America is Business," said President Calvin Coolidge in 1925. Big companies were turning into gigantic corporations such as General Motors and American Telephone and Telegraph (AT&T). Government and the courts tended

FRENCH BLUEBEARD

One of the most sensational murder trials of the interwar years was that of the Frenchman Henri Landru, known as Bluebeard. He went to the guillotine in February 1922, having been found guilty of the murder of ten women and a boy. A notebook found at the time of his arrest contained the names of 283 women who had responded to his advertisements offering marriage, and it is likely that the number of his victims was much greater. Before his execution he asked to be shaved, saying: "It will please the ladies."

to side against organized labor, and membership of the American Federation of Labor fell from 4 million to 3 million in 1929.

The Crash

The stock exchanges of London and the rest of Europe were for professionals and for the social elite who entrusted their spare capital to their stockbrokers. But in the United States, not only millionaires but their chauffeurs and janitors invested on the New York Stock Exchange; working men discussed the market in bars, and as prices steadily rose through the 1920s more and more of them came to see it as a one-way bet. Many invested their life savings in what was seen as the best of all possible investments. Many others bought "on margin," that is, by putting down 10 percent of the price of the stock and borrowing the rest; stock as yet unpaid for but rising in price was used as collateral to buy more stock, which in turn was used to buy still more.

As the decade drew to a close, shrewder investors, aware that average stock prices

NEW YORK, NEW YORK

BRIGHT LIGHTS, BIG CITY   New York at night was aglow with lights—and nowhere were they brighter than on Times Square and Broadway (above). Below: The New York skyline from the East River in 1926.

New York was the world's second-largest city, and one of its wonders. Then as now, it was several cities in one: a great port, where luxury liners unloaded passengers from Europe; an international center of commerce and finance, its might symbolized by the skyscrapers that had been thrusting ever higher since the early 1900s. The gilded tower of the Woolworth Building, 792 feet high, dominated the Wall Street financial district. Farther up town, by the end of the early 1930s the Empire State Building would climb to 1,250 feet, making it the world's tallest structure for the next 40 years.

New York was a city of elegant town houses and apartment buildings, luxurious hotels, restaurants and department stores. It was a center of art and culture, with world-renowned collections and 70-odd theaters in the Times Square area alone. From 1925 on, its sophisticated life was reflected in its own *New Yorker* magazine. At the other end of the scale it was a city of terrible deprivation, whose inhabitants, unemployed or living on sweatshop wages, were crowded into slums as bad as any in the world. It was a tough town of streetwise hustlers, gamblers and racketeers, the Guys and Dolls of Broadway, whose lives would receive their comic memorial in the novels of Damon Runyon. It was also a mecca for artists and writers from all over the country, offering in Greenwich Village an equivalent of the Bohemian quarters of Europe.

Above all, it was a town of immigrants. Of the 5.6 million inhabitants in 1920, just over 2 million had been born in other countries. The most recent and less successful crowded into the ethnic neighborhoods—Chinese, Italian, Jewish, Ukrainian, Polish and others—each as far as possible a replica of the home country. About 200,000 New Yorkers were black, mostly immigrants or the children of migrants from the South. Many lived in Harlem, whose dance halls and clubs, where the best jazz could be enjoyed, were a favorite venue for sophisticates from wealthier parts of the city.

Despite the extremes of wealth and poverty, throughout the interwar years New York was a remarkably safe city. In Manhattan people would sleep out in the parks on hot summer nights; in many districts they did not lock their doors. And on certain festive days, St. Patrick's in particular, New Yorkers rich and poor, in all their ethnic diversity, would come together to celebrate their pride in one of the world's great cities.

THE GREAT CRASH This graph of the Dow Jones Weekly Industrial Averages shows the rollercoaster ride that New York share prices took during the second half of 1929.

had risen far beyond their real value, began to sell. This merely brought more stock into the market and attracted more investors. Others, nervous that the boom might not go on forever but also nervous about the extent of their borrowings, decided to wait for the peak before selling. For them, the peak came too soon and too suddenly.

Although few realized it at the time, it came on September 3, 1929. On that day the volume of transactions on the New York Stock Exchange was 4.5 million shares. U.S. Steel edged up to 261, AT&T was at 302, General Electric at 395, General Motors at 71. The record went unnoticed by the newspapers, because stock market records were no longer news. After that, the market dropped sharply. For weeks it rose and fell and rose again, but its rises always fell well short of the September 3 peak. When it fell, new buyers came in to pick up "bargains." The level of borrowings for stock market purchases actually rose. But as the highs dropped lower and the lows grew still deeper, nervousness began to creep in, and the decline sharpened.

Saturday, October 19, was a bad day on Wall Street; October 21 was worse. By Thursday, October 24, there was full-scale

DEEP DEPRESSION Much of U.S. farming was already in depression before the Crash. Some farmers, unable to sell their produce, had to eat their seed corn to avoid starvation.

panic, with selling orders pouring in by the thousands, and prices falling so fast that the ticker-tape service could not cope. That day some of the biggest U.S. bankers met and agreed to form a pool to support share prices. News of this caused a brief rally, but it was too late. The worst day was October 29, when the volume of trading exceeded 20 million shares. As one newspaper put it: "The present week has witnessed the greatest stock-market catastrophe of all the ages."

The market continued to fall, reaching bottom on November 13. The total loss in value over the weeks of decline and fall added up to some $30 billion.

The consequences

The Wall Street Crash ruined thousands, and its effects continued to spread outward, touching the lives of millions of Americans who had never speculated on the stock exchange as well as tens of millions of other people around the world. The bursting of the speculative bubble had exposed fundamental weaknesses in the world economy, which would strike the United States with

full force only after the tidal wave of the Crash had travelled around the world, wrecking financial confidence. That was when the Great Depression really made itself felt.

The first result of the Crash was a collapse in agricultural prices, first in North America and then around the world. Farmers had to destroy stocks of food because people were too poor to buy. American loans that had financed European imports from the United States stopped abruptly and short-term loans were called in. The effect on the European economic recovery, particularly in Germany and Austria, was devastating.

The Crash had produced a worldwide failure of credit, resulting in a nightmarish paradox where farmers burned food while people starved, and millions were thrown out of work because of a superabundance of goods that could not be sold. One British historian put it this way: "Civilization was choked with its own power to produce abundance, where plenty had actually produced poverty, and where men starved because there was too much wealth." The 1920s thus came to an end with a cataclysm as great as the outbreak of the First World War—one that claimed as many lives and caused as much misery. . . but was more bewildering.

CREATIVE TALENTS

THE REVOLUTION IN THE ARTS THAT BEGAN IN THE 1900S CONTINUED INTO THE 1920S. MODERNISM FOUND A SYMPATHETIC HOME IN WEIMAR GERMANY, BUT LACKED POPULAR APPEAL AND WAS LOATHED ALIKE BY GERMAN NATIONAL SOCIALISTS AND THE RULERS OF SOVIET RUSSIA. MUCH MORE POPULAR WERE THE NEW FORMS OF MASS ENTERTAINMENT, THE MOVIES AND RADIO, AND JAZZ. DURING THE 1930S THE ARTS, LIKE EVERYTHING ELSE, BECAME INTENSELY POLITICAL.

A TALE OF THREE CITIES

PARIS, BERLIN AND PRAGUE WERE CITIES WITH IMPERIAL PASTS THAT NOW FACED AN UNEASY PRESENT AND AN UNCERTAIN FUTURE

STAGE RELIEF Members of the Opéra Comique hand out gifts of food to the poor of Paris. Below: La Coupole in Montparnasse was a favorite haunt of artists and intellectuals.

Paris, Berlin, Prague—the year 1919 brought very different destinies to three great European cities. For Paris it was a year of triumph; France was one of the principal victors of the Great War, its capital host to a glittering procession of world statesmen attending the conference intended to usher in a new era of peace and prosperity. Berlin's plight stood in stark contrast. It had become the capital of a newly unified German Empire only half a century earlier and since then had grown prodigiously until it was the third-largest city in the world. Now its previous triumphs seemed trampled under foot by a combination of defeat, revolution and despair. For the third city, Prague, no less historic than either of the other two, the postwar settlement brought a proud return from relative provincial obscurity. For the first time since the late Middle Ages, it was the capital again of an independent nation: the newly created republic of Czechoslovakia, carved from the collapse of the Habsburg Empire.

The city of lights

At the end of the Great War thousands of young Americans, many of whom had served in France, flocked to visit the city renowned as the heart of European civilization and *douceur de vivre*. The beauty of Paris had faded a little during the war years, but otherwise it had scarcely changed since its massive reconstruction in the 1850s and 60s. It was still a city built on a human scale, ornamented by splendid monuments and refreshed by parks and by the river flowing through its center. The Seine, with its cob-

bled, tree-lined promenades where anglers sat and lovers strolled, brought a breath of country tranquillity, a refuge from the din of traffic in a city that to many seemed the noisiest and most excitable in the world. The great central market, Les Halles, offered all the produce of France fresh every morning. Revellers went there at dawn for onion soup and ended their night by buying the first of the new day's flowers.

Many of the city's visitors were artists and writers. But although Paris was still a mecca of the arts—not least because it was an inexpensive place in which to live in modest comfort—it was no longer the center of the avant-garde; that role had passed to

CAFÉ SOCIETY For rich and poor alike, the café was the focus of Paris life, for discussing politics, art or love, or just watching the world go by.

1922 Fritz Lang's film *Dr. Mabuse*

1925 Kafka's *The Trial* published

1928 George Gershwin's *An American in Paris*; Bertolt Brecht and Kurt Weill's *The Threepenny Opera*

COCO CHANEL: A WOMAN OF STYLE

Gabrielle "Coco" Chanel, the woman who would dominate French fashion for nearly 60 years, was born to poor parents in the Auvergne region of central France in 1883. Little is known about her early life except that as a child she once cut up her aunt's curtains to make a dress for a doll. Whatever her origins, she had an extraordinary intuition for what women would want to wear, even if it was unlike anything they had seen before. She was a genuine revolutionary, creating an entire Chanel "look," whose basis was a simple jersey dress, in utter contrast to the corsetted style of the early 1900s. She introduced women to the pullover and the pleated skirt, made elegant trousers and turned sports clothes into garments that could be worn every day.

In 1913 she opened a millinery shop in the high society seaside resort of Deauville in Normandy. By 1918 her simple jersey look had become high fashion and was making her fortune. More than any other designer in the early 1920s she developed a silhouette that followed the natural line of the body, while emphasizing its slimness. She led the field in shortening the hemline, even for afternoon and evening dresses. Along with Paquin, Patou, Vionnet and Schiaparelli, it was Chanel who developed the essential 1920s look. In 1922 she introduced her scent, Chanel No. 5, whose sales would underpin the rest of her business, which at its height employed 3,500 people. Her friends included Picasso, Igor Stravinsky and Jean Cocteau, and though she never married she had several well-known lovers.

Chanel's business lapsed during the Second World War, and her postwar reputation was clouded by allegations of collaboration. In 1954, however, she reopened the House of Chanel and restored her authority over the world of fashion. She continued to dominate it until her death in 1971.

A NEW LOOK In the 1920s, Coco Chanel rewrote the rules of women's fashion. Here, she wears one of her chic but practical suits.

Berlin. Montmartre had its artists, but the most famous creators of the prewar modernist revolution were moving away. Picasso had prospered and now lived in a more elegant quarter; Matisse was in Nice or travelling abroad; Braque stayed on until 1925 and then crossed the river to the Latin Quarter. Montmartre became a haunt of tourists – as well as the prostitutes and criminals who had favored the neighborhood long before the artists came. Poets and intellectuals gravitated toward the Left Bank: the informality of Montparnasse and the pavement cafés of the Boulevards Saint-Germain and Saint-Michel.

Like any great city, Paris offered contrasts of wealth and poverty. On the west side, the 16th *arrondissement* with its mansions and elegant apartment buildings was almost exclusively the residence of the well-heeled; on the east, the ancient quarter known as the Marais had one of the highest population densities in Europe. In the outskirts, the drab industrial quarters of Belleville and Menilmontant were hotbeds of communism and militant trade unionism. In Paris's working-class quarters, few apartments had inside bathrooms; practically none had plumbing for baths; many lacked even running water.

Between these two extremes the *petit peuple*, the ordinary men and women of Paris, shared the intricate streets and squares of the city's center with the smart, the well-to-do, the artists, the intellectuals and the visiting Americans. A large percentage of the population consisted of self-employed artisans, engaged in the skilled crafts associated with the city's reputation for fashion, elegance and the pursuits of pleasure: embroiderers, glovemakers, jewellers, cabinet-makers, *traiteurs* (caterers) and a thousand other trades. Often they lived over their workplaces. Their homes were cramped, but their home life could spill over into the streets of the *quartier*, where the women met their friends as they did their daily marketing, the men lingered in the cafés and the whole family could eat together in the neighborhood restaurant for little more than the cost of eating at home.

Powerful social tensions did exist in the Paris of the 1920s and 30s—chiefly arising from the extremes of poverty and wealth—and from time to time they erupted in riots. By and large, however, the social fabric held together, partly because of the intricacies of neighborhood, partly because people feared a recurrence of the terrible violence that had

"PILLARS OF SOCIETY" Georg Grosz's painting of 1926 expresses his profound contempt for the Establishment of Weimar society: the Church, the army and the bourgeoisie.

riven the capital twice in its not-so-distant past: during the French Revolution's Great Terror of the 1790s, and again in 1871 when another experiment in revolutionary government, the Paris Commune, was bloodily suppressed. The comparative stability was also due in part to the Parisians' pride in and love of their city, more powerful, if anything, among the poor than the rich.

Babylon-on-Spree

Berlin was the capital of Prussia as well as of Germany, and Prussia—in the minds of non-Prussians, at least—had long been associated with strictness, restraint and moral rigidity. That had never perhaps been entirely true of Berliners, who prided themselves on their skepticism, their laid-back attitude to life's vicissitudes, their brand of gallows humor. But after the end of the Great War, bringing with it the collapse of the kaiser's rule and months of revolutionary chaos, it was as if

1930 Marlene Dietrich in the film *The Blue Angel*

SEX AND SATIRE IN BERLIN

The musical *Cabaret* is based on the novel *Goodbye to Berlin* by the English writer Christopher Isherwood, reflecting the time he spent in Berlin in the 1920s; Isherwood was homosexual, drawn by the city's reputation for permissiveness. The cabarets, mostly occupying smoky cellars, offered an entertainment that would become familiar to non-Berliners through Josef von Sternberg's film *The Blue Angel* (1930), starring Marlene Dietrich. They combined the appeal of scantily dressed young women (or men in drag) with satire of middle-class morality and the solemnities of the political parties, the items being linked by a master of ceremonies. In the late 1920s their writers and performers turned their mockery on the stormtroopers of the National Socialists, and paid for it by being beaten up from time to time.

COME TO THE CABARET At the Palais der Friedrichstadt you could eat, drink, dance and watch the cabaret.

Bertolt Brecht and Kurt Weill's *The Threepenny Opera* (1928) conveys the musical style of Berlin cabaret. Its subject is the city's criminal mafia, the *Ringvereine* or "sporting clubs." Membership in these was limited to men over 21 who had served at least two years in prison. They conducted formal meetings at which the leaders wore top hats, morning coats and silk sashes, and hence were known as the *Zylinderleute* or "top hats." Despite their curious ways, the top hats were brutal criminals, running protection rackets and the drug trade. Because they were generous in their bribes to policemen and politicians, very little action was taken against them for many years. In the late 1920s, however, public demands for action led to an edict banning them and a series of police round-ups.

"THE THREEPENNY OPERA" A 1928 Berlin production of Brecht and Weill's satirical folk opera.

DADA, DADA Dadaists examine and discuss each other's work at their Berlin exhibition in July 1920. Some of them were troubled, however: to hold an exhibition seemed to contradict all they stood for.

Berliners had discovered their shadow side. The city became a byword for sexual license, open homosexuality, alcohol and drugs. Cocaine was peddled on the streets and sold in the famous Berlin nightclubs, which boasted a unique mix of sex, satire and radical politics.

For 15 years, between the fall of the kaiser and the coming to power of Hitler, Berlin was also a home for all that was avant-garde in art. Dada, the most revolutionary and nihilistic movement of them all, flourished there. From its headquarters at the Romanische Café it penetrated every art form, not just painting, but also literature, the movies, the theater and even the cabaret. One of its members, the Marxist artist George Grosz, paraded with a placard that proclaimed "*Dada über Alles.*" His drawings, filled with blistering hatred, showed bloated postwar capitalists, angry scar-faced Prussian officers and the mutilated casualties of the war.

The theater flourished. Berlin offered the magnificent stage productions of Max Reinhardt and, in 1928, Bertolt Brecht and Kurt Weill's *The Threepenny Opera*, based on the city's criminal gangs; this seemed to sum up the black humor of the time. The Berlin film studios, UFA, produced some of the most exciting films of the 1920s and gave employment to directors such as Fritz Lang and Ernst Lubitsch and actors such as Peter Lorre and Marlene Dietrich before they moved on to Hollywood. Berlin musical life enjoyed a golden age. The list of great musicians working there was remarkable: the conductors Erich Kleiber, Bruno Walter, Otto Klemperer and Wilhelm Furtwängler; the soloists Rudolf Serkin, Artur Schnabel, Claudio Arrau and Vladimir Horowitz, to name but a few.

For the majority of Berliners, the city's raffish side and cultural life probably passed them by, embroiled as they were in the business of survival. In working-class areas such as Wedding or Kreuzberg, the poorest lived in vast *Mietskasernen* or rental barracks, often whole families in one room. Only in the late 1920s did they begin to move into modern housing developments, some of the best in Europe, being built in the outer districts alongside modern glass-and-steel factories.

Berlin's lower middle classes, like all Germans of their class, were badly hit by the hyperinflation of 1923. But even before that, in the chaos surrounding the end of the war, they had grown accustomed to buying dickies to wear under their jackets because they could not afford whole shirts, and cigars made of dried cabbage leaves soaked in nicotine.

There was another aspect of the city's life, one that few could have ignored: the sight of marching men in the streets. The right-wing paramilitary Freikorps were disbanded in the early 1920s, but were replaced by uniformed private armies attached to different political factions: the *Rotfrontkampferbund* of the communists, the *Reichsbanner* of the socialists, the *Sturmabteilung* (SA) of the Nazis. In the early 1920s the last of these was the smallest; by 1930, however, it outnumbered them all. After 1933 the Nazi government swept away the features that had made Berlin a German Babylon. They cleared the streets of crime, while planning crimes of a quite different magnitude.

The first Bohemia

Bohemia, the region that gave its name to artists' quarters and an "artistic" lifestyle everywhere, ceased to exist as an independent country when it was absorbed into the Habsburg Empire in 1526. In 1919 its capital, Prague, came to preside over the whole of Czechoslovakia. It had a population of well under a million, making it much smaller than Paris or Berlin, but it had a strategic position, lying at the heart of Europe where the Slav and Germanic worlds met. Reflecting this, its citizens spoke both Czech, a Slavonic language, and German. Its great Charles University, founded in the Middle Ages, was one of the oldest in Europe. In the 16th and 17th centuries Prague had been a center of Renaissance learning, attracting scholars, artists, even occultists; according to a popular legend, it was in Prague in the early 17th century that a Jewish rabbi and mystic, Rabbi Judah

GRACIOUS LIVING Prague is a picture of baroque elegance in this photograph of 1936 (below). It was a city of craftsmen, whose wares could be bought on the street (right).

Löw, was supposed to have invented the Golem, a robot magically endowed with life. The noble houses and churches built at that time had earned it the name, "the city of 100 spires," and made it one of the most beautiful cities in the world.

By the beginning of the 20th century, Prague was also an industrial center, notable for its ironworks and engineering and textile factories, as well as its famous Bohemian glass. By the 1920s the new Czechoslovakia had a democratic constitution and a government set on modernization. But Prague's

PLENTY IN PRAGUE

Milena Jesenska's *A Stroll through Everyday Life* gives a sense of how Prague came out of the First World War better than Vienna and Berlin:

"If you'd been abroad for a while and then returned to Prague, you'd be amazed at the quality of our food shops, at the variety and color. I don't think there's anywhere like it . . . We perhaps do not see it, but for visitors Prague is first a city of exquisite romantic streets of olden times, and then a town of salami, sausages, smoked meats, bacon dumplings, crisp bread and whipped cream. Nowhere else can people eat so well and so cheaply. Nowhere do they eat so much . . .

"I found myself wondering where all this food comes from . . . I began my search at Mr. Mysak's, the Prague baker, whose huge shop you will know. There is an ice machine, a sugar mill, a coffee mill, an ice cream machine, a fantastical cellar with huge, modern machines . . . And then there is the Cake Hall . . . A shop assistant serves the most wonderful things— preserves and creams, chocolates, nuts and fruits preserved in sugar, and more cakes. Some are cheerful, with cherries and almonds; others are melancholy, with chocolate buttons or little biscuits. One cake has an 'avant-garde' look, with constructivist chocolate-covered chestnuts, and a red rose in the middle!"

GOOD SOLDIERING Jaroslav Hasek's comic creation, the Good Soldier Svejk, makes his way through the trials and absurdities of life in the former Austro-Hungarian army in this illustration for the four-novel sequence, published between 1920 and 1923.

modern industry was located in its suburbs; the city itself had changed little in the 20th century, and its shape dictated a lifestyle that dated from earlier times.

Like Paris, it was a city of hard-working small craftsmen. For many of its inhabitants the day started early and ended at 2 pm. In the afternoons the men dropped into the *kavarnas* or coffee rooms to linger over conversation or the newspapers. The *kavarnas* were like clubs, each with a recognized clientele: of medical men, say, or lawyers, or supporters of a particular political party. In the evenings they provided music, often played by gypsy musicians. Much of Prague's social and intellectual life was conducted in these coffee rooms or in wine cellars and beer cellars (Prague's beer was famous even then), some of which dated back several centuries. Its cobbled, winding streets tended to be unfriendly to the automobile, and although it had electric tram cars, its cabs were still horse-drawn; several of the city's drinking places had outside bars where the cabmen could consume something warming, distilled from the peach or the plum, on cold winter nights.

When countrymen came in, they wore sheepskin hats, sheepskin jerkins and gartered felt leggings sewn on in the autumn and not removed until spring. The city had a thriving Jewish community—boasting one of the oldest synagogues in Europe—among whom the older men wore beaver hats and coats reaching to their ankles.

Prague in the 1920s was a rich cultural center. The composer Leos Janácek worked there until his death in 1928, and the city was home to both Cubist and Surrealist artists. Among its many writers, two would become world-famous. Jaroslav Hasek, a Bohemian in both senses of the word, who had fought with the Bolsheviks in the Russian Civil War, was writing *The Good Soldier Svejk*. Svejk (or Schweik in German) would come to represent the Czech people as Cervantes's Don Quixote stood for the Spanish—except

ALIEN VISION Franz Kafka created some of the most disturbing symbolic works of the 20th century, including *The Castle*, *The Trial* and *Metamorphosis* (in which the central character wakes up as a giant cockroach).

that Svejk, with his antiheroic qualities, was closer in character to Don Quixote's attendant, Sancho Panza, than to the Don himself. Hasek was writing in Czech; the Jewish author, Franz Kafka, earning his living in the insurance business when he was not disabled by tuberculosis, was writing in German. Two of his novels, *The Trial* and *The Castle*, published after he died in 1924, would come to be seen as representing the anxiety and sense of alienation of 20th-century man. *The Castle* was thought to have its location in Hradcany Castle, which loomed over Prague.

In many ways the two novelists represented complementary aspects of their country. Svejk, a simple man obliged to fight for the Austro-Hungarian army during the First World War, represented its past, and its hopes for an independent existence. Kafka's antiheroes, facing an implacable but faceless enemy, represented what was to be the country's future for many years.

A NEW ORDER IN THE ARTS

IN PAINTING, MUSIC AND ARCHITECTURE, THE MOST CREATIVE MINDS OF THE 1920S AND 30S WERE ENGAGED IN MAKING A NEW KIND OF ART

TIME WATCH Combining a metronome with a photograph of a human eye, this piece was titled *Indestructible Object* by its creator, the Surrealist photographer Man Ray.

The 1920s were a decade of self-conscious modernism, and nowhere more so than in defeated Germany and revolutionary Russia. In both countries there was a passionate, even violent rejection of the bourgeois values and comfortable aesthetics of the previous regime. In Russia, for a handful of years, avant-garde artists and architects attempted a revolution as extreme as the one that had taken place in the political world. As it turned out, their ideas were not to the taste of the apparatchiks of the new order, and by the end of the 1920s their experimentalism had given way to the rigidities of Socialist Realism.

The United States, in other respects the most advanced country in the world, was relatively conservative in aesthetic matters. American newspapers were virulent in their mockery of modernism in music and art. Britain also lagged well behind, and France yielded to Germany its leading role as a sympathetic home for the avant-garde. It was as if the victor nations were content to dust off their old institutions and attempt to return to things as they were before, while others, devastated and traumatized by defeat and revolution, were ready to turn their backs on the past, return to first principles and embrace the new almost as a form of therapy.

At the same time, the artistic revolution that had started before the war continued.

In part, at least, this was a reaction to the stalemate reached at the end of the 19th century when photography began to overtake painting as the logical means of portraying three-dimensional reality. In Cubism the Spaniard Pablo Picasso and the Frenchman Georges Braque set out to depict the essential, almost geometrical forms that underlie perceived reality. They still started from external subject matter—landscape, still life and portrait—but their work and that of other similar artists represented a fundamental rethinking of what painting was about. Before long this led to the notion that no external reference was necessary—that a painting's subject could simply be itself, just as a piece of music refers to nothing but itself. It led, in other words, to pure abstraction.

Another reaction to the challenge of photography was to take representation into a realm that painting could reach more readily than photographs—the realm of the unconscious and the irrational. This was Surrealism, practiced by artists such as Salvador Dali and Joan Miró and in many ways the dominant movement of the 1920s. It grew out of Dadaism. But whereas Dada was a negative, nihilistic movement, a revolt against rationality, especially popular in postwar Germany, Surrealism was more positive. It set out to explore the world of dream and

SURREAL FANTASY The Catalan artist Joan Miró painted *Dialogue of Insects* in 1924-5, shortly after his "conversion" to Surrealism. His work during the 1920s shows an exuberant joy in the freedom from strict representation.

WHAT'S SO FUNNY, FAT-HEAD?

The Dadaists took delight in shocking the public. In his memoirs, the artist George Grosz recalled some of the exploits of the Berlin Dadaists in the 1920s:

"We held Dadaist meetings, charged a few marks admission and did nothing but tell people the truth, that is, abuse them. We never minced our words, and would say things like: 'You . . . the one with the umbrella, you silly ass!' or: 'What's so funny, fathead?' If anyone answered back . . . we would bawl: 'Shut your trap or you'll get a kick up your arse!' And so it went on . . .

"The news spread quickly and soon our meetings . . . were sold out, crammed with people wanting to be scandalized or just after fun . . .

"There had never been anything like Dada before. It was the art (or the philosophy) of the dustbin. A leader of the 'school' was a certain Schwitters from Hanover, who walked about collecting anything he could find on rubbish dumps . . . rusty nails, old rags, toothbrushes without bristles, cigar boxes, old bicycle spokes, broken umbrellas. All the useless things people had thrown away were piled up on old planks, stuck on to canvas or tied on with wire or string, and then exhibited as so-called 'Merz collages' and even sold. Many critics, who wanted to be 'in' at all costs, praised this send-up of the public and were completely taken in by it. Only ordinary people, who know nothing about art, reacted normally, calling Dada art garbage, rubbish and muck—which was exactly what it was."

fantasy, uniting the unconscious with the conscious in what André Breton, one of its founders, called "an absolute reality, a surreality." The Surrealists had a group exhibition in Paris in 1925, but the movement was also international, with important centers in Berlin and Prague. The major painters, apart from Miró and Dali, included Jean Arp, Paul Delvaux, Max Ernst, Paul Klee, René Magritte and Yves Tanguy. All were highly individual artists but, broadly speaking, their work fell into two types. On the one hand, there were works by painters such as Miró and Ernst that presented indeterminate but highly suggestive shapes that the viewer could interpret or complete in his or her own mind; on the other hand were pictures by Delvaux, Magritte or Dali that depicted, in a realistic, carefully detailed way, scenes or situations that made no sense—or only the sense that we understand in dreams—and were full of ambiguity and paradox.

AMERICAN REALISM A man or woman isolated in an urban landscape is a theme that appears again and again in Edward Hopper's work, though he also manages to instill beauty into such scenes, as here in *Automat*.

PRECISIONISM Charles Demuth painted the American landscape in a cool, unemotional style—he and his colleagues were also known as the "Immaculates." He called this painting of grain elevators *My Egypt*.

The Surrealists did not limit themselves to painting. There were Surrealist poets, such as André Breton and Paul Eluard; the movement also extended into photography and the movies, as in the films of the Spaniard Luis Buñuel.

Art in America

Another response to the new was to preserve a basically realistic technique but to apply it to subject matter that earlier art had tended to ignore, especially to an unsentimental view of low-life urban existence. This movement was particularly strong in the United States, where it produced the Ashcan School of realist painters. Among them were George Bellows, who depicted prize fighters, and Edward Hopper, whose work expressed better than anyone's the sense of urban alienation. Another American movement was Precisionism, which took as its subject matter the modern industrial landscape and treated it in a cool, careful style reminiscent of precision engineering. Charles Demuth was its leading exponent.

American modernist art suffered from an almost total lack of public support and patronage; rich collectors such as Peggy Guggenheim

1900

1919 Bauhaus founded

1921 Picasso's painting *Three Musicians*

1922 T.S. Eliot's *The Waste Land*; James Joyce's *Ulysses*

1923 Scott Fitzgerald's *Tales of the Jazz Age*

1924 Thomas Mann's *The Magic Mountain*

1925 Virginia Woolf's *Mrs. Dalloway*

1928 Evelyn Waugh's *Decline and Fall*

1929 Remarque's *All Quiet on the Western Front*

SKYSCRAPER CONTEST There were 260 entries from 23 countries for the 1922 competition to design the Chicago Tribune Building. One of the rejected entries was Adolf Loos' vast Doric column (above left). In the end, the judges favored John Mead Howells and Raymond M. Hood's design (above right).

bought modernist works—but French ones. Yet the United States had a vigorous artistic culture, with its own Cubists and Surrealists, producing works—by Stuart Davis, Patrick Henry Bruce and Henry Dove, for example —that would still look fresh 50 years later. The photographer Alfred Stieglitz, who had almost single-handedly won recognition for photography as an art, also led the way in introducing modernist ideas to the United States through his Gallery 291 in New York. But even he struggled to maintain any kind of public interest in his protégés, who included his wife, Georgia O'Keeffe.

As a photographer, Stieglitz's subject matter was the astonishing urban landscape being created by the skyscraper, itself an American art form. Since the 1890s, clusters of giant buildings had been shooting up in the centers of nearly all the larger cities, especially Chicago and New York. Innovative though the skyscrapers were in their engineering, they were still decorated in the 19th-century manner. The new ideas about style reflecting function that were emerging, chiefly in Europe, made little impact. In a competition in 1922 for the Chicago Tribune Building the startling functional design of the Finnish architect Eliel Saarinen came second to one by Raymond Hood and John Mead Howells that treated it as a neo-Gothic cathedral. Architects such as Louis Sullivan and Frank Lloyd Wright protested at the decision, but it was only in the 1930s, as emigré designers and architects from Hitler's Germany arrived in North America, that modernism gained a secure foothold there.

Like their counterparts in Europe, American artists in the 1920s and 30s were in pursuit of the new. But they had an additional aspiration: to break free of the cultural

PICASSO, TOWERING GENIUS

The man who would dominate the art world through much of the 20th century was born in Málaga in Spain in 1881. Showing extraordinary precocity as an artist, he was admitted to art school in Barcelona at the age of 15 and had settled in Paris by 1904.

In the early 1900s he went through his Blue and Pink periods, named from their dominating hues. In 1907 he completed *Les Demoiselles d'Avignon*, the first Cubist painting and one of the most revolutionary art works of all time. With his friend Georges Braque, he spent the next few years developing Cubism. In the mid 1920s he came under the influence of Surrealism, and although never a surrealist himself, an element of symbolism entered his work. Central to this are the figures of the bull and the minotaur, which appear in *Guernica*, painted as a memorial to the Basque city destroyed by Hitler's bombers in 1937 during the Spanish Civil War.

Picasso stayed in France during the German occupation in the Second World War, but was unable to show his work and experienced severe poverty. After the Liberation he joined the Communist Party. From then on he lived mainly in the South of France, working in sculpture and pottery as well as painting, drawing and print-making. His art constantly developed, expressing at times political commitment, at times existential despair, at times sheer playfulness. At his death in 1973 he left more than 20,000 works.

"GUERNICA" Picasso was already at work on this huge symbolic canvas when he heard of the bombing of the Basque city.

1930
W.H. Auden's
Poems

1932 Aldous
Huxley's *Brave
New World*

1933 George Orwell's
*Down and Out in
Paris and London*

1935 Jazz
music banned
in Germany

1937 Picasso's
Guernica

1939 John
Steinbeck's *The
Grapes of Wrath*

house should look like a machine for living in, and not a Tudor cottage; an electric lamp that was well designed for its purpose could look beautiful—it did not need to look like a piece of ecclesiastical furniture.

These ideas were not particularly popular —people liked the comforting associations of the old-fashioned styles, and the new designs seemed cold and austere. At the government level, however, among the social democratic regimes of Europe, in particular, they got a better reception. One of the first acts of Germany's new Weimar Republic was to establish the school of applied art, architecture and design known as the Bauhaus or

dominance of Europe. In music they had considerable success. The development of jazz reversed the direction of cultural exchange across the Atlantic and was a major influence on "serious" European composers such as Ravel and Stravinsky. American music-lovers were discovering the glories of their folk music, in particular the Negro spiritual. They were developing a sophisticated style of popular song and musical comedy that was self-confidently and distinctively American rather than an imitation of Viennese operetta. In George Gershwin, they had a composer who seemed to bridge the gap between jazz and classical music and who was earning international recognition.

In the years after 1933 the government moved into the arts in the United States. As part of its public spending program, the Roosevelt administration set up the Federal Arts Project, which paid artists to create murals depicting everyday life on public buildings in over 1,000 American cities.

The Bauhaus and the new architecture

The tide of revolution had also engulfed architecture and design. Now that concrete, iron-frame construction and industrial production techniques were replacing the stone carver and the handcraftsman, architects and designers believed that there should be a new machine aesthetic, one in which form reflected function. A factory should look like a factory and not like a medieval guildhall; a

A DESIGN REVOLUTION The Bauhaus design school pursued clean, uncluttered lines and applied its principle of form following function to everything from buildings to table lamps to typography. The geometric wooden interior above is Walter Gropius's Treppenhaus, which was commissioned by a Berlin building contractor, Adolf Sommerfeld. It was built in 1921-2 using teak rescued from a wrecked battleship.

DIEGO RIVERA: MEXICAN GENIUS

North Americans discovered the Mexican painter Diego Rivera in 1932 when he had a show at New York's Museum of Modern Art. Earlier he had travelled in Europe and lived for a while in Paris, where he came under the influence of the Cubists and the primitivism of Henri "Le Douanier" Rousseau. By the 1920s he had developed a distinctive style, combining modernism with the brilliant palette of native Mexican painting. In his homeland he was commissioned by the government to produce frescoes with a propagandist message for public buildings such as the Ministry of Education, where his *Ballad of the Proletarian Revolution* appeared in 1928.

"MAKING TORTILLAS" 1927 Rivera combined Mexican folk art and scenes of everyday life with a strong political message.

EXILE IN CHICAGO The Nazis hated the Bauhaus and all it stood for. Walter Gropius (on the left, beside the pointing figure) was one of many designers and artists who left Germany in the 1930s, taking their ideas with them.

"House of Building." Its first director was Walter Gropius, who had been developing his own functional, geometrical style of architecture since before the Great War. The school was originally set up in Weimar, but later moved to new buildings in Dessau designed by Gropius. Its teaching covered carpentry, ceramics, metalwork, textiles, graphic design and typography. Each subject had two teachers, one a practical artisan, the other an artist, the idea being that the synthesis of the two would produce the best possible design for practical production by machine methods.

Apart from Gropius, the school attracted as teachers artists who subsequently became famous names in the history of modern art and design, including Paul Klee, Wassily Kandinsky, Laszlo Moholy-Nagy, Lyonel Feininger and Marcel Breuer. It produced designs for furniture, tableware, fabrics, advertising posters, all with a distinctive Bauhaus stamp.

The ideas behind the new, functional style seeped through gradually. In Germany in the early 1920s they were temporarily displaced by the style known as Expressionism, exemplified by Fritz Hoeger's Chilehaus in Hamburg and by Erich Mendelsohn's Einsteinturm in Potsdam, buildings that looked almost like sculptures. By 1925, however, the functional style had been accepted throughout central Europe for almost every kind of building. In France it was adopted by a group of architects led by Le Corbusier —but he had only a small clientele. It made some progress in Soviet Russia until rejected by the Stalinists. In Britain and the United

Following the New York show he was asked to paint murals for the Detroit Institute of Arts, one of which, entitled *Vaccination*, was denounced as blasphemous because it looked like a caricature of the Holy Family. In 1933, he was commissioned to produce a giant mural, *Man at the Crossroads*, for Rockefeller Center in New York. There was a public outcry when it was found that Rivera, a Marxist, had introduced a figure of Lenin into the work. The mural was left unfinished and eventually remounted in Mexico City. With its message of protest against injustice, Rivera's work had a strong influence on the painters of the Federal Art Project, part of Franklin Roosevelt's WPA or Works Progress Administration.

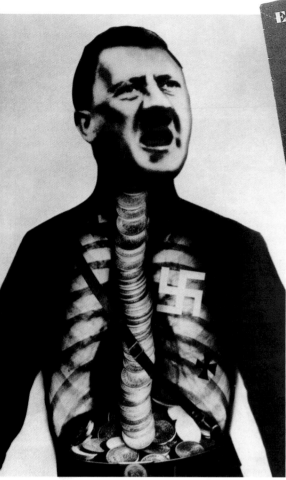

ANTI-ART OR ANTI-NAZI Above, a catalogue for the 1937 Nazi exhibition of "Degenerate Art," which denounced the modernism they hated. The German Dada satirist John Heartfield used photomontage for anti-Nazi propaganda (left).

of Socialist Realism applied to all the arts, including music and literature, and those who dared to offend against them risked, at best, deprivation of income and, at worst, imprisonment and death. Thousands of artists, writers and intellectuals, like the poet Osip Mandelstam, died in Stalin's camps; others, like the composer Shostakovitch, lived in constant fear.

For the Nazis, modern art was part of the conspiracy of Jews and Bolsheviks against the traditions of the German *Volk*. In 1937 they mounted an exhibition of "Degenerate Art," which included works by Picasso and Chagall as well as by leading modern German artists, all denounced in a passionate speech by Hitler. German avant-garde artists who had not already left the country now did so or ceased to produce work.

Exhibitions of "Great German Art"—that is, Nazi-approved art—were shown regularly.

States, it made virtually no progress at all until the early 1930s; after the first refugees from Nazi Germany began to arrive, it began to be widely adopted for public and commercial buildings, though only rarely for domestic ones. These emigrés included Walter Gropius himself and others such as Marcel Breuer and Erich Mendelsohn, all fleeing a regime that was determined to turn back the architectural clock.

Art and the dictators

It was ironic that Hitler, who loathed modernism, played a major part in spreading it around the world. In his efforts to drive it out of Germany he followed a course already taken by Stalin's henchmen in the Soviet Union. For them, avant-garde art was a bourgeois aberration, elitist and neurotic; art should serve the people by offering positive representations of the heroic achievements of workers and peasants under socialism in a manner comprehensible to all. The canons

TOTALITARIAN ARCHITECTURE A huge statue of Lenin surmounts Moscow's Palace of the Soviets, built in the 1930s. Nazis and Stalinists had remarkably similar ideas about what made good art and architecture.

DARK REVELATIONS D.H. Lawrence shocked many of his contemporaries with his frank depictions of sex and the passions. *The Plumed Serpent* (1926), which is set in Mexico where he travelled for some years, includes a human blood-drinking scene.

This favored scenes of peasants and industrial workers as its subject matter, and placed a great emphasis on the family, with the roles of the sexes clearly differentiated. It also added to the repertoire celebrations of athleticism and militarism and portraits of the Führer. Hitler patronized the crude neoclassicism of sculptors such as Arno Breker and the grandiose projects of his favorite architect, Albert Speer, who designed much of the pageantry of Nazi ceremonials.

In the end, the art of communist Russia and Nazi Germany in the 1930s was curiously similar. The subject matter might differ to some extent, but the manner was much the same, reflecting the essentially bourgeois and peasant tastes of the men who had taken control in both countries.

Literature between the wars

Probably the most internationally successful novel of the 1920s was about the Great War: Erich Maria Remarque's *Im Westen nichts Neues* (*All Quiet on the Western Front*). Although written from the German point of view, its antiwar sentiment could be shared by all. It was first published in Germany in January 1929 and had sold almost a million copies of the German edition by the end of the year, as well as another million in the British, American and French editions.

Comparable literary stardom was enjoyed in the United States by the young F. Scott Fitzgerald, whose novel *This Side of Paradise* was published in 1920. Along with *The Beautiful and Damned* (1921) and *The Great Gatsby* (1925), it came to symbolize the generation who had been born with the century —their frantic pursuit of happiness and their underlying despair. In Britain, Aldous Huxley, Virginia Woolf, D.H. Lawrence and Evelyn Waugh were producing novels of an entirely new kind which, in the case of Huxley and Waugh, at least, were almost immediately recognized as representative of their times.

The 1920s were an age of literary experiment which produced in one year—1922— James Joyce's *Ulysses* and T.S. Eliot's *The Waste Land*, both representing a break with the literary forms of the past. The period's anxieties were also expressed in major European works such as Thomas Mann's *The Magic Mountain* (1924), Jules Romains' 27-volume novel sequence *Men of Good Will* and the novels of André Gide. All conveyed the sense that Western society was in crisis, searching for new values and new ways of expressing them.

Social consciousness was more prominent among the writers of the 1930s. In the United States, Sinclair Lewis had blazed the trail in the previous decade with novels such as *Main Street*, *Babbitt*, and *Elmer Gantry*, portraying small-town life in the Midwest; he won the Nobel prize for literature in 1930. John Dos Passos in his *U.S.A.* trilogy (1930-6) chronicled his sense of the hollowness and wastefulness of the pre-Depression years; the novels of William Faulkner took as their material the perplexities of the American South. In Britain, social consciousness turned to political commitment for writers such as George Orwell, one of many who fought in the Spanish Civil War (1936-9), and the poet W.H. Auden. By contrast, the circle of writers and intellectuals around Virginia Woolf, known as the Bloomsbury Group, seemed to be strangely aloof from the concerns of the masses. Though leftist in sympathies, they maintained an almost Edwardian cultivation of the individual sensibility.

IRISH GENIUS James Joyce with his publisher Sylvia Beach, who published his *Ulysses* in Paris on February 2, 1922, Joyce's 40th birthday. It was banned as obscene in both Britain and the United States.

FREEDOMS AND FASHIONS

**IN THE 1920s WOMEN WORE BOYISH CLOTHES THAT REFLECTED THEIR NEW-FOUND
FREEDOMS, BUT BY THE 1930s THEY WERE REVERTING TO A MORE "FEMININE" LOOK**

In the 1920s young women in the Western world wrought an extraordinary change in their appearance, probably the most dramatic since the French Revolution. Before the Great War women had worn their hair long and elaborately dressed; in the 1920s they had it cut short in a "bob" or even cropped like a boy's. Prewar women cultivated a voluptuously curved look, their waists nipped in and their bosoms thrust out by elaborate corsetry; postwar women dispensed with corsets, tried to make their figures as boyish-looking as possible, and wore their skirts shorter and shorter until, in 1926, they barely covered the knees. Prewar women had worn several layers of clothing; fashionable women could scarcely dress themselves without assistance. Young women in the 1920s dressed so skimpily, especially in the evenings, that textile manufacturers, as well as moralists, became gravely worried. Increasingly, too, they were wearing lipstick and make-up, something that only disreputable women had done before the war.

These changes reflected an equally dramatic change in their status. By the early 1920s, women through much of the Western world had been granted the vote and the right to serve on juries. This reflected the contribution that many thousands of women had made to the war effort by taking jobs previously done only by men. In the postwar years many of these jobs—in engineering, transport and printing, for example—reverted to men, but the experience of working outside the home had changed women's expectations. The enormous increase in business activity also meant that employers now depended on women for secretarial and clerical work; trained typists and stenographers were greatly in demand. Many thousands of women were employed as teachers; thousands of others were finding work in the retail trade and in the newer light industries. The universities and professions were being opened to them, and the numbers of women doctors and lawyers sharply increased.

The most liberated young women of the 1920s were known as "flappers." Although they had short haircuts and slim, boyish figures that went with the clothes of the period, it was the youthfulness of the flapper look that was perhaps most important. The male contemporaries of the flappers were young men who had survived the war. They were weary and disillusioned; they had seen their friends die, and had known fear. But despite the horrors that had made them grow up beyond their years, in most cases they had little or no experience of women. Consciously or unconsciously, the flappers offered a femininity that was unthreatening, a period of light-hearted fun before the responsibilities of marriage. They were also asserting their own independence, their right to enjoy the company of men without falling into the subservience of the Victorian marriage.

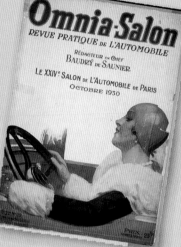

AT THE WHEEL A French motoring magazine of 1930 invites independent young women to enjoy the freedom of the roads.

The manners of the flappers shocked conservatives. They used slang, and even cursed freely. They smoked in public, and appeared to drink heavily. They danced very close to their partners. And they were, or at least they made a show of being, much more relaxed in their sexual morals than their Edwardian forebears had been. Sexual manners and morals among young middle- and upper-class people were certainly freer in the 1920s. But perhaps they were also simply more honest than in the period when "to be found out was the greatest sin."

Fashions changed in the 1930s.

Hemlines dropped in 1929 and the flapper look gave way to clothes that drew attention to the curves of the mature female body; waists and bosoms were back, emphasized by rubber girdles and uplift brassieres of American design. Clothes were more modest but also more elaborate and more glamorous; a day dress that required 2 yards of material in the 1920s needed 5 yards by 1938. The Depression and the desire to compensate for the grimness of the times helped to explain the change. Also, the women who influenced fashion had grown a decade older.

In manners and morals there was a similar change. The pendulum that had swung so sharply away from Victorian values and led to world-weary cynicism and talk of "free love" now began to swing back, not to the old puritanism, but toward a romantic view of life, a celebration of the difference between the sexes, and a renewed appreciation of marriage and family life. As hemlines fell, so did the divorce rate.

HIGH FASHION AT THE RACES Philadelphia heiress Frances Munn photographed at the Belmont Park races in November 1936. By now, women's fashion was assuming more flowing lines.

THE ENTERTAINERS

WITH THE GROWTH OF MOVIES, RADIO AND POPULAR DANCE MUSIC, THIS WAS A GOLDEN NEW AGE OF MASS ENTERTAINMENT

On the evening of October 31, 1938, listeners to CBS radio throughout the northeastern United States heard disturbing reports. Punctuating what seemed to be a normal dance music program, these told of a mysterious meteorite shower heading toward Earth from the direction of the planet Mars. As the evening wore on, the reports became more numerous and more detailed. The meteorites were spacecraft from Mars; they had landed at several places in New Jersey and were disgorging an invasion army of hideous creatures equipped with death rays. By this time, much of the area between Boston and Philadelphia was in the grip of panic; telephone lines were choked and traffic jams built up in Jersey City and New York as the inhabitants tried to flee westward.

The police descended on CBS and discovered the culprits: Orson Welles, John Houseman and their Mercury Theater Company were staging an avant-garde production of *The War of the Worlds*, a science fiction fantasy by the popular English author H.G. Wells.

POWER OF THE UNSEEN Orson Welles demonstrated the power of radio—and of the human imagination—one Halloween night in 1938, and with it the potential of the new medium to entertain the public.

The War of the Worlds broadcast revealed the extraordinary power of radio by the late 1930s. Indeed, the rise of broadcasting had been as dramatic and influential as the rise of movies. In 1922 radio sales in the United States had amounted to $60 million; by 1929 the figure was over $800 million. By 1939 there were over 40 million sets, and 90 percent of Americans were listening in.

Europe lagged behind somewhat. Even so, in Britain, within the space of two weeks in November 1922, more than a million people bought licenses that would entitle them to tune in to the new British Broadcasting Company when it started daily transmissions on November 14. Under its general manager, John Reith, the company became a national institution—King George V made the first royal broadcast in 1924—and in 1927 it received a royal charter, becoming the British Broadcasting Corporation: the BBC. The 1930s saw a dramatic increase in the private ownership of radios in Britain, particularly London and the south. By 1939 roughly two-thirds of households in the country had access to a "wireless," which was what the British called radio.

In Germany, meanwhile, Joseph Goebbels pressed ahead with the production of the *Volksempfanger*, a reliable cheap radio, when he became Nazi minister of enlightenment and propaganda in 1933. By 1939 the number of private radio sets in Germany had quadrupled, from over 2 million to nearly 10 million.

In common with other regimes across the world—democratic and anti-democratic alike—not to mention commercial advertisers, the Nazis had spotted radio's potential as a medium for persuasion and the spread of propaganda.

The earliest radio sets had been crude, requiring some skill to tune in, but within a few years crystal sets and headphones gave way to cabinet sets with built-in loudspeakers that formed a prominent feature in the average living room. In the early days the stations offered a diet of news, talks, religious programs, children's programs and music. Before long they had added outside broadcasts, plays and comedy shows.

Radio in the United States, which ran on commercial lines and was supported by advertising, was less high-minded than the BBC—John Reith, who now had the grander title of director-general of the BBC,

THE MANY FACES OF RADIO Radio programs during the 1930s took many forms, from (clockwise from bottom right) Big Band dance music broadcast from the Radioland shell at the Great Lakes Exposition in Cleveland in 1937; the brilliantly acerbic wit of Fred Allen; the chillingly manipulative broadcasts of Nazi Propaganda Minister Joseph Goebbels; to the casual drama of Madame Dussane of the Comédie Française, 1936. Center: a popular push-button model found in many homes.

theless, in the 1930s, it was among the most listened to programs on the radio.

Entertainment for all

The interwar years were the first age of mass entertainment. The radio and the record player brought it into people's homes; movies and spectator sports brought it as public entertainment. These were also, especially for the young, the dancing years. People danced in restaurants and nightclubs and dance halls; they danced at home to the record player. In the 1920s they shocked their elders as they danced the shimmy, the Charleston and the Blackbottom. In the 1930s they reverted to the more sedate rhythms of the foxtrot, the quickstep and the tango. On the stage and later on screen, the debonair Fred Astaire and his different partners, most famously Ginger Rogers, showed them how to dance with elegance and grace. In the late 1930s young Americans were provoking their elders again with the jitterbug, though it would take another war to bring that craze to Europe.

Latin American rhythms had already been popular before the Great War and remained so throughout the 1920s and 30s. But the favorite beat of the times was the beat of

insisted that announcers should wear formal dress in the evenings, even though their audience could not see them.

On commercial American stations morning and afternoon schedules were largely given over to "soap operas," serials mainly sponsored by soap manufacturers. In the early evening there were adventure serials for the young, often based on favorite cartoon strip characters such as Buck Rogers, Dick Tracy, Little Orphan Annie and Superman; the Lone Ranger also figured largely. Later in the evening there were family comedy shows, featuring performers such as Jack Benny and George Burns and Gracie Allen. One of the most popular was *Amos 'n' Andy*, a situation comedy featuring two black characters played by white actors that perpetuated black stereotypes and could today be considered distasteful. Never-

1922 British Broadcasting Company formed; *Reader's Digest* founded

1923 *Time* magazine founded; *Radio Times* first published

1925 Josephine Baker makes her Paris debut

1926 Romberg's operetta, *The Desert Song*

1927 Jerome Kern's musical, *Show Boat*, first performed

1929 Cartoon characters Popeye and Tintin appear for first time

FACE TO FACE, BACK TO BACK Radio listeners enjoyed the home-spun sparring of Fibber Mcgee and Molly (Jim and Marian Jordan). Below: German dancers demonstrate the Blackbottom.

jazz. In the early years of the 20th century New Orleans jazz was spreading throughout all of North America as black workers, including musicians, moved from the South to the North and from the country to major cities such as Chicago, New York and Kansas City, in search of work. American soldiers in the First World War had helped to introduce the new music to Europe, and as soon as the war was over American bandsmen were finding engagements in all the European cities. British and Continental dance bands, already familiar with ragtime, were soon playing jazz, while often giving it a distinctively British or French or German stamp.

In America, one of the black musicians who made the journey north was Joe "King" Oliver, who moved from New Orleans to Chicago in 1918. In 1922, by now a successful bandleader, he sent to New Orleans for a young jazz trumpeter he had worked with there, Louis Armstrong. Within a few years Armstrong was making classic recordings with his groups, the Hot Five and the Hot Seven. With his extraordinary talent and attractive personality, he was a Broadway star and a national and international figure, whose fame helped enormously to spread the popularity of jazz.

Thanks to Armstrong, Chicago became the new center of jazz, and it was there that the basic style was established—beginning and ending with ensemble playing, with solo variations by trumpet, clarinet and trombone in between. While jazz continued to be dominated by blacks, in Chicago white musicians rapidly took it up, among them three of the greatest: the cornetist and pianist Bix Beiderbecke, the trombonist Jack Teagarden and the clarinetist Benny Goodman.

In the 1930s the tight syncopations of traditional jazz gave way to the looser, swinging rhythm that became known as "swing." This was usually arranged for big commercial dance bands with large brass sections, in which the saxophone came into its own. The outstanding bandleaders of the swing era

KINGS OF JAZZ Joe "King" Oliver (third from the right) poses with his band in 1920s Chicago. Louis Armstrong is on his right. The clarinetist is Johnny Dodds, another jazz legend.

1931 Pearl S. Buck's novel, *The Good Earth*

1936 Margaret Mitchell's *Gone with the Wind*

1938 Orson Welles's *War of the Worlds* broadcast

1939 Ivor Novello's musical, *The Dancing Years*

were Benny Goodman, Tommy Dorsey, Artie Shaw, Gene Krupa, Count Basie, Duke Ellington and Glenn Miller. Most of the bands featured vocalists and in the 1930s these were increasingly singing in the soft, sentimental style known as "crooning." The first successful crooner was Rudy Vallee, succeeded by Bing Crosby and, at the end of the decade, the young Frank Sinatra.

Jazz was one of the factors that led to U.S. dominance of the commercial popular music industry, based on sales of sheet music and records. Tin Pan Alley—from the slang "tin pan" for anything noisy or tinny—had been an American term for both the popular music industry and the district of any city where it was based since the mid–19th century. By the 1920s Tin Pan Alley, in other words American popular music, was firmly established as a world leader.

Popular song

The countries of Europe, meanwhile, held on to their own popular musical traditions. Paris and Berlin had their cabaret songs, witty, sardonic or sentimental. The French and German-Austrian light opera and operetta tradition continued to thrive. Although the Parisians loved jazz, their favorite stars were still singers such as Yvette Guilbert, Mistinguett and Maurice Chevalier.

The European operetta tradition also took root in the United States thanks to two highly successful immigrants: Rudolf Friml, born in Prague, and the Hungarian

A TUNE FOR CROONING Yale-educated Rudy Vallee developed the singing style known as "crooning" with his band the Connecticut Yankees. His successors included future megastars Bing Crosby and Frank Sinatra.

JOSEPHINE BAKER: J'AI DEUX AMOURS

The African-American woman who became the toast of France was born, illegitimate, in St. Louis, in 1906. By 1923 she was working on Broadway and at the Plantation Club in Harlem. In 1925 she went to Paris with the *Revue Nègre*; later that year she starred at the Théâtre des Champs-Elysées and caused a sensation when she appeared as a solo act wearing only a bunch of bananas as a skirt.

Although she performed near-naked in those years—her hair straightened and lacquered into a black cap with a curl on her forehead—it was not her eroticism that appealed as her grace and humor. She would turn her knees inwards, make her eyes cross, and the audience would convulse in laughter. She took up an old song, "*J'ai deux amours, mon pays et Paris*" ("I have two loves, my own country and Paris") and it became her signature tune. She became wealthy, and enjoyed her wealth, strolling along the Champs-Elysées with a pet leopard.

She made a return visit to the U. S. in 1936, but her mix of sexuality and humor was not appreciated in her native country. In 1937 she was naturalized as a French citizen. During the Occupation she worked for the Red Cross. After the war she devoted much of her time to her estate in southwestern France, which she made a home for adopted children of all nationalities, her "rainbow family." She died, much loved and much honored, in 1975.

THE TOAST OF FRANCE Josephine Baker, here shown wearing more than usual for a performance. She fell in love with Paris, and Paris with her. She eventually would become a French citizen.

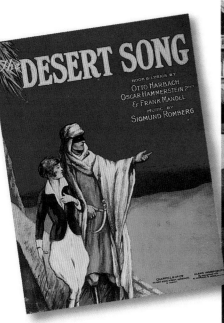

LIGHT OPERETTA *The White Horse Inn* (above right) typified the German tradition of operetta. Hungarian-born Sigmund Romberg helped to introduce it to English-speaking audiences with Broadway hits such as *The Desert Song*.

Sigmund Romberg. These two produced some of the greatest hits of the 1920s: Friml's *Rose Marie* (1924) and *The Vagabond King* (1925), and Romberg's *The Student Prince* (1924) and *The Desert Song* (1926). In Britain the same tradition produced the musicals of Ivor Novello, notably *Glamorous Nights* (1935), *Careless Rapture* (1936) and *The Dancing Years* (1939).

In the 1920s, a distinctive kind of musical show, the "musical," had begun to emerge. Two of its early successes were George Gershwin's *Lady be Good* (1924) and Jerome Kern's *Show Boat* (1927). In the 1930s Irving Berlin, Cole Porter, Richard Rodgers and Lorenz Hart were producing the musicals of a golden age. Numbers from their shows became many of the most popular songs of the period and some of the most enduring songs of all time, not just in North America but in Britain and beyond. The year 1928 alone produced "When Day is Done," "My Blue Heaven" and "Ol' Man River."

Words and pictures
Popular newspapers and magazines were part of the entertainment industry. In Britain, in particular, there was a huge increase in the circulation of popular newspapers. In 1930

five British dailies had circulations of over a million; by 1937 two Sunday papers, *The People* and the *News of the World*, were selling well over 3 million. In the United States, the first tabloid, the *New York Daily News*, founded in 1919, soon had the largest circulation of all the country's newspapers.

Newspapers carried more and more illustrations. American Sunday papers were accompanied by full-color comic papers in which characters such as Dick Tracey, Li'l Abner, Popeye and Blondie ran year after year. There was nothing like them in Europe until 1929, when the Belgian illustrator

MARION ANDERSON AT THE LINCOLN MEMORIAL

On April 9, 1939, the great American contralto Marion Anderson sang to a crowd of thousands at the Lincoln Memorial in Washington. She was widely regarded as the finest singer of the day—Toscanini told her, "A voice like yours comes but once in a century"—but she was black, and subject to the same humiliations as other black musicians in 1930s America. She had planned to give a concert in Constitution Hall, but it belonged to the Daughters of the American Revolution (DAR), an elite and exclusively white organization of women claiming descent from families who had fought against the British in the War of Independence. They barred her from appearing there. When the president's wife, Eleanor Roosevelt, and the secretary of the interior, Harold Ickes, heard this news, they decided to take action. Mrs. Roosevelt resigned from the DAR, and both she and Ickes took the matter up with the president, who instructed them to give the biggest free concert possible. In the end the audience numbered 75,000 for a program that began with "America" and ended with the spiritual, "Nobody knows the trouble I've seen." At the end, the rush of the crowd toward the great singer threatened to turn into a stampede. Despite this triumph, entrenched racist attitudes would prevent Anderson from making her debut at New York's Metropolitan Opera House until 1955.

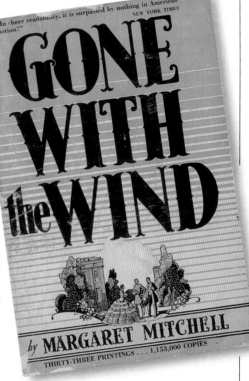

Hergé (Georges Rémi) introduced Tintin and his dog Snowy to the world in the pages of *Le Petit vingtième*, a weekly children's supplement to the Brussels newspaper, *Le Vingtième siècle*.

Photographs and graphic illustrations made an increasing impact in magazines. Women's magazines, such as *Good Housekeeping* in the U.S., *Woman* in Britain and *Marie-Claire*

PULP HERO Dick Tracey was one of several cartoon characters who appeared in the "funnies" of American Sunday newspapers in the 1920s and 30s. There was nothing like them in Europe until Tintin, the Belgian boy detective, arrived in 1929.

in France, flourished, as did specialized magazines devoted to every conceivable interest. Among general-interest periodicals one of the greatest successes was *Reader's Digest*, started in 1922. Another was the weekly news magazine *Time*, founded in 1923. *The New Yorker*, founded in 1925, appealed to America's sophisticates. The first magazine to present news events purely through photographs, *Life*, appeared in the U.S. in 1936. It was followed soon after by *Look*, and the British *Picture Post*.

The motion pictures and radio did not crush the reading habit; book sales quadrupled in the period. Inexpensive paperback books appeared in the late 1930s when the English publisher, Allen Lane, issued his pocket Penguins in 1935. But even if people had to borrow from libraries, reading was still a popular pastime for all.

The 1930s especially were a period when a handful of books in the English-speaking world caught the popular imagination in an unprecedented way and sold in record numbers—the term "bestseller" appeared just before the Great War but came into its own around this time. John Steinbeck's deeply serious novel, *The Grapes of Wrath*, headed the lists in 1939 and

won the Pulitzer prize. It was a bestseller but it was also exceptional among popular fiction in dealing with a recent, painful experience. Most of the fictional successes of the Depression years offered not only superb storytelling but also some kind of escape from contemporary reality. Another Pulitzer Prize winner, Pearl S. Buck's *The Good Earth*, took its readers to China—and helped Buck win the Nobel prize for literature in 1938, as Steinbeck would do later, in 1962. Charles Morgan's *The Fountain* (1932) offered a path from the harshness of contemporary experience to an inward spirituality. Hervey Allen's enormous novel *Anthony Adverse*, the lead seller in 1933 and 1934, offered escape to the past. So, too, did Margaret Mitchell's colossal success, *Gone with the Wind*, which sold a million copies in the first six months after publication in 1936; 70 years after the end of the Civil War, Americans, living in a bleak time, were able to romanticize the charm and glory as well as the hard times of the Old South.

THE MOVIES COME OF AGE

BOTH AS AN ART FORM AND A MASS ENTERTAINMENT MEDIUM, MOVIES WERE TRANSFORMED BY THE COMING OF THE TALKIES IN 1927

By 1919 the motion pictures were no longer a novelty; they were an established form of entertainment, popular with all classes throughout the developed world. Until 1927 films were silent, and when sound was first introduced, there were some who thought it a gimmick that would soon disappear. The art of telling a story in moving pictures, with only occasional text captions or with no text at all, had been brought to a considerable degree of sophistication. Piano accompanists supplied music to underline the dramatic mood of what was happening on the screen. The need to add a dialogue soundtrack was not apparent—rather, in the opinion of serious students of film, it would vulgarize what they saw as an art form.

Moreover, because films were silent, they were international;captions were easily altered to the language of any country in which they were shown. The dominant provider for this international market was the United States, which in the first nine months of 1921 alone exported 112 million feet of film. British film-makers lagged behind and found it hard to sell their productions as distributors bought up scores of American movies in advance, sight unseen; they had no room for the more modest British films of the period. Many fine British actors, such as Ronald Colman and George Arliss, moved to Hollywood as a result.

French films in the 1920s were technically of poor quality, grainy and grey rather than black-and-white, and although France had some much-admired avant-garde directors, French audiences preferred the highly polished American movies. Only a handful of films, notably René Clair's delightful comedy, *The Italian Straw Hat* (1927), suggested the greatness to come a few years later. Even

MASTER OF SUSPENSE Alfred Hitchcock's thriller *Blackmail,* starring Anny Ondra, was the first British feature film with sound, released in 1929.

Abel Gance's extraordinary epic *Napoléon* (1927), which was four hours long and took its hero only to the beginning of his military career, was not a commercial success. It was not until the 1930s that France entered a cinematic "golden age" with such masters as Clair, Jean Renoir and Marcel Carné producing films that delighted audiences at home and abroad. Jean Renoir's *La Grande illusion* (1937) and *La Règle du jeu* (1939) are two of the great masterpieces of the period.

Only Germany came close to challenging the United States as a large-scale international producer of films in the interwar years. (In the 1930s Japan was the biggest film producer in the world, but few of its films were exported.) In the mid 1920s there were nearly 300 German film companies, and unlike any other country Germany exported a considerable number of films to the United States; it was able to offer high-quality productions at very competitive prices. German directors specialized in studio work, shooting many outdoor scenes indoors and making dramatic use of light and shadow. An outstanding example of their

FACE OF HORROR Robert Wiene's 1919 horror film, *The Cabinet of Dr. Caligari,* was the leading example of Expressionism in German cinema, making powerful use of photography's capacity for visual distortion.

ANGEL SHE AIN'T Director Josef von Sternberg's *The Blue Angel* (1930) was the film that shot Marlene Dietrich to stardom. Both Sternberg and Dietrich were immediately signed up by Hollywood.

technique was Robert Wiene's strange masterpiece of 1919, *The Cabinet of Dr. Caligari*; others were F.W. Murnau's version of the Dracula story, *Nosferatu* (1922), and Fritz Lang's futuristic fantasy, *Metropolis* (1926). The German film industry was also capable of producing polished comedies and costume dramas that went down well with American audiences. Later, in the age of the talkies, it was the 1930 German film *The Blue Angel*—with German and English ver-

sions shot simultaneously—that brought Marlene Dietrich to the attention of Hollywood. Under the Nazis the German film industry continued to produce comedies and historical dramas, reserving most of its propaganda activity for the newsreels.

The Russian film industry was wholly state-owned, generously financed and devoted to education and propaganda. It was Soviet directors who developed the technique of "montage," juxtaposing shots to convey meaning and dramatic emotion without words. The greatest exponents were Vsevolod Pudovkin and, above all, Sergei Eisenstein, whose *Battleship Potemkin* appeared in 1925. He adapted well to sound, producing two other masterpieces, *Ivan the Terrible* and *Alexander Nevsky*. Eisenstein's films were devoted to the service of the Soviet state, distorting history and justifying the tyranny of Stalin, but they showed a mastery of the language of cinema that has rarely been surpassed.

Hollywood

The United States had a number of advantages over other countries. It had the capital to finance large-scale film-making, much of it diverted from the liquor business after Prohibition. Its film industry started with a

huge home market. In California it also had the perfect climate for outdoor shooting. With all these benefits behind it, it attracted the best directors, the most photogenic actors and actresses, the best technicians.

American film-making was devoted to box-office success through entertainment, not experiment, but this did not necessarily mean a lowering of standards. American

"THE GOLD RUSH" Cold and hunger are Charlie Chaplin's great foes in this film made in 1925. It is one of Chaplin's masterpieces, and the film he himself wished to be remembered for. In 1942 he reissued it with added soundtrack.

films had a technical polish that European films often lacked, while the best Hollywood directors, themselves European immigrants more often than not, had a well-developed intuition for story lines that would enthrall audiences from China to Peru.

It was Hollywood that produced the film serial, most successfully in *The Mark of Zorro*, with Douglas Fairbanks, and *The Perils of Pauline*, in which Pearl White made thrilling escapes from apparently catastrophic situations. These appealed mainly to the unsophisticated, or youthful, people who went to the movies in their early days. By the 1920s, however, movie audiences embraced all ages and classes, and the movie theaters themselves were growing more comfortable, even luxurious, to appeal to them. There was a demand for more substantial fare. To the basic stock of Westerns and comedy shorts were added more "seri-

GRAND-SCALE CINEMA Cecil B. DeMille's 1923 religious epic, *The Ten Commandments*, was made in response to a newspaper competition for film ideas. A number of scenes were shot on location in Egypt.

1919

1919 Robert Wiene's *The Cabinet of Dr. Caligari*   1921 Valentino's debut in *The Four Horsemen of the Apocalypse*   1922 Robert Flaherty's *Nanook of the North*   1923 Cecil B. DeMille's *The Ten Commandments*   1925 Sergei Eisenstein's *Battleship Potemkin*   1926 Fritz Lang's *Metropolis*   1927 Al Jolson in *The Jazz Singer*

TAKING TO THE TALKIES *The Jazz Singer*, starring Al Jolson, was the first synchronized sound feature film. Thanks largely to Jolson's huge popularity, it was an immediate success when it opened in New York in October 1927 and revived the fortunes of Warner Brothers.

ous" films—biopics such as *Disraeli*, starring George Arliss, or versions of successful novels like *The Four Horsemen of the Apocalypse*, which created the Valentino cult. Cecil B. DeMille made vast Biblical epics, notably *The Ten Commandments* and *King of Kings*, which were, or at least were believed to be, the movie industry's tribute to religious belief. The Austrian-born patrician Erich von Stroheim, the enfant terrible of the day, made films such as *Greed* that were full of elegant sexuality, starring in some of them himself. Robert Flaherty created more or less single-handedly the genre of the documentary with his classic *Nanook of the North*, which portrayed the daily life of a real Inuit fisherman.

Hollywood also produced two film comedians of genius, Charlie Chaplin and Buster Keaton, and two others, Harold Lloyd and Harry Langdon, who at the time equalled them in popularity. Chaplin's *The Gold Rush* (1925) and Keaton's *The Navigator* (1924) and *The General* (1926) are enduring classics. A genius of a different kind was Walt Disney, who made his first animated sound film, starring Mickey Mouse, in 1928 and his feature-length masterpiece, *Snow White and the Seven Dwarfs*, in 1937.

Talking pictures

There had been attempts to marry a synchronized soundtrack to film since the earliest days, but in the 1920s the pace of experiment accelerated and some films had brief sound sequences. The Germans developed a good recording system early on, but because of the country's economic problems could not put it into immediate use. In 1926 Warner Brothers released *Don Juan*, with full-length sound effects and musical score. Although it starred John Barrymore, considered by the studios a big box-office draw, it was seen as no more than an interesting novelty. In April 1927 William Fox launched Fox Movietone News on sound film, again without causing any great excitement.

Then, in October 1927, an almost bankrupt Warner Brothers brought out *The Jazz Singer* with the popular singer Al Jolson in the title role. The film's soundtrack consisted only of a few songs and some snatches of dialogue, but the rapturous reception it received from audiences made it clear that sound, having arrived apparently overnight, had come to stay. Warner Brothers netted a huge profit and followed up with the all-talkie *Lights of New York* in 1928. Their head start in sound made them one of Hollywood's biggest and richest studios, able, for instance,

GARBO: A LEGEND IN HER LIFETIME

One of the greatest of all cinema stars was born Greta Gustafsson in Sweden in 1905. She began her career as a salesgirl in a department store for which she made advertising films. Then in the early 1920s she trained as an actress at the Royal Dramatic Theatre School in Stockholm. There she was discovered by the director Mauritz Stiller, who changed her name to Garbo and put her into the film *Gösta Berlings Saga* (1924). The American producer Louis B. Mayer, talent-spotting in Europe, saw the film and enticed both Stiller and his protégée to Hollywood.

Before long Stiller returned to Sweden. Without him, Garbo was lonely and ill at ease, but Metro-Goldwyn-Mayer, recognizing her star quality, built up her loneliness and sense of isolation into a myth in which she figured as the woman of mystery eternally wanting "to be alone." The studio carefully chose roles for her in which she appeared as the tragic heroine, notably in *Anna Christie* (1930), *Grand Hotel* (1932), *Queen Christina* (1934), *Anna Karenina* (1935) and *Camille* (1936). The soundtrack loved her husky Scandinavian accent, just as the camera adored her ethereal beauty, accentuated by the subtle overhead lighting of which Hollywood had developed complete mastery.

Her comedy film, *Ninotchka* (1939), was a commercial failure, and by the early 1940s she had effectively retired, well provided for as the result of careful investment. She lived quietly, mainly in New York, until her death in 1990, quite literally a legend in her own lifetime.

FACE OF THE THIRTIES Garbo had an extraordinary beauty which bloomed in the intimacy of the close-up. Her famous line, "I want to be alone," was spoken just once, in *Grand Hotel*.

1940

1931 Charlie Chaplin's City Lights | 1933 King Kong | 1934 Frank Capra's It Happened One Night | 1935 Greta Garbo in Anna Karenina | 1937 Walt Disney's Snow White and the Seven Dwarfs | 1939 Gone with the Wind

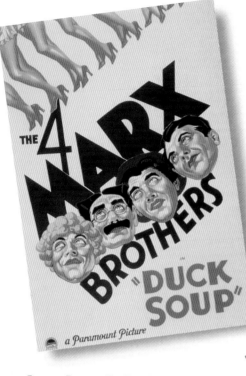

men and women who regularly appeared in them became familiar to tens of millions of people. These were the "stars," who acquired a degree of fame that no one in history had ever enjoyed before. To moviegoers in small-town America, not to mention places much farther afield, they seemed to be godlike creatures, known to live fabulous-

WHAT'S IN A NAME

Name changes were common practice for would-be Hollywood stars of the 1920s and 30s. As far as the studio bosses were concerned, Latin names such as Rudolf Valentino or Carmen Miranda were fine for performers who played exotic roles, but generally they wanted all-American, preferably Anglo-Saxon names, with the occasional French flavor. Thus, Claudette Chauchoin became Claudette Colbert, Ethel Zimmerman became Ethel Merman, Margarita Carmen Cansino became Rita Hayworth and Archie Leach became Cary Grant.

ly glamorous lives in luxurious houses with swimming pools and tennis courts in a heaven-on-earth called Hollywood.

Hollywood made stars, and made sure that press offices spread suitable tales of their off-screen doings—the first fan magazine had been published in 1915. The wedding in 1920 of two of the biggest stars, Douglas Fairbanks and Mary Pickford, seemed the perfect fairy-tale marriage (until they divorced in 1934). On the other hand, Hollywood would have been glad to suppress the squalid story of the film comedian "Fatty" Arbuckle, charged with rape and murder, in 1920.

FUN AND FROLICS The Marx Brothers—Harpo, Groucho, Chico, and Zeppo—were a successful stage act in the 1920s, and started making films after the advent of sound. Their zany antics belied the brilliance of their writers and directors. "Duck Soup," for example, was written and directed by Leo McCarey.

to buy a large share of many of America's premier movie theaters.

Audiences made their preferences clear, choosing talking pictures over silent ones, irrespective of their other merits or lack of them. Warner Brothers' competitors hastily followed their example, borrowing capital to equip their studios and theaters for sound. By 1929 the changeover was virtually complete, and relatively few silent films were made after that date. The film musical, a natural next step and a new genre, rapidly followed, offering lavish spectacles that rivalled anything to be seen on the stage. Technicolor arrived in 1934.

Since American films were seen by audiences all round the world, the faces of the

When stars are born

If potential stars, such as Greta Garbo and Marlene Dietrich, emerged in other countries, Hollywood enticed them over with fabulous salaries. It was stars who sold films and as a result they could command massive earnings. In 1926, the biggest Hollywood stars in order of earnings were Harold Lloyd, Tom Mix, Charlie Chaplin, Douglas Fairbanks,

OH SO CUTE! Born in 1928, Shirley Temple (left) was Twentieth Century-Fox's biggest asset until she retired from child roles at the age of 12. Below: Fred Astaire and Ginger Rogers, dancing partners throughout the 1930s, go through their paces in the 1935 classic, *Top Hat*.

A NATION'S SWEETHEART The daughter of a stallholder in London's Berwick Street market, singer and dancer Jessie Matthews started her career on the stage. In the 1930s she became a great favorite in British film musicals, such as *The Good Companions* and *Evergreen*.

John Barrymore, Mary Pickford, Buster Keaton, Lilian Gish, Gloria Swanson, Norma Talmadge, Colleen Moore, Adolphe Menjou and Reginald Denny—Rudolf Valentino would have been among them but he had died that year. At the top, Harold Lloyd and Tom Mix were making over $400,000 a year (several million in today's values), but Chaplin, Fairbanks and Pickford, who had formed United Artists, were also earning a percentage of profits.

When sound arrived film stars' voices were tested for the first time. There were tales of beautiful actresses who had looked utterly convincing as 18th-century French countesses but who were doomed after 1927 because they could not lose the accents of Brooklyn or West Virginia. In fact, most of the principal stars made the transition with ease. Greta Garbo resisted sound at first, but her husky, Swedish-accented voice was seen as a positive asset. Likewise, voices like Ronald Colman's or Marlene Dietrich's added a new dimension to the stars' sex appeal. Only Chaplin and Keaton, recognizing that their genius lay in the silent movie, remained silent. Chaplin went on making silent films until 1940. Keaton made no more films of his own after 1928.

PERFECT FORMATION Busby Berkeley was famous for his cinematic vision and inventive camerawork. This flower of chorus girls from the film *Gold Diggers of 1933* was typical of his extravagant choreography.

In the era of the talkies there were new stars. One of the biggest was Shirley Temple, who made her debut in 1932; by the time she was six in 1934 she had replaced Mae West at the top of the box office. Mae West had represented blatant sexuality; Shirley Temple was promoted as the model of wholesomeness and innocence. In her very different way, she became the center of a cult almost as big as the one that had grown around Rudolf Valentino in the 1920s.

These were the Depression years, when Hollywood's response was not to confront the issues of the day. Instead, it offered escape from anxious lives into a world of glamor and excitement; cowboys fought "redskins," gangsters died with a snarl on their lips, and the rich danced through life with unrequited love as their only worry. Some of the milestones of this golden age were Chaplin's *City Lights* (1931); *42nd Street*, with choreography by Busby Berkeley (1932); *King Kong* (1933); Frank Capra's romantic comedy *It Happened One Night*, with Clark Gable and Claudette Colbert (1934); *Top Hat*, with Ginger Rogers and Fred Astaire (1935); *Anna Karenina*, starring Greta Garbo (1935); the Marx Brothers' *A Day at the Races* (1937); and the film version of Margaret Mitchell's *Gone with the Wind* (1939).

THE HOLLYWOOD STUDIO

The early silent film studio was a large building divided into three-sided compartments that could be lit and furnished individually for interior shots, with a single camera placed on the open side to photograph the action. In a studio like this, several films could be made simultaneously; since they were silent there was no problem with the sound from one film intruding into that of another. The same interiors, with minor variations in props and furnishings, appeared in countless films. Outside on the studio lot, sets were erected to simulate different kinds of streets for filming exterior shots. They were permanent structures and again appeared, with small variations in paintwork, time after time. All these were good enough for Hollywood's bread-and-butter movies. When, however, directors like Cecil B. DeMille made their multi-reel epics, they moved out of the studios. DeMille filmed parts of *The Ten Commandments* (1923) on location in Egypt.

As budgets grew larger, and films more lavish and sophisticated, studios would be stripped to build a single, large set—a ballroom, for example, or the interior of a Western saloon—with multiple camera positions. The era of the talkies required, in any case, the building of "sound stages" on which only one movie could be made at a time. Cameras were mounted on wheeled "dollies" so that they could be moved smoothly to pan across the scene being filmed or in and out of it for long shots and close-ups. Lights and sound-recording equipment were slung on gantries. A whole hierarchy of technicians, from cameraman, sound recordist and make-up artist to "grip" (to adjust sets and props) emerged around the central figure of the director. At the same time, as movies developed from being simply filmed dramas using a single camera, to cinematic narratives using a variety of angles, close-up and deep-focus shots, fade-outs and other devices, they were increasingly created, not only on the studio floor, but also by editing in the cutting room.

In time the word "studio" came to mean the company dedicated to the whole business of making and selling movies, from the initial concept to distribution, and including the planning of the stars' careers and the cultivation of their public images. The men who dominated the studio system, like Adolph Zukor, Louis B. Mayer or the Warner brothers, were the moguls of the age, wielding enormous power over thousands of men and women. It was to win back some control of their own affairs that D.W. Griffith, Chaplin, Douglas Fairbanks and Mary Pickford had founded United Artists in 1919, but they were the exceptions. Throughout the 1920s and 30s many stars were little more than highly paid prisoners of the studios.

HERO ON HORSEBACK Shooting an outdoor scene in *The Virginian*, Paramount Studio's first all-talkie movie made in 1929. The film would make Gary Cooper a star.

PROMOTION PIECES The French loved Hollywood films. This issue of the magazine *Mon Film* (top) shows George Raft and Carole Lombard in the musical *Rumba* (1935).
Above: A poster for Frank Capra's 1934 comedy *It Happened One Night,* which won five Oscars.

Among the male stars of this period, James Cagney and Edward G. Robinson supplied the favorite villains for the ever-popular gangster movie, while stars such as Gary Cooper, James Stewart and Henry Fonda represented the quiet heroes, slow to resort to violence, whom Americans of the 1930s admired. But the biggest male star of all at the end of the decade was Clark Gable, who had learned his craft from his first wife, Josephine Dillon, a former actress. He epitomized the perfect mixture of virility and charm. By then he was known as "the King" and the big question of 1939 was who would play opposite him in *Gone with the Wind*. After a long search by producer Daniel O. Selznick, the role was given to the stylish and sexy British actress Vivien Leigh.

SPORTING POWERS

FOR PLAYERS AND SPECTATORS ALIKE, SPORTS CAME INTO THEIR OWN IN THE INTERWAR YEARS AND PROFESSIONALS BEGAN TO REAP REWARDS

DOWNHILL THRILLS Skiing grew in popularity in the 1920s and 30s. This poster advertises the university skiing championships of 1934 to be held at the Swiss resort of Wengen.

Working people in the developed world had more leisure time to occupy in the interwar years than ever before. By the 1920s most finished work on Saturdays at midday; by the 1930s Americans especially

THE GREAT OUTDOORS A small crowd encourages a competitor on a mountain stretch of the 1937 Tour de France. Bottom: Members of the Nazi's *Bund Deutscher Mädel* (League of German Girls) display "Strength through Joy" at a summer camp in 1939.

were growing accustomed to having the whole day off. Flocking to football games or baseball games was one of the ways in which working men occupied their Saturday afternoons. At the same time, the cult of fitness and slimness in the 1920s encouraged men and women of the middle class to take part in active sports. Ownership of a tennis court or membership in a tennis club became a badge of middle-class status and tennis parties a familiar feature of weekend social life. Taking part in sports also fit with the post-First World War determination to "have fun," which went from the pursuit of excellence at golf or bridge at one end to ping-pong, roller-skating and such short-lived fads as the pogo stick at the other.

For those who could afford it, skiing became a popular winter sport, encouraged by the example of enthusiasts such as Britain's Arnold Lunn, son of the Methodist missionary turned travel agent, Sir Henry Lunn. In 1922 Arnold Lunn invented the modern ski slalom technique; in 1924 he made the first ski ascent of the Eiger in the Swiss Alps. He wrote numerous popular books on skiing (as

well as on religion), and for more than half a century, from 1919 to 1971, edited the *British Ski Year Book*. The pioneering activities of men like him bore fruit in an ever higher profile for skiing. The first Winter Olympics were held at Chamonix in the French Alps in 1924. From the early 1930s onward, devices such as the chair lift helped to open up resorts in Europe and North America, and later Australia and New Zealand, to still greater numbers of skiers.

In the United States, meanwhile, Roosevelt's New Deal helped to democratize sports.

TAKING A HIKE A French family heads for the railway station equipped for a serious walking vacation. In general, the British and Germans were more enthusiastic walkers than the French.

The public works projects financed by the Roosevelt administration in the 1930s included the building of public swimming pools, ice rinks, tennis courts and golf courses. The number of municipal golf courses in the United States grew from 184 in 1925 to 576 in 1935, while membership of private clubs fell sharply in the Depression years.

AT THE NET Two stars of the tennis world during the 1930s were Helen Moody (below, left) shown at Wimbledon in 1938 and W.T "Big Bill" Tilden (right), at Wimbledon in 1935.

National attitudes to participation in sports varied more than they do today. Frenchmen followed bicycle racing with the same devotion that Britons gave to soccer or Americans to baseball. But apart from a gentle game of *boules* or *pétanque*, the French regarded talking in the local café as a more sensible leisure pursuit than any form of exercise. Germans, on the other hand, were encouraged by the Nazi regime from 1933 onward to develop physical fitness through pursuits such as gymnastics and swimming—ironically, the poliomyelitis epidemic of the 1930s hit Germany especially hard because the disease was transmitted in swimming pools. Organized walking in the countryside was popular with German youth throughout the interwar years; in the 1930s this had a political dimension—it was encouraged by the Nazi regime as a way of shedding urban intellectuality and rediscovering the grand simplicities of the German soil and the German *Volk*.

In Britain, walking and bicycling were probably the most common active leisure pursuits of the working class, especially in the industrial North, where hill country was often no more than a short tram or cycle ride from the mills and factories.

Youth hostels, which had originated in Germany, spread throughout Europe, offering young people with little money the chance to extend their rambling over several days. Railway companies in Britain ran "Ramblers' Specials" with low fares to take hikers from the cities to country destinations. Thousands of the unemployed in the Depression years found some consolation in exploring the countryside on foot. In Britain, too, there was a subtle political dimension in the form of organized mass rambling. This took place along rights of way that crossed great estates and tacitly questioned the property rights of private landowners.

DOUBLE CHAMPION One of the all-time greats of golf, the 28-year-old American Bobby Jones, won both the British and U.S. amateur and open championships in 1930.

1920 Babe Ruth joins New York Yankees

1924 Paris Olympics

MONOPOLY HITS THE SHOPS

The game Monopoly, in which fortunes are made and lost through real estate, was invented in the United States in the Depression. Its creator was an unemployed engineer, Charles Darrow. In 1933 he had 5,000 sets made, and the game began to catch on. He also offered it to Parker Bros., the games' manufacturers. At first they rejected it, but then reconsidered, launching Monopoly nationally for Christmas 1935. By January it had become a runaway success.

The popular press, meanwhile, was devoting more and more space to the spectator sports, and combined with movie newsreels and the radio to make stars of the leading players. Cigarette cards and bubble-gum wrappers featuring portraits of sports heroes, such as the Australian cricketer Donald Bradman, the English soccer star Stanley Matthews or the American baseball player Babe Ruth, fed the adulation of the young.

Seeing stars

In tennis, crowds of thousands watched the championships at Wimbledon or Forest Hills. The media allowed millions more to follow the fortunes of the French stars Suzanne Lenglen and Jean Borotra (known as "the bouncing Basque"), of the Americans Helen Wills and William Tilden, and of the British-born player Fred Perry. Lenglen, one of the greatest woman tennis players of all time, was the women's champion of France through most of the 1920s and had several victories at Wimbledon. Borotra won the men's singles at Wimbledon in 1924 as well as the French and Australian championships. Helen Wills, who became Helen Wills Moody after her marriage, succeeded Suzanne Lenglen in the 1930s as the leading woman player and won eight singles championships at Wimbledon and seven U.S. championships. Big Bill Tilden was the seven time winner of the U.S. amateur championship and three times singles winner at Wimbledon. Fred Perry, originally a table-tennis champion, dominated the men's game in the 1930s, winning every major amateur title, including the singles at Wimbledon and the U.S. singles, each three times.

Golf had its heroes, too. Among the greatest were the Americans Walter Hagen and Bobby Jones and Britain's Henry Cotton. Walter Hagen led the Americans to triumph after triumph in the early 20s. Bobby Jones pulled off a quadruple triumph in 1930 when he won the British and the U.S. amateur and open championships. Henry Cotton saved Britain's honor on a number of occasions; he overcame the American challenge to win the British Open in 1934 and 1937.

Hagen, Jones and Cotton were not just superb players of their chosen game, but also models of courtesy and sportsmanship. These were virtues proverbially associated with the game of cricket, but cricket's reputation was severely blemished during a British team's tour of Australia in 1933, when the captain instructed his men to deliberately pitch the ball toward the batsman's body rather than the wicket.

Controversy of a quite different kind arose during the 1924 Paris Olympics. The deeply religious Scots runner Eric Liddell refused

HITLER'S SHOWCASE—THE 1936 OLYMPICS

Hosting the Olympic Games in Berlin was an important coup for Germany's National Socialist government. As far as possible the event was turned into a Nazi spectacular; Hitler's favorite film-maker, Leni Riefenstahl, was commissioned to shoot it, with brilliant results. The Games were also the first to be televised, although only broadcast to a relatively small audience in the Berlin area.

Four thousand athletes from some 40 nations attended, but the 1936 Olympics are chiefly remembered for the triumphs of the black American athlete Jesse Owens. He won gold in the 100 m, the 200 m, the 4 x 100 m relay and the long jump—to the reported disgust of Hitler, who had hoped for an unblemished display of Aryan athletic superiority. Nevertheless, Germany could count the 1936 Games as a success, winning the greatest number of medals overall. Countries such as Hungary and Finland also performed well relative to their size. The British, by contrast, had only modest success.

From their origins in ancient Greece the Olympic Games were dedicated to peace and peaceful competition. Three years after Berlin, many of the competing nations were at war. The next Olympic Games were not held until 1948.

NON-ARYAN CONQUESTS The U.S. athlete Jesse Owens (left) triumphed four times at the 1936 Olympics. Hitler (below) was happier with German success.

1930 Bobby Jones wins U.S. and British amateur and open championships

1934 Italy wins World Cup

1935 Malcolm Campbell breaks 300 mph on land

1936 Berlin Olympics

1938 World heavyweight champion Joe Louis defeats Max Schmeling

NEVER ON A SUNDAY Back in Edinburgh, the Scots runner Eric Liddell is raised aloft after winning gold and bronze at the 1924 Olympics in Paris.

to run the 100 m race, for which he was the favorite, because the heats were to be run on a Sunday. The race was won by another Briton, Harold Abrahams. Liddell went on to win the bronze medal in the 200 m; in the 400 m, a distance over which he was not very experienced, he won the gold in a world record time of 47.6 seconds. Liddell stood out for his own strict notion of integrity at a time when the Olympic ideal of amateurism was being undermined by commercial pressures.

Soccer, whose rules had been established at the British public schools in the 19th century, was now the favorite spectator sport for working men throughout the world, except North America. In 1930 the Fédération Internationale de Football Association (FIFA) had 40 members. Britain was not one of them, having declined membership, but was regarded as the international authority on the rules of the game.

At the level of the top teams soccer was now almost entirely a professional game, although remuneration for the players was extremely modest by today's standards. The wages of British players were fixed at a level comparable with those of skilled industrial workers. By the 1930s players were regularly being "bought" from other teams or even from other countries. Italy, for example, found many of its top players in Argentina and even fielded them in its winning 1934 World Cup team.

In Britain soccer was a passion. The FA Cup Final at the new Wembley Stadium in 1923 attracted a crowd estimated at 150,000, and on a Saturday afternoon the streets of all industrial towns were thronged with men on their way to support their local teams. Of the game's heroes, two stand out: Dixie Dean in the 1920s and Stanley Matthews in the 30s and early 40s. Dixie Dean, an engine-driver's son from Birkenhead, scored an astounding 349 goals in 399 games; at the end of his career he held the record of 60 League goals in one season. Stanley Matthews, born in Stoke-on-Trent, played mainly for Stoke City and Blackpool. In the course of a long career—he would still be playing professional soccer in his forties in the 1960s—he won 54 international titles.

"...At the ol' ball game"

Meanwhile, scandal had struck the game of baseball in 1919 when eight members of the great Chicago White Sox team were accused of deliberately losing the World Series in return for bribes. They were indicted in 1920 on a charge of fraud and suspended for the 1921 season while an investigation went forward. In August that year a jury found them not guilty, but they were

THE DEAN BROTHERS Two brothers pitching for the St. Louis Cardinals, Dizzy and Paul Dean, became the sensation of the 1934 baseball season, capping off a spectacular year by winning two games each against the Detroit Tigers in the World Series.

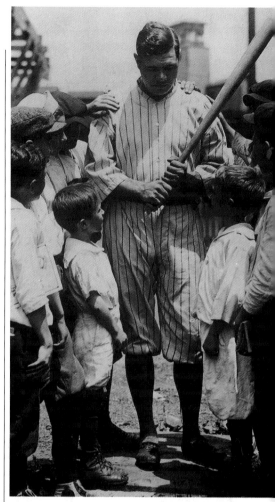

HERO WORSHIP Small boys worshipped leading sportsmen, as their older sisters worshipped film stars. Baseball stars Babe Ruth (left) and Ty Cobb (right) were revered in spite of less-than-exemplary personal lives.

nonetheless banned from organized baseball for life.

In time, baseball overcame the stain left by the "Black Sox" scandal, mainly because of the stellar play of the game's remarkable athletes. Ty Cobb, for example, had thrilled crowds with his mastery of every aspect of the game. Having played 22 of his 24 years as a professional baseball player for the Detroit Tigers, he ended his career with an astounding lifetime batting average of .367.

If baseball rose to preeminence in the 1930s it was largely because of one man, George Herman Ruth, known around the world as "Babe" Ruth. In 1920 the owner of the Red Sox needed some quick cash to finance a musical (that never made it to Broadway), so he traded Ruth to the New York Yankees for $125,000. Ruth remained with them until 1935. Standing 6 feet 2 inches tall and weighing 215 pounds, he was a left-

hander. In his early years he was an excellent pitcher, but from 1918 he was known as the most powerful hitter the game had ever seen. He set a record of 60 home runs in 1927, a record that stood unchallenged for 30 years, and a total record of 714 home runs in 22 major league seasons. New York's Yankee Stadium was dubbed "the house that Ruth built," but in truth, Babe Ruth had elevated all of baseball in America's consciousness, making it a game of larger–than–life heroes—a game worthy of being called "America's pastime."

By the early 1930s Ruth's hard living took its toll and he was being matched run for run by his less flamboyant teammate Lou Gehrig, another mighty hitter. At the end of the 1930s another great baseball star was emerging—Joe DiMaggio, who would later win a different kind of fame by marrying Marilyn Monroe. Men like Lou Gehrig gave the game a heroic dimension that even Hollywood had trouble rivaling. After setting records for endurance and consecutive games, Gehrig—having earned the epithet "the iron horse"—succumbed to a fatal neromuscular disease. His tearful farewell in Yankee Stadium on July 4, 1939, in which he

HEROES OF THE GAME Baseball fans outside New York cursed Yankee luck when a new hero, "Joltin' Joe" Dimaggio (below, at the plate) succeeded Ruth in the clean-up spot. Meanwhile, Lou Gehrig lent stature to the game, highlighted by his emotional farewell in 1939.

declared himself to be "the luckiest man on the face of the earth," is one of the defining moments in the history of baseball, and, in fact, in American history between the wars. Baseball had undergone a transformation in the 1920s and 1930s—from the scruffy, hard hitter sandlotters to American idols and larger-than-life royalty.

Another sport, a subculture of its own, was boxing, which also attracted a large following, despite a somewhat disreputable status. Although largely promoted in the United States, boxing was not entirely dominated by American fighters. Georges Carpentier of France, Primo Carnera of Italy and the German Max Schmeling, world heavyweight champion from 1930 to 1932, were all important figures in the interwar years.

The two great American fighters of the 1920s were Jack Dempsey, heavyweight champion from 1919 to 1926, and Gene Tunney, who defeated him in 1926 and again the following year. Both Dempsey and Tunney were white, but the arrival on the scene of Joe Louis in 1935 heralded the emergence of the black boxers who would soon dominate the sport. For them, as for the poor white immigrants to America who had taken to boxing before them, the ring offered a short cut to affluence and status.

Louis was an immensely popular heavyweight champion from 1937 to 1949. In 1936 he was defeated by Max Schmeling by a technical knockout in the 12th round. In 1938 he knocked Schmeling out in the first round. By that time, the match had become political, as had most things by that time. Schmeling was at the time an admirer of Hitler, although he later became a courageous opponent of the Nazi regime.

HEAVYWEIGHT CONTENDERS Boxing had an international profile in the 1930s. Frenchman Georges Carpentier (left) was world light heavyweight champion from 1920 to 1922. Below, German Max Schmeling is beaten by American Joe Louis in June 1938 .

IN PURSUIT OF SPEED

SPEED KING Malcolm Campbell peers from the cockpit of his car *Bluebird* before his successful attempt on the 300 mph land-speed record in 1935.

One of the great record breakers of the 1920s and 30s was the British motorist Malcolm Campbell. He had been a pilot in the Royal Flying Corps during the Great War, and then took up automobile racing, devoting himself to record-breaking with single-minded devotion. Between 1924 and 1935 he established nine world land-speed records: from 146.16 mph in 1924 to 301.129 mph in 1935. The last of these, the first to break the 300 mph barrier, was set at Bonneville Salt Flats, Utah, still a favorite venue for speed trials.

Campbell's strongest competitor in the 1920s was another British driver, the hugely popular Henry Segrave, who won the Grand Prix de France in 1923. He established his own world speed record of 231 mph at Daytona Beach, Florida, in 1929, driving his 1,000 horsepower car, *Golden Arrow*. Segrave, however, was killed in 1930 while attempting a world speedboat record in his boat *Miss England II* on Lake Windermere. Still alive when pulled out of the water, he just managed to ask, "Did we do it?," and see his rescuers nod in the affirmative before he died. On the last run before the accident he had achieved 101 mph.

Campbell also took to the water and captured a new record in 1931 when he reached 129.5 mph. His record of 141.74 mph, set at Coniston Water in 1939, was still unbroken when he died in 1948.

All of Campbell's cars and speedboats were named *Bluebird*. His son Donald was killed in 1967 on Coniston Water in the English Lake District while attempting a new record in a jet-propelled hydrofoil of the same name.

SCIENCE AND TECHNOLOGY

BETWEEN THE WARS, THE TECHNOLOGICAL REVOLUTION OF THE START OF THE CENTURY WAS HAVING DRAMATIC EFFECTS ON EVERYDAY LIFE

In the years just before and after 1900 there had been an astonishing revolution in science and technology. Then came the war of 1914-18 that in some respects halted, in others sharply stimulated, the process. While men died or were mutilated as a result of improved technology, technology itself, because of the need for vast amounts of efficient weaponry, developed more rapidly than it might otherwise have. This was especially true in fields such as powered flight, wireless communication, precision engineering and the application of electrical power and mass-production techniques. The scale of the casualties, meanwhile, stimulated advances in surgical techniques and medical procedures.

The electrical revolution, which had begun at the end of the 19th century, was thoroughly established by the 1920s, transforming not only the industrial workplace but also the landscape.

With electricity, industrial development was possible in places where it had not been possible before because they lacked local supplies of coal, timber or fast-running streams. Lenin had announced that "Communism was Soviet Power plus Electrification," and Soviet Russia duly embarked upon a program of bringing electrical power to regions that had never known any power source more potent than the ox or the horse. In the advanced capitalist world, too, electricity ushered in a second industrial revolution; when the power needed was obtained not from a single prime mover, but from multiple electrical sources, it was possible to build factories that were not

INDUSTRIAL SPRAWL The Zenith radio factory in Chicago, then the largest in the world, provided jobs for thousands after the depression.

SHEDDING LIGHT Adapted from the engineering drafting table, the Anglepoise lamp, invented by George Cardwardine and launched in 1933, was an ingenious example of functional design and an instant success.

CONSUMER ELECTRICALS By the mid 1930s domestic electrical goods were becoming familiar and inexpensive household items.

ELECTRICITY – BEST ALL WAYS

THE 'COUNTY' FIVE

CASH PRICE 11/6

CASH PRICE 33/-

CASH PRICE 19/6

CASH PRICE 19/6

CASH PRICE 13/9

The COUNTY OF LONDON ELECTRIC SUPPLY Co Ltd

Obtainable at Local Showrooms

ZENITH RADIO CORPORATION

only cleaner but also more flexibly designed. The new, purpose-built factories that sprang up in the 1920s and 30s were based on electricity, with its capacity for clean, efficient, flexible, 24 hour operation.

There was, of course, a downside. With electrification, and the mass-production techniques it made possible, came an increasing division of labor, with one operative repetitively making or assembling one part of a product. What resulted was a new kind of industrial enslavement and the decline and death of older forms of craftsmanship. Not surprisingly, boredom, exhaustion and lack of job satisfaction—combined with a sense that workers were not getting a fair share of the profits of their labors— were causes of unrest during the interwar years throughout the industrialized world.

Meanwhile, cities were being transformed by electric streetlighting and electrified transport systems. In the 1930s neon lighting was increasingly used for advertising displays, changing the face of urban nightlife. Pylons, carrying national electricity supply networks, began to stride across the countryside from the mid 30s onward. Homes and social life were also changed—the rise of motion pictures to take just one example,

SCIENCE AND LIFE Popular science
magazines like this French publication
proliferated throughout
the 1920s.

could not have happened without electricity. In the U.S. in the mid 20s, only about 3 million homes were wired for electricity; by 1939 the figure was about 7 million.

A scientific age

"It is science, ultimately, that makes our age different . . . from the ages that have gone before," wrote philosopher Bertrand Russell in 1923. "And science is capable of bringing mankind into a far happier condition than any that he has known in the past."

People in the 1920s were aware that they were living in a scientific age, that scientific progress was accelerating rapidly, that it had changed their lives, mostly for the better, and that it would continue to change them even more dramatically. The great scientists of the 19th century had for the most part been amateurs, funding their own research; only medicine and mathematics had support from academic institutions. This was still to some extent true in the 1920s when there was room for solitary scientific researchers and inventors such as the Scot, John Logie Baird. Working entirely on his own, Baird developed, among other things, a form of radar and a mechanical television system. In 1926 he demonstrated the television in a room above a restaurant in London's Soho. Experimental television broadcasting using the Baird system began in the United States two years later, by which time Baird had made the first transatlantic television transmission and had begun working on color television.

At the same time, in such fields as chemistry and electronics some, though by no means all, of the world's great universities had set up research institutes, and the larger industrial corporations were increasingly funding their own research laboratories. The development of high-grade motor and aviation fuels and of the first plastics and the rapid improvement of wireless receiving equipment were just some of the results.

Although most schools taught science only at the most elementary level—and most public elementary schools, for example, more or less ignored it—knowledge of the latest advances spread widely among amateur enthusiasts, who were responsible for the proliferation and success of popular science magazines in the United States.

In the imagination of most people the scientist was still a strange figure, eccentric and

probably absent-minded. Albert Einstein, who seemed to fit that bill, was a figure of worldwide fame, the first scientist in history whose name would be known and his face recognized anywhere in the Western world. He was famous even though very few of those who had heard of him would have understood anything about his Theory of Relativity or the implications for the future of the world of his celebrated formula, $E=mc^2$.

Even less comprehensible to most people was the work being done on radioactivity and atomic theory; the leading figure in this field was the New Zealand-born Ernest Rutherford working in England at Manchester University and the Cavendish Laboratory in Cambridge. When J.D. Cockcroft and E.T.S. Walton split an atom of lithium at the Cavendish in 1932 the experiment reached the headlines, but very few people, even among scientists, grasped what it might lead to.

Science and disease

By the mid 1930s infant mortality rates in the Western world had dramatically decreased compared with those of the 19th century. Life expectancy, meanwhile, had increased to an average of 60 years compared with 48 in 1900. The mere fact that people were having far fewer children on average than their parents indicated a new confidence; they could feel reasonably certain that all their children would survive to adulthood. These greatly improved mortality statistics, however, were still due largely to improvements in

1919

1919 Rutherford
produces first
nuclear reaction

1924 Willem Einthoven
wins Nobel prize for his
electrocardiograph

1926 Baird
demonstrates
television

1927 Lindbergh
makes first solo
flight across Atlantic

1928 Alexander
Fleming discovers
penicillin

1929 Barcelona
Exhibition

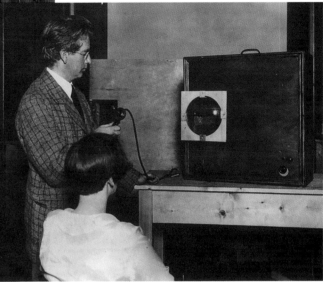

EARLY DAYS TV pioneer John Logie Baird carries out an experiment on the roof of the Television Company's offices. Watching him from a deck chair is British stage star Jack Buchanan, who would later perform for the new medium. Below: Baird with his "televisor." He holds a telephone to direct the person whose actions are being transmitted.

public health—in such basic matters as the provision of safe drinking water and efficient sewage systems. In the 1920s hospitals were still to some degree regarded as places where the poor went to die, but in the course of the 1930s brighter, more hygienic hospitals were built throughout the advanced industrial world—though many buildings from the 19th century and earlier remained in use.

In the face of many diseases medicine was still impotent, but new understanding of chemistry and biology made a growing contribution. People had been vaccinated against smallpox since the late 18th century, but by the interwar years the increasingly widespread use of vaccination had virtually eliminated many of the formerly fatal diseases of childhood such as diphtheria and

TECHNOCRATS IN CHARGE

In the early 1930s, in the depths of the Depression, a "technocracy movement" arose in the United States. Its basic premise was that technicians, whose achievements in industry were manifest, would be the best people to run government. Their managerial efficiency would replace the incompetence and self-interest of the governing class, producing an age of abundance. In those dark days the movement seemed to offer a dream of hope, but technocracy, condemned by its critics as too materialistic, had dropped out of the headlines by 1933 and was largely dead by 1936.

whooping cough. One great missed opportunity of the period was the discovery of the antibiotic penicillin. Sir Alexander Fleming made his almost accidental discovery in 1928 and announced it in 1929, but it did not come into use until the needs of war stimulated its adoption in the 1940s.

X-rays, still regarded by many as virtually miraculous, were in widespread use for medical diagnosis and the treatment of cancers—they were even used to measure children's feet in shoe shops. But the radiation hazards attached to them were not fully understood, even though many of those who worked with x-ray machines had suffered burns or even lost limbs because of constant exposure to them.

The application of electricity to medical technology produced other important diagnostic aids, such as the galvanometer, a forerunner of the electrocardiograph, to measure the electrical impulses of the heart and detect any irregularities. Another new aid was the electroencephalograph, invented in 1929, to trace the pattern of brainwaves.

Taking to the air

The Great War had transformed aviation. Planes were now much better designed; their manufacture had been industrialized, and there were large numbers of trained and experienced pilots. Commercial air services

went into operation almost at once, though many of the routes still had to be pioneered. Flight was still a matter of excitement, romance and danger.

Three of the great pioneering flights took place in 1919. In June two Britons, Captain John Alcock and Lieutenant A. Whitten Brown, flew a Vickers Vimy across the Atlantic from Newfoundland to the coast of Ireland in just under 16 hours and were knighted for their exploit. In July the British airship *R34* crossed and recrossed the Atlantic in 11 days, keeping in constant radio contact with the Air Ministry in London. In November the Australian brothers Keith and Ross Macpherson Smith, with two sergeant mechanics, J.M. Bennett and W.H. Shiers, flew another Vickers Vimy from England to Port Darwin in Australia, taking 27 days; the Smiths also were knighted.

Another pioneer was Alan Cobham. In November 1925, he set off from London's Croydon airport—then not much more than a field and a collection of huts – bound for Cape Town. He flew over territory that no one had ever before seen from the air, and reached his destination, to a tumultuous welcome, on February 17 the following year. Also in 1925, the Italian Commander de

Pineda flew from Italy to Australia and back, via Japan, in a single-engined flying boat. In 1926 the Norwegian explorer Roald Amundsen flew over the North Pole in an airship. In the same year, the American naval pilot Richard Byrd claimed also to have flown over the North Pole—in a plane—though his claim was later disputed. Another feat of 1926 was a further journey by Alan Cobham—from Britain to Australia and back again.

The greatest flying sensation of all in the 1920s, however, was Charles Lindbergh's solo crossing of the Atlantic—the first ever—in 1927. Paris seemed to empty and the roads around Le Bourget airport were blocked when the 25-year-old's monoplane, the *Spirit of St. Louis*, arrived there on May 21. The flight, without any communication with land, had taken just over 33 hours. The welcome he received from a crowd estimated at half a million was ecstatic. Soon after, a similar crowd greeted him at Croydon in England.

In the years following his flight, the modest Lindbergh, more than any other flying pioneer, achieved a godlike status. Later, he would become a controversial figure because of his involvement with right-wing politics and was much criticized in 1938 for accepting a decoration from Germany's Nazi government. As a leading member of the isolationist and anti-Semitic America First movement, Lindbergh lost much credibility after Pearl Harbor, but in the earlier, postwar years, he seemed to embody an angelic link between the youthfulness and hope of the New World and the weariness of the Old.

PIONEERS OF THE AIR American Amelia Earhart (below) sitting on her plane in 1928. American Polar aviator Richard Byrd poses with his sextant (right).

The pioneering continued. In 1928 Amelia Earhart became the first woman to fly the Atlantic—later she would fly it solo. With the help of her husband, publisher George Putnam, she became one of the most famous and admired women in the world. In 1929 the *Graf Zeppelin* made the first round-the-world airship flight. In the same year and again in 1933 Richard Byrd flew over the Antarctic, seeing vast areas of territory for the first time. In 1930, Amy Johnson was the first woman to fly solo from Britain to Australia—she would be killed in an airplane crash in 1941, ferrying a military plane from a factory to an RAF base.

In 1931 the Texan Wiley Post and his Australian navigator, Harold Gatty, made the round-the-world journey in just under nine days; in 1933 Post completed the course solo in seven. In 1933 the Italian air minister, Italo Balbo, led a flight of 24 planes from Italy to Chicago, returning via New York. In 1937 Amelia Earhart disappeared mysteriously somewhere in the Pacific in the course of an attempted round-the-world flight.

FLYING HERO Charles Lindbergh's plane is photographed as it leaves Long Island on its historic flight (right); the reception Lindy received upon his return was considerably better attended as he is treated to a ticker-tape parade down New York's Broadway. Most photos of Lindbergh (left) were taken after his successful flight to Paris.

IN-FLIGHT ENTERTAINMENT
Travellers in an English passenger
aircraft in 1925 watch an early
experiment with in-flight movies.
Above: Germany's Lufthansa was
founded in 1926.

however, and worldwide routes continued to expand. By 1939 Pan American Airways and Imperial Airways were opening up passenger services between Europe and North America, while French, German and Italian airlines flew regularly between Africa and South America.

One feature of 1920s and 30s aviation was the air race over a fixed course. The most prestigious event of this kind was for the Schneider Trophy, established in 1912 by the French industrialist Jacques Schneider, a keen amateur balloonist and pilot until he was injured in an accident. It was a race for seaplanes only and took place over a course of 212 nautical miles (roughly 245 miles), starting and finishing in the same place. The aviation club that won it one year would hold it the next.

Among the general public, the Schneider aroused huge enthusiasm and excitement, regularly drawing crowds of more than a quarter of a million spectators. Competition was intense, and although no pilot ever died during the race, at least ten—two Americans, one Frenchman, two Britons and five Italians—were killed while training for it.

Commercial air traffic had followed the pioneers. One of the first airlines was the Dutch KLM, which flew its first scheduled flight from Croydon to Amsterdam in May 1920. By 1924 Britain's Imperial Airways was claiming in its advertising that it was the only British line to the Continent that offered cushioned seating, a lavatory, luncheon and a radio in every plane. In 1926 Imperial started scheduled flights to India. Lufthansa, Air France, Swissair and the Italian line, Alla Littoria, were also established in the 1920s. By 1929, there were 48 regular air routes in the United States, serving 35 cities and with a combined length of 20,000 miles.

At the same time enterprises such as the French Compagnie Latécoère based in Toulouse were establishing international airmail routes. Latécoère's most famous pilot was the impoverished aristocrat Antoine de Saint-Exupéry, author of *The Little Prince*, who would turn his experiences into classic novels such as *Vol de nuit* (*Night Flight*).

In the 1920s the airship was seen as a safe, pleasant and economical alternative to the plane for leisurely travel. The tragic crash of the British *R101* in 1930, with the loss of 46 lives, shook public confidence. But the Germans would carry on with airships until the disaster of 1937 when the *Hindenburg* exploded as it docked at Lakehurst, New Jersey, effectively bringing the age of the airships to an end. People still trusted the plane,

HILLSIDE TRAGEDY On October 5, 1930, the British airship *R101*—at that time, the world's biggest airship—crashed into a hillside near Beauvais in France. It was en route for India. Heavy rain had soaked the ship, causing it to lose height.

STREAMLINING—THE MODERN LOOK

THE DOMINANT AMERICAN DESIGN STYLE OF THE 1930s HAD MORE TO DO WITH STIMULATING CONSUMER DEMAND THAN WITH AERODYNAMIC EFFICIENCY

T he 1930s saw the rise of the industrial designer; at the same time, the public began to accept, even demand, modernism in the way goods were made, packaged and presented. The idea of industrial design had been developed at the Bauhaus in Germany in the 1920s, but its principles were perhaps too pure and spartan for popular tastes. In the 1930s, the initiative passed to the U.S., where industrial design was developed as a marketing tool, its purpose to stimulate consumer demand with annual model changes and by varying product design.

Among the leading figures were Norman Bel Geddes and Raymond Loewy, both associated with the style known as "streamlined." They modelled designs for aircraft, locomotives, automobiles and ships. By the mid 30s, under their influence, the American automobile had acquired the voluptuous curves and chrome speed-lines that distinguished it from most European vehicles. The style arose out of the principles of aerodynamics, but it was applied indiscriminately to objects with no need for speed—city buses, vacuum cleaners, refrigerators, electric irons, even buildings. The style had much to do with a modernist appearance and persuading consumers not to hold on to serviceable goods but to buy the most up-to-date product. Functionally, however, streamlining did lend itself to manufacturing in the new form of molded plastic known as Bakelite.

The new style was displayed at the Chicago and New York World's Fairs of 1934 and 1939. Streamlining had some influence on European manufacturers: Dr. Porsche adopted a streamlined outline for Hitler's projected "People's Car," the *Volkswagen*. But throughout the 1930s the style continued to epitomize America's huge lead over the rest of the world in innovation and mass consumerism.

DYNAMIC DESIGN Raymond Loewy's 1934 Hupmobile (above) pioneered the rounded appearance of automobiles. It would become the classic 1930s look of American cars.

MR. STREAMLINE In 1936, Loewy stands on a streamlined locomotive, one of a series he designed for the Philadelphia Railroad. The new aerodynamic style was applied even to objects that would never move, such as this Loewy-designed pencil sharpener.

3768

Some of the high-powered, single-seat planes developed to compete were forerunners of the fighters of the Second World War. The winner of the 1931 Schneider, for example, was a British Supermarine S.6B, ancestor of the Spitfire. The Supermarine's pilot was 30-year-old RAF officer John Boothman—later Air Chief Marshal Sir John Boothman. He clocked up an average speed over the whole course of 340 mph, the fastest so far achieved.

The engineers

Both the democracies and the dictatorships engaged in huge engineering projects in the interwar years. In the United States the building of bridges and dams was an important part of Roosevelt's New Deal. These projects were designed to provide employment and revive the flow of money in the economy, as well as to improve communications and provide flood control and hydroelectric power. The Grand Coulee Dam

SHOWCASE BARCELONA

On May 18, 1929, in the presence of the Spanish king, Alfonso XIII, Barcelona's International Exposition was opened. Built on the slopes of the hill called Montjuïc and on the park below, its organizers—led by Spain's dictator, General Miguel Primo de Rivera—had envisaged the exhibition as a showcase for Spanish enterprise. But the show was stolen by a handful of foreign pavilions, especially those of Germany, Sweden and Yugoslavia. Of these the most striking was the German, designed in a pure geometrical modernist style by Miës van der Rohe. Never intended as a permanent structure, it was demolished after the exhibition closed and is now known only from photographs. But it is still regarded as a milestone in the history of 20th-century architecture. Miës van der Rohe also designed for his pavilion the famous "Barcelona chair," constructed in stainless steel, leather and foam rubber. The celebration of Spanish national identity, meanwhile, was reflected in the *Pueblo Español*, a village whose buildings were modelled on the vernacular styles of all the regions of Spain, and in which "villagers" could be seen practicing their regional crafts; it had taken three years to research. It is still on Montjuïc—although now called, in the Catalan language, the *Poble Espanyol*—as is the Olympic stadium, remodelled for the 1992 Olympiad.

FASTEST IN THE AIR The race for the Schneider Trophy was held in most years until 1931. It was restricted to seaplanes, though the technology was applied to aircraft of all kinds.

in the state of Washington was at the time the largest structure ever built by man. Two of the other great engineering triumphs of the period were the Sydney Harbor bridge, completed in 1932, and San Francisco's Golden Gate, completed in 1937. The great arch of the Sydney Harbor bridge was considerably shorter than the Golden Gate's 4,200 feet span, but it boasted immense carrying capacity; both were hailed as brilliant engineering achievements.

In the realm of private enterprise the years following the Wall Street Crash saw the culmination of the skyscraper boom with the construction of New York's Chrysler Building (1930) and the Empire State Building (1931). No attempt was made to match the height of these enormous structures until after the Second World War. At 1,250 feet, the Empire State would remain the tallest building in the world until the 1970s.

In 1935 Stalin inaugurated the building of the Moscow Metro, whose stations, with their lavish mosaics and chandeliers, were designed as underground people's palaces. The Russians also built dams, railways and canals on a massive scale, often in the most bitterly inhospitable parts of the country, using slave labor from the prison camps and with huge loss of life.

Mussolini's Italy led the world in the construction of its autostradas or highways. Another remarkable

achievement was the draining of the Pontine marshes in the Lazio region, a task that had defied popes and emperors for centuries. Infested with malaria, the area was inhabited only by a handful of shepherds. After clearing it, the Italians built several new towns and brought millions of acres into cultivation, making it one of the most productive parts of the country. In land reclamation the only comparable feat was the Zuiderzee dam in the Netherlands in 1932.

Nazi Germany followed Italy's example by building a network of *autobahnen*, but Hitler's promised "People's Car," the *Volkswagen*, did not go into mass production before the outbreak of war in 1939.

BRIDGING THE BAY Pedestrians swarm over San Francisco's new Golden Gate Bridge on May 27, 1937. It opened to traffic the following day, and remained the longest suspension bridge in the world until 1964.

THE ROADS TO WAR

NO COUNTRY IN THE WORLD ESCAPED THE EFFECTS OF THE GREAT DEPRESSION. IT DAMAGED PEOPLE'S FAITH IN DEMOCRACY AND CAPITALISM, HELPED TO BRING HITLER'S NATIONAL SOCIALISTS TO POWER IN GERMANY, BOOSTED MUSSOLINI'S IMPERIAL AMBITIONS, DISTRACTED WORLD ATTENTION FROM STALIN'S TERROR IN THE SOVIET UNION AND STIMULATED THE RISE OF NEW DICTATORSHIPS. ITS EFFECTS ENDED ONLY WHEN PREPARATIONS BEGAN FOR ANOTHER WORLD WAR.

THE WORLD IN DEPRESSION

THE COLLAPSE OF THE WORLD'S FINANCIAL SYSTEM LED TO MASS UNEMPLOYMENT, DESPERATE POVERTY AND POLITICAL EXTREMISM

The effect of the Wall Street Crash of October 1929 was to drag down the economy of the whole world, creating the Great Depression of the 1930s. It had exposed a global crisis of overproduction, in which more manufactured goods, food and raw materials were being produced than the markets could absorb. Too many goods chasing too few buyers brought the threat of deflation as prices tumbled. American loans to just about every other country on the globe had disguised the worst of the problem—until the Crash. Then the loans were severely curtailed, and later ceased altogether. U.S. demand for goods produced in other countries fell sharply, then slumped further in 1930 when President Hoover introduced high tariffs on imports. The effect was to strike a blow at already fragile economies, and to start a rapid downward spiral of recession. The flow of world trade began to dry up. Everywhere industrial production fell as factories closed or laid off workers.

For the workers of the industrial world this meant unemployment on a massive scale. The effects also reached less industrialized countries such as Australia, Canada and Argentina and the undeveloped countries of Africa, Asia and Latin America. Farmers and miners all over the world who had never heard of Wall Street found themselves unable to obtain a fair price for what they produced. Among the results were some cruel paradoxes. While the amount of starvation in the world increased, farms were abandoned or reduced to subsistence level, grain stocks were used to fuel railway engines and coffee crops were dumped in the sea.

In Britain matters were at their worst in the winter of 1932-3, with 3 million people—a quarter of the work force—unemployed. In the United States, where industrial production fell by 45 percent in the years between 1929 and 1932, the unemployment figure stood at over 15 million. France, with a more self-sufficient economy, was less badly hit at first, but the worldwide crisis had caught up with it by 1933. After that unemployment increased steadily and remained high for the rest of the decade. In Germany there were 5.6 million registered unemployed, almost a third of the work force,

THE BONUS ARMY ON CAPITOL HILL **Members of the "Bonus Expeditionary Force"—veterans of World War I— march on Washington in 1932 demanding payment of their war bonus.**

and probably another million unregistered unemployed. Australia reached the point where one worker in three was out of work.

These figures do not, however, represent the full scale of the problem. They do not include the millions of small farmers everywhere facing ruin, the employed workers on short hours and reduced wages, the small tradespeople whose businesses were devastated by the drop in working people's spending, or the teachers, policemen and other public employees forced to take salary cuts.

Most industrialized countries paid some form of unemployment benefit, but generally only to male industrial workers, not to women, farmworkers, domestic servants or the self-employed. Where benefits were paid they were barely enough to keep families above starvation level. And generally they were strictly means-tested; inspectors visited the homes of claimants to ensure that they had no other source of income or any goods that could be sold.

FINANCIAL GLOOM **Left, anxious faces of men crowding an employment agency during the Depression in search of work. In most cities, nearly the only areas of secure employment was in the public sector and civil service.**

1929 Wall Street Crash

The humiliation of the means test was just one of the psychological effects of long-term unemployment. Others were the feelings of hopelessness and apathy that gripped entire communities as they were engulfed in general impoverishment and shabby neglect. Such sentiments were particularly devastating in the United States, where people had grown used to the idea that hard work would always be rewarded and life would grow steadily more prosperous for all. Many reacted with guilt and shame as if blaming themselves for being unemployed; the bewildering shock of the Depression appeared to have destroyed the American Dream.

American working people of all classes were reduced to poverty. In 1932 *Fortune* magazine calculated that 34 million Americans had no income whatsoever. Millions of children were showing the effects of severe malnutrition. Soup kitchens, organized by private charity to provide the unemployed with at least one hot meal per day, were set up in cities and the lines there were long. Former professional men and "white collar" workers could be seen begging, selling apples or matches on the street, or searching trash cans for food. As people lost their homes because they were unable to pay the rent, shanty towns grew up on the outskirts of cities. Some 2 million Americans took to the roads in a desperate search for any kind of work. For the first time in the country's history, emigration actually exceeded immigration—including thousands of Americans who emigrated to the Soviet Union.

Financial collapse

The worldwide collapse of trade and industry was both cause and effect of a breakdown in the world's financial system. The American banking network consisted of large numbers of mostly small banks with very modest reserves. The recession forced them to call in their credits, from both local businesses and foreign borrowers. Even after taking these measures, some 9,000 American banks failed in the first three years of the Depression.

The withdrawal of U.S. capital and the demand for debt repayment put a severe strain on the banks of the major European countries, themselves large-scale creditors of poorer countries in Europe and beyond. The banks of Germany and Austria came under particularly heavy pressure from 1929 on, and finally broke in 1931 when Bolivia defaulted on its foreign debts, followed by other Latin American countries. In May that year the largest Austrian bank, Creditanstalt, failed, creating a domino effect among other European banks. The German government had to move to purchase stock in its country's banks to prevent their total collapse.

DOWN AND OUT The shanty towns that grew up in American cities, like this one in New York, were known as "Hoovervilles" in mocking allusion to President Roosevelt's predecessor. Right: A white collar worker reduced to selling apples in the streets.

1931 Creditanstalt fails

1932 World unemployment levels at their highest

1933 Roosevelt becomes president; Hitler becomes German chancellor

FALLING STANDARDS

Before 1914 world trade was based on the gold standard. Countries such as Britain and the United States, with strong currencies and large gold reserves, had an internal gold standard, which meant that paper currency could be exchanged for gold coins. There was also an international gold standard by which international debts were settled using either gold or a gold-backed currency such as sterling. The system helped trade by providing stable exchange rates; it also disciplined governments by discouraging them from the inflationary practice of printing paper money not backed by real assets.

The gold standard collapsed during and after the Great War as countries printed money to pay for supplies and reconstruction. It was restored in the mid 20s, but gold coins were no longer in wide circulation and the ability to exchange paper for gold was largely theoretical. The disadvantages of the system now became apparent. World currencies were fixed at parities that the economies of most countries could not sustain, damaging their export trade. Gold flowed into the United States in settlement of international debts, where it sat inert rather than producing liquid wealth to finance trade. Also, the system bound national economies too tightly together, so that when one collapsed the others fell with it, which is what happened in the years following the Crash. Britain went off the gold standard during the crisis year of 1931. France, the Netherlands and some other countries stayed in for a few more years, but by 1937 the system had expired worldwide.

WORTH ITS WEIGHT By the time this German banker was photographed perched on a stack of gold bars in 1938, the gold standard was a thing of the past.

In Britain, the gold reserves of the Bank of England shrank, and parliament voted to take the country off the gold standard—suspend the bank's obligation to exchange sterling for gold. This had the effect of reducing the pound's value against the dollar by a third. Other countries followed suit, effectively devaluing their currencies in a desperate bid to give their export trade a competitive edge. In April 1933 newly elected president Franklin Roosevelt took the dollar, too, off the gold standard.

Taking action

The measures adopted by most governments were arguably the exact opposite of those appropriate to the crisis. Basically, they set out to balance their budgets and to reduce their indebtedness and the outflow of capital by cutting public spending. In effect, they used deflationary methods to combat what was essentially a problem of deflation, cutting demand when they should have been encouraging it to grow. In fairness, they felt obliged to do this because of the problem of world indebtedness to the United States which had arisen during the Great War. At the same time, governments intervened to protect their economies by controlling the outflow of

STREET VIOLENCE A poster on the wall advertises an organ recital, but events on the street are more violent as London policemen fight left-wing demonstrators during a march of the unemployed in 1930.

foreign exchange and by introducing tariffs and import quotas. This further inhibited world trade at a time when it needed to be stimulated.

The measures adopted by the German government of Chancellor Brüning were representative of those taken in other countries.

Income tax and unemployment insurance contributions were increased and taxes were raised on such basic items as sugar, coffee, tobacco and tea. Public sector pay was cut, as were pensions and other social security benefits and government investment generally. This was part of an overall plan to reduce Germany's expenditure on the welfare schemes introduced in 1919. Brüning also announced that for the time being Germany would not be able to keep up with reparations payments to the wartime Allies. The measures did not succeed in curing Germany's economic problems, and as unemployment grew so did support for extremist groups, notably Hitler's National Socialists.

From 1933 onward, Hitler in Germany and Roosevelt in the United States both, in their different ways, reversed these conservative economic policies by using large-scale state intervention to restore employment. In the United States the improvement was steady but slow. In Nazi Germany, where the methods were more radical, unemployment dropped rapidly, not least because of a program of rapid rearmament. Elsewhere, it was not until the end of the 1930s, when the world began to prepare for war, that the Great Depression finally came to an end.

PROPHET OF THE NEW ECONOMICS, JOHN MAYNARD KEYNES

IN FAVOR OF SPENDING According to Keynes, governments should spend more in times of recession in order to stimulate the economy.

The Englishman John Maynard Keynes (1883-1946) was one of the most influential economists of the 20th century. He was educated at Eton and Cambridge, where he demonstrated brilliance in both mathematics and classics. On graduation he joined the civil service and in 1919 attended the Paris Peace Conference as an economic adviser to the British prime minister, David Lloyd George. This experience led to the publication later that year of his devastating critique, *The Economic Consequences of the Peace*, in which he denounced the punitive terms imposed on Germany and predicted their disastrous consequences.

In the early 1930s he confronted the tragedy of the Great Depression and the failure of classical laissez-faire economics to solve the problem of mass unemployment. According to laissez-faire theory, governments should not intervene in such crises; instead, they should leave things to the market, which would automatically correct itself as workers accepted lower wages and businessmen reduced prices to restore sales. In the early 1930s this was clearly not happening; for millions there were no jobs to be had even at the lowest wages. In his *Theory of Money* (1930) and his major work, *The General Theory of Employment, Interest and Money* (1935), Keynes argued that in periods of severe recession governments must intervene to stimulate demand by substantial public investment, even if this meant going into deficit. Keynes' arguments had a great influence on Roosevelt's New Deal and have influenced governments ever since, although they began to be called into question in the 1970s.

Keynes' abilities as an economist were by no means purely theoretical. He enriched himself and King's, his Cambridge college, through shrewd investment, conducted while he breakfasted in bed. He was also a man of great charm and wide culture, a member since his undergraduate days of the circle of writers and artists known as the Bloomsbury Group.

FOOD HANDOUTS Unemployed men in rural France in 1932 have a meal provided by a local Church, but the faces show their resentment at having to rely on charity.

ROOSEVELT'S NEW DEAL

THE NEW DEAL FOR AMERICANS MEANT FEDERAL INTERVENTION ON A MASSIVE SCALE AND ACCUSATIONS OF COMMUNISM

On March 4, 1933, Franklin D. Roosevelt was inaugurated as 32nd president of the United States. In his election campaign he had already promised the American people a "New Deal." He now promised them prompt action to get people back to work. He would fight the Depression as if it were a war, and in order to do so he would demand emergency powers for himself from Congress. The American people, he told them, had "nothing to fear except fear itself."

Even before his inauguration, Roosevelt had kept an election promise to start the process of repealing Prohibition. He now embarked on his first "hundred days" of emergency legislation. With the U.S. banking system close to collapse, his first act was to declare a compulsory four-day bank holiday while the government took steps to restore stability, chiefly by eliminating the weaker banks and reinforcing the stronger. The Emergency Banking Act was passed through Congress in the single day of March 9, 1933. The Securities and Exchange Act of 1934 was one of several measures taken to prevent any repetition of the speculative boom that had produced the Wall Street Crash. Before long Roosevelt had taken the dollar off the gold standard and set out on a deliberate policy of devaluation. This was designed to encourage inflation, which he and his advisers believed would reduce the debt problem and stimulate the economy.

Apart from restoring financial stability, the main purpose of the New Deal was to tackle the problems of unemployment in industry and low prices in agriculture, and to provide relief for those for whom jobs still could not be found. Though far from being a socialist, Roosevelt was ready to abandon America's almost religious belief in laissez-faire and economic individualism. The advisors who poured into Washington, mainly academics rather than businessmen, created a program with diverse influences, from the socialist idea of state economic planning, to the corporatist ideas of Mussolini's fascism, to the central idea of the British economist, J.M. Keynes—that governments should "spend their way back to prosperity." Such ideas were anathema to conservatives and to large numbers of businessmen. For many of them Roosevelt became a deeply loathed figure.

The hundred days

The new administration was revolutionary in spirit and dynamic in action. The legislative program of the hundred days was massive; the resulting expenditure of federal funds and degree of federal involvement in business affairs were quite unprecedented.

The Federal Emergency Relief Administration, set up in May 1933, gave federal funds to state and municipal governments to help them to provide relief programs for the unemployed. The Unemployment Relief Act created the Civilian Conservation Corps which enlisted thousands of young men to work in reforestation, soil conservation and road-maintenance projects across the country.

The biggest public enterprise of all was the setting up, also in May, of the Tennessee Valley Authority. This put under public control the hydroelectric and other resources of

DRAGON SLAYER A 1934 cartoon from the German satirical magazine *Simplicissimus* depicts Roosevelt as chivalrous defender of the little man against the big financiers.

CAMPAIGN TRAIL Roosevelt shaking hands with a miner in West Virginia during his 1932 election campaign. He offered the American people hope, and they rewarded him with a landslide victory.

PLANTING FORESTS FOR THE FUTURE Young men of the Civilian Conservation Corps clear land in Virginia. Nearly 2 million men had been employed in the CCC by 1940.

a vast area, embracing parts of seven states. The project involved the construction of dams, power plants and power transmission lines. It provided electricity for the farms and townships of the area at prices that served as a benchmark against which the electricity prices of private companies could be compared. It also incorporated important measures of flood control and the production of nitrate fertilizers. As an example of large-scale public ownership and federal intervention in state affairs, the project was denounced by the administration's critics as something very close to communism.

In June 1933 came the Home Owners' Loan Corporation. This provided $2 billion to refinance the mortgages of people who were at risk of losing their homes because they could not make interest payments. The same month saw the biggest, most controversial piece of legislation, the National Industrial Recovery Act (NIRA), which created the National Recovery Administration (NRA). This set out to revive business and reduce unemployment by requiring employers to draw up voluntary codes on prices, wages and working hours which, when they were approved by the president, would become compulsory. The codes included provision for matters such as the abolition of child labor. The NRA was run by Hugh Johnson, a tough former brigadier general, and firms participating in it dis-played the agency's symbol, the Blue Eagle. At the same time NIRA officially guaranteed the right of employees to bargain collectively through labor unions. The NIRA also established the Public Works Administration (PWA) which, by 1939, had spent some $5 billion on such nationwide construction works as roads, schools, hospitals, bridges and dams.

The Civil Works Administration (CWA), created in November 1933, provided jobs for around 4 million men in projects such as road repair and park improvement.

A new deal for farmers

The Agricultural Adjustment Act of May 1933 set out to restore farm prices by subsidizing farmers in order to reduce production. The cost of the subsidies was met by a tax on processing companies such as flour millers

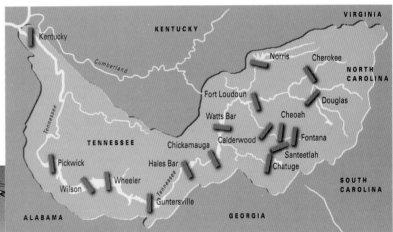

PUBLIC ENTERPRISE Designed to bring relief to an impoverished area, the Tennessee Valley Authority project was immense. The construction of a network of dams provided hydroelectric power and flood control.

and meat packers. The Farm Credit Act of June provided loans to farmers, who were in danger of losing their land to the banks and insurance companies that had provided them with credit and held their mortgages.

Such actions were much needed, for the farming crisis was particularly severe. Farming in the United States had already been depressed in the 1920s. During the Great War, it had become more intensive and increasingly mechanized to meet growing demand abroad. With the war over, demand fell; prices dropped, and kept on dropping, to the point where in many cases they fell

SCARS OF EROSION Years of overgrazing and overcropping, combined with hot, dry summers, led to the erosion of the topsoil over much of the Great Plains, turning it to dust.

below the cost of production. With no income, many farmers went into debt and lost their farms. These passed into the hands of banks, insurance companies, the Internal Revenue Service or other creditors, who rented them to tenants. Part of the dream on which the American republic was founded was of men working their own land in sturdy independence from great landowners and state officialdom. By 1935, 42 percent of American farms were worked by tenants, and less than two-thirds of these tenants had occupied their farms for more than one year.

IN THE DUST BOWL

In 1933 R.D. Lusk, a reporter on the *Saturday Evening Post*, described the first of the dust storms as it blew across the Karnstrum family's farm in South Dakota:

"By mid-morning a gale was blowing, cold and black. By noon it was blacker than night, because one can see through night and this was an opaque black. It was a wall of dirt one's eyes could not penetrate, but it could penetrate the eyes and ears and nose. It could penetrate the lungs until one coughed up black. If a person was outside, he tied his handkerchief around his face, but he still coughed up black; and inside the house the Karnstrums soaked sheets and towels and stuffed them around the window ledges, but these didn't help much.

"They were afraid, because they had never seen anything like this before . . .

"When the wind died and the sun shone forth again, it was on a different world. There were no fields, only sand drifting into mounds and eddies that swirled in what was now but an autumn breeze. There was no longer a section-line road fifty feet from the front door. It was obliterated. In the farmyard, fences, machinery and trees were gone, buried. The roofs of sheds stuck out through drifts deeper than a man is tall."

WIND AND DUST Dust storms like this one, photographed in Oklahoma in April 1936, obliterated farms and created a dust bowl across much of the American Midwest.

The record of the Agricultural Adjustment Agency was patchy, and in some cases it actually exacerbated the situation. When it offered money for reducing acreage, the larger farmers were tempted to take the check and use it to buy tractors, throw tenants and share-croppers off the land, and run their farms mechanically with the help of day laborers. The purchase of a single tractor commonly displaced two tenants and their families from the land and the rate of displacement could be much higher.

Thousands of displaced tenants became day laborers, or moved to the towns in search of relief. Some of them set off to try to earn wages in the fruit-picking fields of California. On the road these migrants met thousands of other farmers who had been displaced by a catastrophe of a different kind. Their farms had blown away.

The farms that blew away

One of the provisions of the Agricultural Adjustment Act had been to pay farmers to plant grasses on untilled land so as to secure the topsoil and prevent dust storms. But by then—1933—it was too late for many. That year saw the first of the huge dust storms that blew across many states of the Great Plains from Montana in the north to Oklahoma and Texas in the south.

For much of the 19th century the grasslands of the Great Plains had been cattle country. Before the end of the century they had been damaged by overgrazing. By the time of the Great War much of this land had been ploughed up and turned over to wheat. The region seemed to be one of great promise, a great new breadbasket for the nation. In the 1920s there were years of unusually high rainfall, disguising the underlying problem—that the Plains were hot, dry and windy. Decades of overgrazing and overcropping had destroyed the thick mat of grass and grass roots that held the topsoil together. In the hot dry summer of 1933 this topsoil turned to dust and began to blow away.

In November of 1933 the first of several great dust storms swept across the country. In 1934 and 1935, the drought continued and the winds blew again. In 1936, a farmer, watching a dust storm through his window, said that he was counting the farms of Kansas as they came by. Farms in Oklahoma became great dunes of drifting sand. Vast tracts of country were turned into an enormous dust bowl. Refugees from the dust bowl, their land now uncultivable, loaded their families and their possessions into their vehicles, often battered old Model-T Fords, and headed for California, leaving behind them an abandoned country.

For thousands of migrants, whether "Okies" from the dust bowl (particularly Oklahoma, hence their name), or evicted tenants or sharecroppers, or former industri-

HEADING WEST Thousands of farming families had no choice but to load up their possessions on their old jalopies and head for California in the hope of finding work.

al workers, California was the land of promise. In reality, what it gave them was, at best, day labor picking fruit or vegetables on its great industrialized farms—and even that could not be guaranteed. Much of the work was already done by "fruit tramps," formerly Mexicans or Japanese but now mostly Native Americans. As more and more of the new migrants poured in, the labor market became glutted. Many were unable to find work and were forced to settle into cardboard shanties or live in their cars by the roadside.

The immigrants received a poor welcome. Those who did find work were paid minimal wages and housed in camps consisting of lines of cabins that offered only the most basic

INDUSTRIAL WARFARE Workers, police and strike-breakers clash in Minneapolis in 1934 (right). Blockades were set up during the General Motors strike of 1937 (below).

accommodation. When, as many did, they tried to organize in order to improve wages and conditions, they were attacked and driven out by armed police or local vigilantes. For such people the immigrants were not fellow Americans suffering from economic and natural disaster but a dangerous, possibly communist-inspired, rabble. In the 1930s, for thousands of American farmers and their families, the move to California was a move from one tragedy to another.

A second term

In the congressional elections of 1934 the American people gave the Roosevelt administration a generous endorsement, but the honeymoon of the hundred days was over. The Civil Works Administration and its successor the Works Progress Administration were providing public sector employment for between 3 and 4 million workers. But these were meant to be only temporary measures until the economy revived. In any case, they carefully avoided any kind of productive work that competed with private industry. The employment picture as a whole remained gloomy.

Industry was reviving, but only to the extent that factories returned to full-time working with the existing work force; new jobs

were still hard to find. Through greater efficiency and speeded-up working, employers had learned to produce more goods with fewer workers. Many employers used their right under the NIRA to fix prices but

declined to raise wages to the agreed minimum levels or to recognize labor unions. Industrial relations grew ugly, sometimes violent. A new agricultural policy, which sought to raise prices by creating scarcity, came too little and too late for farmers who had already lost their farms or were so hard stretched that they had to eat the seed corn for the next harvest.

In May 1935 the Supreme Court ruled against the National Recovery Agency. The justices declared that it was unconstitutional for the federal government to interfere in what the court judged to be the internal state matters of setting wages and working hours. Roosevelt was enraged at the notion that the federal government must be impotent in dealing with national economic problems, but for the moment he could do nothing.

In 1936, when Roosevelt was campaigning for his second term, there were still 10 million unemployed Americans. One-third of the population was, in Roosevelt's words, "ill-housed, ill-clothed, ill-nourished." Most businessmen regarded the president with intense hatred. He had destroyed business confidence, they declared, through interference and overregulation. They believed that

THE LINDBERGH BABY

On the evening of March 1, 1932, the infant son of Colonel and Mrs. Charles Lindbergh was kidnapped from their home in Hopewell, New Jersey. The aviator and his wife were the most admired couple in the United States; their house, newly built and remotely situated, had been designed to provide them with some refuge from the public. The story of the kidnapping was nationwide headline news. President Hoover issued a statement; the Lindberghs received over 100,000 letters of sympathy from members of the public.

Through an intermediary the parents handed $50,000 to a man calling himself "John" who provided evidence that he was the kidnapper. "John" handed over a note describing a location on the island of Martha's Vineyard where the baby would be found. Lindbergh flew there twice and found nothing. On May 12, the child's body was discovered buried not far from the Lindbergh house.

In September 1934, Bruno Hauptmann, an illegal immigrant from Germany, was arrested and charged with the kidnapping and murder of the Lindbergh baby. He was electrocuted in April 1936. Amongst the evidence against him was the fact that $14,600 in marked bills from the ransom money had been found hidden in his garage. And part of the wooden ladder used to climb to the child's bedroom exactly matched a piece missing from a floorboard in his attic, right down to the placing of the old nail holes.

MOTHER LOVE Ann Morrow Lindbergh with her baby.

PULLING AMERICA OUT OF DEPRESSION
A *Punch* cartoon comments on Roosevelt's fight to rescue the New Deal from the U.S. Supreme Court, which had ruled some of his measures unconstitutional.

he had breached the Constitution and defied the rights of private businesses and of individual states. The federal deficit was huge, yet much of it wasted, in the opinion of the conservatives, on pointless projects that had come to be known as "boondoggles."

The Press, almost entirely anti-New Deal, predicted victory for Alfred Landon, the Republican candidate. Yet Roosevelt won a second landslide, taking every state of the Union except Maine and Vermont. Despite the hostility of their newspapers, despite the continuing problems, the American people felt admiration and trust for Roosevelt, the silver-voiced aristocrat who spoke to them in his fireside chats on the radio. His New Deal had helped them personally, and he seemed to be their ally against the forces of business greed and selfishness that had driven them out of work and into poverty.

Election victory in 1936 brought no instant solution to America's problems; indeed, matters rapidly got worse. During Roosevelt's inauguration in 1937 there was a sit-down strike at General Motors that looked as if it would turn into armed warfare. In the end the dispute was settled peacefully, but other disputes of the late 1930s were met with extreme violence as employers and unions flexed their muscles; ten picketers were killed and 90 wounded in south Chicago during strikes by workers at three steel companies which, unlike the U.S. Steel Corporation, resisted signing contracts with the unions.

A new recession

In the spring of 1937 Roosevelt took on the Supreme Court when he tried to enlarge its membership from nine to fifteen by appointing six sympathetic new justices. This scheme to "pack the Court" was defeated in Congress but the Court got the message and adopted more liberal positions, favorable to extending federal power.

Business had revived, but mainly among the big corporations; small companies were losing money. In 1937 a quarter of all corporate profits in the United States were made by six companies: General Motors, American Telephone, Standard Oil, U.S. Steel, Du Pont and General Electric. That autumn the stock market fell and the economy slipped again into severe recession. By the spring of 1938 American trade and industry had lost two-thirds of the growth it had made since the beginning of the New Deal. Some 2 million people were once again out of work.

Roosevelt was now reluctant to increase deficit spending, and tried to balance the budget to calm the business world. He then changed his mind and in April 1938 told of a further $3 billion of public spending.

GETTING ORGANIZED Steel workers stare at the camera with a mixture of aggression and apprehension. In the 1930s the unions engaged in a bitter, often violent struggle with the steel companies.

THE WOMAN BEHIND THE PRESIDENT

Eleanor Roosevelt was also her husband Franklin's distant cousin; her uncle was the earlier Roosevelt president, Theodore. She was the first presidential wife to take on a major public role in her own right, partly because she was used to being the "eyes and ears" of a husband stricken by polio in 1921. Probably more left-wing than her essentially pragmatic husband, she toured the country, speaking on issues such as child welfare, youth unemployment, slum clearance and the rights of racial minorities. From 1936 she had a syndicated newspaper column, "My Day." Though she and Franklin presented themselves as a devoted man-and-wife team, in private they led largely separate lives, he with a devoted mistress, she with a circle of close friends. After his death in 1945 she continued an active life of travelling and lecturing until her own death in 1962.

FIRST LADY Mrs. Roosevelt was an active campaigner with many causes of her own.

Business began to revive, but the beginning of arms manufacturing for a 1939 European war brought the Great Depression to an end.

Economists still debate whether it would have ended anyway. As historian Frederick Allen said: "Of all the economic medicines applied to the U.S. as a whole during the 1930s, only two had been of proved general effectiveness, and both of these have a habit-forming tendency and may be lethal if too often repeated: these two medicines are devaluation and spending." What was certain was that at the end of the Depression government in the United States had grown larger and more costly, and the agencies of federal government had a degree of power over the individual states that would have been unthinkable to an earlier generation.

STALIN'S TERROR

BETWEEN FORCED COLLECTIVIZATION AND INCESSANT PURGES OF ALL POSSIBLE OPPOSITION, STALIN DESTROYED MILLIONS OF LIVES

IRON HAND, IRON GLOVE
An admiring Soviet cartoon of 1938 shows secret police chief Nikolay Yezhov destroying opposition. The next year he himself fell victim to another round of Stalin's purges.

In the 1930s, as the world struggled through the Great Depression, intellectuals in the West published books in praise of the achievements of Russian communism—in particular, of Stalin's first Five Year Plan for the economic development of his country. The British communist John Strachey wrote: "To pass from the capitalist world into Soviet territory is to pass from death to birth." In those years Joseph Stalin, now master of the Soviet Union, was establishing his own unassailable authority and creating a socialist state free of the last vestiges of capitalism. To achieve this he was imposing on the Russian people a reign of terror whose victims would be numbered in the millions.

From 1929 on, he had three chief projects: the rapid industrialization of the Soviet Union on a massive scale; the collectivization of agriculture; and the elimination of his enemies, both real and imagined, in a huge

FATHER OF HIS PEOPLE Like the tsars of old, Stalin was presented as the father of his people, here with representatives of the Soviet Union's many nationalities.

purge of the Communist Party, the armed forces and the population at large.

The brutality of Stalin's regime derived in part from ideology—the fanatic element in Bolshevik beliefs, in which all means, including murder, were justified by the higher end of bringing communism into being. But it also stemmed from the character and motives of Stalin himself. The leading Bolshevik, Bukharin, who became one of his victims, wrote of him: "This is a small, vicious man; no, not a man, but a devil." Others of his contemporaries noted that he was obsessed with his own small stature; seven portrait painters who produced unflattering likenesses of him were shot. His wife Nadezhda committed suicide in 1932 after denouncing him before witnesses for his treatment of the peasants. His daughter later wrote that she believed that the last spark of human kindness died in him with this event.

He surrounded himself with men of exceptional cynicism and inhumanity, such as Yezhov and Beria, his

police chiefs; Molotov, who became Russia's foreign minister; and Vyshinsky, the vicious prosecutor at the show trials. At the same time he organized a cult of personality in which he was the Man of Steel, the Granite Bolshevik, the Iron Soldier, the Universal Genius who could bend anything to his will.

The great hunger

The peasants of Russia had in effect brought the Bolsheviks to power through their support of the Reds in the Civil War. This was based on the promise that they would be given the land they farmed. But millions of small peasant holdings, many still worked by wooden ploughs, could not produce the surpluses needed both to feed the workers of a greatly expanded industrial base and to be sold abroad to earn currency to buy capital equipment. By 1928 the problem had become urgent; there was food rationing in the towns and a desperate shortage of foreign currency. What was needed, the Bolshevik authorities believed, was industrialized farming on a large scale and under state control.

By the late 1920s they had determined on a gradual and partial collectivization, including the elimination of some 10 million of the wealthier peasants, or *kulaks*—the "moderate" Bukharin argued that they could be mown down with machine guns. In 1929 Stalin, having denounced this as too harsh and got rid of those who advocated it, announced that collectivization would be immediate and total. His slogan was "Liquidate the kulaks as a class," but in truth he was declaring war not just on the kulaks, but on 100 million peasant farmers.

1929 Trotsky
expelled from
Soviet Union

Police and Red Army units went into the country to impose the policy with utter ruthlessness. The kulaks, most of whom were far from wealthy by Western standards, were shot, driven into exile on barren land, or sent to the labor camps now spreading far and wide in the remoter parts of the country. The small and "middle" peasants were driven into the new collectives. Those who resisted violently were machine-gunned.

By the end of 1933 collectivization had been established. The result was famine on a massive scale, probably the first large-scale, man-made famine in history. While the Soviet state stepped up its exports of grain and butter, millions of peasants starved to death, some 4 million in the Ukraine alone. Meanwhile, the executions and deportations went on. As a party official put it: "It took a famine to show them who is master here. It has cost millions of lives, but the collective farm system is here to stay. We have won the war." The peasants who survived the war were now forbidden to change their place of domicile without state permission. Serfdom, abolished by Tsar Alexander II in 1861, had been re-established.

The numbers of those who died during the years of collectivization will never be known for certain. Stalin himself told Churchill in 1942 that he had "dealt with" 10 million

FAMINE AND SLAVERY Starving children were among the millions who suffered as a result of the Soviet state policy of "reforming" agriculture. Millions of others, like these Uzbeks (right), photographed around 1930, became slave laborers for the state.

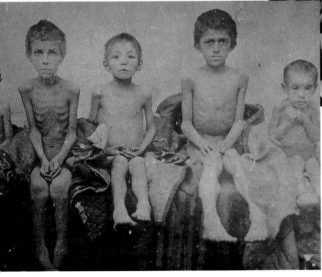

peasants. Probably more than that number died as the result of being executed on the spot, killed in fighting when they resisted, from starvation, or in the labor camps.

The crash program of industrialization went forward with equal ruthlessness. Workers were packed into ramshackle barracks alongside the factories they were building. Since they were using unfamiliar machinery for which they were untrained, fatal accidents were frequent. A system of internal passports prevented them from leaving their place of work. Food rations were controlled by factory managers and depended on achieving productivity targets. There were strict penalties, including death, for any dereliction.

1932 Stalin's wife commits suicide

1933 Millions of Russians die in great famine

1934 Murder of Kirov

1936 Trial and execution of Kamenev and Zinoviev

1937 Yezhov becomes head of NKVD

1938 Yezhov replaced by Beria and murdered

THE WEIGHT OF THE STATE

The accused at Stalin's show trials confessed to the most monstrous crimes. Mironov, a leading investigator, later described the pressure put on them:

"'You think that Kamenev may not confess?' asked Stalin, his eyes slyly screwed up.

"'I don't know,' Mironov answered. 'He doesn't yield to persuasion.'

"'You don't know?' inquired Stalin with marked surprise, staring at Mironov. 'Do you know how much our state weighs, with all the factories, machines, the army, with all the armaments and the navy?'

"... Mironov smiled, believing that Stalin was getting ready to crack a joke. But Stalin did not intend to jest . . .

"Mironov shrugged his shoulders and, like a schoolboy undergoing an examination, said in an irresolute voice: 'Nobody can know that, Yosif Vissarionovich. It is in the realm of astronomical figures.'

"'Well, and can one man withstand the pressure of that astronomical weight?,' asked Stalin sternly.

"'No,' answered Mironov.

"'Now then, don't tell me any more that Kamenev, or this or that prisoner, is able to withstand that pressure. Don't come to report to me,' said Stalin to Mironov, 'until you have in this briefcase the confession of Kamenev.'"

The Five Year Plan on which this program was based set targets for the whole industrial economy. Since local officials were terrified to admit that they had failed to meet their targets, the results claimed were largely a matter of fantasy. Yet progress was undoubtedly made, and on a giant scale. Not only factories were built but also roads, railways, dams and canals. Many of them, notably the Baltic-White Sea Canal, were built in the most inhospitable of conditions in Arctic or sub-Arctic regions. For such projects the government negotiated labor contracts with the security police, the OGPU and later the NKVD, who controlled the labor camp system. In their paranoia, Stalin and his henchmen had arrested a significant percentage of

NOW YOU SEE HIM, NOW YOU DON'T Stalin with delegates at a conference of collective farm "shockworkers" in 1935. The figure seated on Stalin's right has been purged from the photograph, as from life.

the population, providing an army of slave laborers for just this kind of work.

Millions lived and died in the camps of what came to be known as the *Gulag*—from the Russian initials for Main Administration for Corrective Labor Camps. They were the submerged part of a great iceberg of arrest, imprisonment and execution. Its visible tip was represented by the public show trials of the 1930s.

The great terror

From 1929 onward the Stalin regime conducted a campaign of terror against supposed enemies of the people. It involved highly publicized, stage-managed show trials in which the accused made carefully rehearsed confessions and were then publicly interrogated by Vyshinsky and other prosecutors. Under interrogation the accused would incriminate others, while the

spectators shouted their outrage at their crimes and well-drilled groups of "work-ers"marched up and down outside the court chanting calls for the death penalty.

The accused, almost all party members, were invariably found guilty of crimes that ranged from plotting to murder the leadership to trying to restore capitalism, from conspiring with foreign powers to the commonest "crime" of all—"wrecking" or sabotage. The entire spectacle was designed to prove that a vast conspiracy pervaded the whole of Soviet society. This, in turn, justified the arrest of thousands of others in what became a frenzy of denunciation.

The most notorious show trial began after the murder of Leningrad party boss Sergei Kirov in December 1934. Stalin—who had almost certainly ordered the murder of a man whose popularity threatened him—used the killing as a pretext for turning on other enemies. Those immediately involved were executed and 40,000 Leningraders sent to the labor camps. Two weeks later Zinoviev and Kamenev, survivors of the old Bolshevik leadership, were arrested. In 1936 they were put on trial and confessed, having been promised that their lives would be spared and their families left alone. In fact, both were shot immediately after the trial, along with 5,000 party members arrested at the same time. Bukharin, the last of the old leadership, was arrested and shot the following year.

BERIA, ARCHITECT OF TERROR

Lavrenty Beria, Stalin's most notorious henchman, was born in 1899 and joined the Communist Party in 1917. By 1921 he had begun the career he found most congenial, as a secret policeman. In 1938 Stalin brought him from Georgia to Moscow to replace "the bloodthirsty dwarf," Yezhov, as head of the Commissariat of Internal Affairs, NKVD. Beria at once initiated a purge of the police under his control; Yezhov himself disappeared, almost certainly executed.

Under Beria the public show trials came to an end, but arbitrary arrests were kept up to maintain an atmosphere of terror. For the next 15 years he ran the vast apparatus of the state security system, including its espionage operations and labor camps. In the postwar years he stage-managed a new series of purges for his increasingly insane master.

Stalin died in March 1953. Three months later Beria was arrested. Officially he was tried and executed in December that year, but Nikita Khrushchev later circulated a story that he was either strangled or shot by prominent party members immediately after his arrest.

FAITHFUL SERVANT Beria maintained the terror for Stalin, but did not long survive his master.

No one was safe from the Great Terror, and the accusers often became the accused. In 1937, when Stalin's crony, Yezhov, became head of the NKVD, 3,000 of the officers who had served under his predecessor Yagoda were shot and hundreds of others committed suicide at the moment of arrest. In the same year 90 percent of provincial prosecutors were executed. Yezhov himself was murdered and replaced by Beria in 1938. In that same period some 30,000 senior army officers were put to death, accused of conspiring with Nazi Germany. Of 150 delegates representing Leningrad at the 17th Party Congress, only two escaped death. The victims also included large numbers of foreign communists, many of whom were taking refuge from persecution in their own countries. The Marxist historian Roy Medvedev wrote that "most European communist leaders and activists who lived in the U.S.S.R. perished, while most of those who were in prison in their native lands in 1937-8 survived." Many victims of the purge died under torture.

The total death count of the Great Terror may never be known. Stalin personally signed death lists with the names of over 40,000 persons, but these were the more prominent cases. The total number of party members arrested was over a million, of whom the majority were executed at once or died in the camps. But the purge spread far beyond the party to engulf millions of people, arrested for a careless remark, or because local officials had a quota for denunciation and were fearful of arrest if they did not meet it.

The "islands" of what the writer Alexander Solzhenitsyn would later call the "Gulag archipelago" occupied thousands of square miles in the most rugged parts of the country. From the mid 1930s until Stalin's death in 1953 their population never fell below 10 million. The average death rate was over a million people a year, from exhaustion, disease, cold and hunger or from beatings and shootings by the guards. In the camps of the Arctic regions the death rate was well above that average. Today, estimates of the total number of deaths in the camps range between 8 and 15 million.

PURGED FROM POWER In 1922 Grigory Yevseyevich Zinoviev (left) and Lev Borisovich Kamenev (above) had shared the supreme leadership with Stalin. In 1936 they were summarily shot after a show trial.

THE THOUSAND-YEAR REICH

ONCE IN POWER, HITLER ABOLISHED DEMOCRACY, BEGAN TO IMPOSE HIS RACIAL POLICIES AND PREPARED GERMANY FOR AGGRESSIVE WAR

It was the Depression and fear of communism that brought Adolf Hitler and his National Socialist Party to power in Germany. In 1929 the party had only 120,000 members; just a year later, it became the second largest party in the Reichstag, with 107 seats, the Communists being third with 77. By 1932 it had almost 800,000 members and its private army, the *Sturmabteilung* (SA), numbered half a million. The business community's fear of a communist revolution ensured that it was well financed.

Political instability brought two sets of Reichstag elections in 1932 in both of which the Nazis came out as the largest party. They won 230 seats in July; in November their share fell to 196, against 100 for the Communists, but the election was still a convincing victory. The army and the political Right now offered

FLAMES IN THE NIGHT The burning of the Reichstag, the German parliament building, gave Hitler the pretext he wanted to establish himself as dictator of a totalitarian state.

Hitler an anti-communist coalition, believing that they could use him. Hitler's price was the top post in the government.

On January 30, 1933, he became chancellor. That night he put on the first of the Nazis' political spectaculars, a six-hour torchlight parade of SA men before the Chancellery. At this point he had only two fellow Nazis in his government, Hermann Goering and Wilhelm Frick, but together they controlled the German interior ministry and therefore the police. Goering ordered an immediate expansion of the Gestapo, or Secret State Police, under Nazi officers and added 50,000 SA members as police auxiliaries. Using Hitler's constitutional powers as chancellor they began breaking up opposition political parties and newspapers.

On the night of February 27, 1933, less than a month after Hitler came to power, the Reichstag burnt down. This was probably the work of a demented loner, Martinus van der Lubbe, but it gave Hitler the pretext he needed to bring in an Emergency Decree, which effectively abolished all constitutional civil rights. Hitler ordered yet another round of elections for March 1933 in which the Nazis won 288 seats with 43.9 percent of the votes. They had won power democratically, but Hitler's Enabling Act a few weeks later brought German democracy formally to an end, establishing in its place a totalitarian state with Hitler as dictator. Germany still had a constitutional president, the First World War hero Field Marshal Paul von Hindenburg. When he died in August 1934 Hitler merged the two offices of president and chancellor into that of *Führer* ("Leader").

Meanwhile, all non-Nazi political parties had been dissolved. Members of left-wing parties were hunted down and then beaten, imprisoned or in some cases murdered. Those who escaped fled the country or went underground.

The first concentration camps were set up; for the moment, they were there only for the internment of political dissidents. They were placed under the control of another of Hitler's henchmen, Heinrich Himmler, and his black-uniformed *Schutzstaffel* or SS.

Originally formed as Hitler's personal bodyguard, the SS had been greatly enlarged. It now had its own military units and its own internal security organization, the *Sicherheitsdienst* (SD) under Reinhard Heydrich. It saw itself as an elite body, a new order of chivalry very different from the ruffianly SA; its ranks included members of the German nobility as well as lawyers, doctors and civil servants.

Night of the Long Knives

In 1934 the brownshirted SA had an active membership of a million men, and was both a threat and a source of political embarrassment to Hitler. Its leader, Ernst Röhm, went back to the earliest days of National Socialism and, with a huge private army at his back, had never fully accepted the supremacy of the Führer. His men saw themselves as the ones who had won the revolution that destroyed the Weimar Republic. They now expected their reward in the shape of a second, socialist, revolution that among other things would allow them to take over the German army and nationalize the German economy. Their socialist aims were disturbing to German business interests and their thuggish behavior was deeply offensive to the mass of respectable citizens. Above all, the German army, whose support Hitler desperately needed, had given him its backing on condition that the SA was cut down to size.

Having come into power, Hitler had to bring his street fighters under control. He set out to decapitate the SA, taking the opportunity to remove other enemies at the same time. His instruments were the SS and the Gestapo. Publicly, Hitler usually took pains to observe the legalities of a civilized society, but the purge of June 30, 1934, the "Night of the Long Knives," was an act of sheer gangsterism worthy of Al Capone. Hitler was both its planner and an active participant. Having signed the execu-

GUN RULE In March 1933, Nazi stormtroopers stand guard over suspected opponents of the new regime.

tion lists of those involved in an alleged "SA conspiracy," he flew to Munich. There, carrying a whip, he led the group that arrested Ernst Röhm at the Bavarian lake resort of Bad Wiessee. Other groups led by Himmler, Heydrich and Goering moved against the SA in Berlin and elsewhere. Röhm survived until July 2, but scores of other SA leaders
continued on page 92

NEW POWER The SS, led by Heinrich Himmler (left), became a state-within-the-state. With its death's head and lightning flash badges (top), it saw itself as a new order of chivalry.

BROWNSHIRTS Röhm (right), his face puckered with bullet wounds from the Great War, built up the SA (above) to a force of a million men.

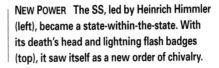

1933 Hitler becomes chancellor

1934 Night of the Long Knives

1935 Nuremberg Laws promulgated

1936 German troops march into the demilitarized Rhineland

1938 *Anschluss* with Austria

AN EVIL MAGIC

Mussolini's Italy helped to teach Hitler the importance of political spectacle, while the example of Stalin encouraged him in promoting a cult of personality. But he did not need too much teaching in either subject, for he had a strong instinct for both aspects of totalitarian showmanship. In his youth he had been an artist and a bohemian; at one point he described himself as "the greatest actor in Europe." He had promised the German people that he would abolish politics; in its place he offered them participation in a Wagnerian national drama in which he was the central figure. He was ably assisted by Goebbels, his propagandist, and Speer, his favorite architect.

Spectacle therefore became central to the creation of the "National Socialist Idea" and the Hitler cult. As soon as they had taken power the Nazis introduced a program of public ceremonies—state visits, memorial days, services for Nazi "martyrs," all splendidly choreographed. The effect of forests of blood-red flags and torches, the columns of marching men, the bands, the chants of acclamation was overwhelming. Several foreign observers noted that at the high moments of these ceremonies they longed to become Nazis and join in themselves. The center of the new Berlin that Hitler was planning with Speer and his other architects was designed not for commerce or administration, but for ceremony and symbolism on a colossal scale. The most magnificent of the regular festivals were the annual eight-day Nuremberg party rallies. At the climax of the 1937 rally, 30,000 flag-bearers advanced toward the grandstand and the beams of 150 searchlights shot into the sky around the vast arena creating "a cathedral of light" at the moment of Hitler's arrival. Then the searchlights were lowered inward as he began to speak. His oratory, as always during this period, was spellbinding.

The purpose of these ceremonies was to give the party and the people an intense sense of belonging. They were part of a Germany that had been wronged at Versailles but was now triumphant—thanks to Adolf Hitler. He was the "man of the people," the simple front-line soldier, chosen and inspired by Providence to give their lives new meaning. Behind this idolatry lay a magic that worked for millions of Germans, at least until the war it would draw them into began to go wrong.

A CAST OF THOUSANDS **Rallies with thousands of uniformed men marching in step had a key part in building up Nazi mystique. They were particularly effective at night, lit by torches and searchlights.**

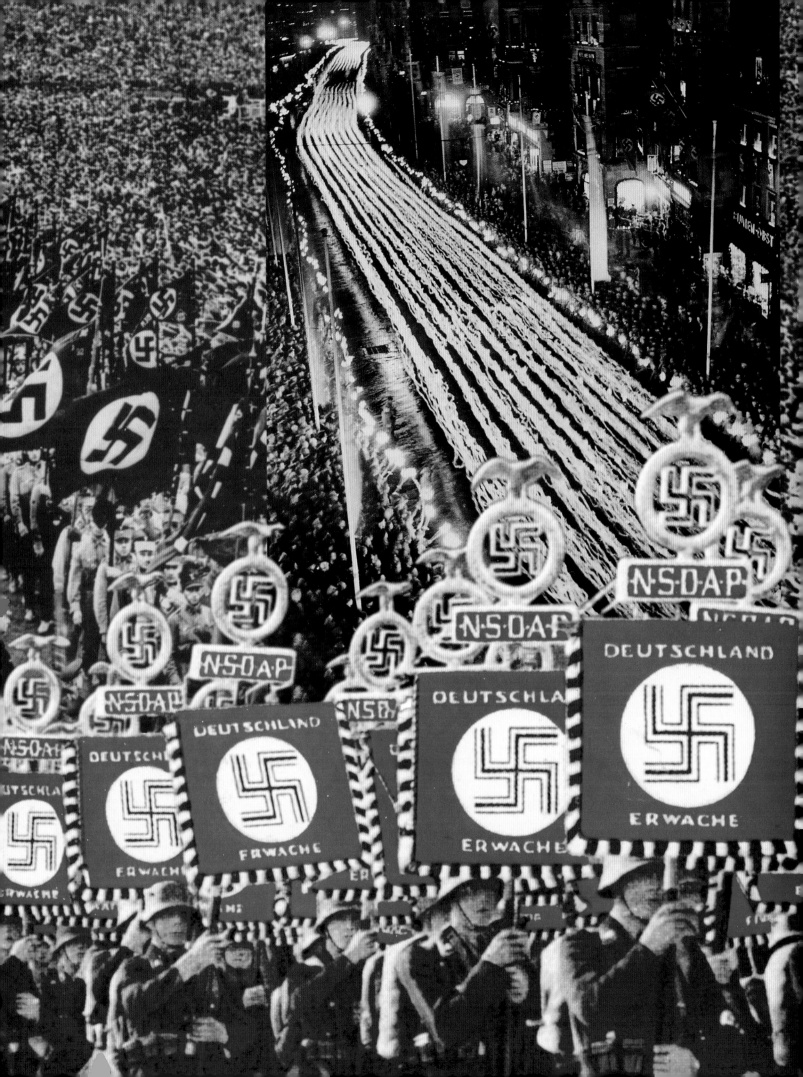

were arrested and shot that same night. Some of them, bewildered, died crying "*Heil Hitler!*" Apart from the SA, those murdered included a rival Nazi leader, Gregor Strasser, and prominent anti-Nazis such as the former chancellor, General von Schleicher, and his wife, both killed in their Berlin apartment.

In his purge Hitler had emulated the worst excesses of the Bolsheviks—serving in his turn as a model for Stalin's purges later in the 1930s. Yet the Night of the Long Knives, by clipping the unruly Brownshirts' wings, increased his popularity in the country as a whole. In August all officers and men of the army took an oath of obedience to the Führer. Later that month, 84.6 percent of Germans gave him their support in a plebiscite.

Nazi government

The National Socialists had promised the restoration of full employment and public order, but apart from establishing their own savage kind of order, they had few systematic policies. Nazi government was based on the

overlapping empires of men like Goering, Goebbels, Ribbentrop and Himmler, who loathed and distrusted each other. Hitler himself, who deliberately fomented the rivalries of his chieftains, was uninterested in the administrative detail of domestic policy.

Even policy toward the Jews was unsystematic in the early years. Individual Jews were murdered, humiliated and stripped of their property. But the Economics Ministry dissuaded Hitler from keeping his promise of smashing Jewish-owned businesses, fearing that this would lead to mass unemployment and attacks on big business in general. Jews began leaving Germany in large numbers, but for the moment there was no policy of enforced emigration or mass arrests.

In 1935 the Law for the Protection of German Blood was announced at a party rally in Nuremberg. It outlawed marriage and sexual relations between Aryans and non-Aryans—that is, Jews, Gypsies and other racial minorities. Jews were also denied citizenship. In 1938 pressure intensified. Jewish passports were stamped with a "J". Jewish men were

FINANCIAL WIZARD Hjalmar Schacht addressing a meeting in 1934, his neat civilian clothes striking an incongruous note among the uniformed figures around him. As minister of economics from 1934 to 1937, he played a major part in the Nazis' economic success.

obliged to add the name Israel to their given names; Jewish women had to add Sara. Jewish doctors, dentists and lawyers were forbidden to offer their services to Aryans.

On November 9, 1938, came the terrible pogrom of *Kristallnacht* ("Night of Broken Glass"), the opening salvo in a campaign of systematic violence against Jews and their property; it was instigated by Hitler's propaganda chief, Joseph Goebbels. On that night, 91 Jews were murdered and 20,000 sent to concentration camps; synagogues were burnt down and Jewish shops had their windows shattered. Thereafter, efforts were stepped up to drive Jews out of German society and the German economy. But Hitler had to wait for war before embarking on his long-term aim of destroying European Jewry altogether.

Nazi economic policy was one of state-directed capitalism. Hitler had no intention of making Lenin's mistake of removing those who knew how to run business and industry. Although he called himself a socialist, his notion of socialism was one in which individuals and groups should be compelled to work in the national interest. As he put it: "Why should we need to socialize the banks and the factories? We are socializing the people." Free trade unions were abolished and replaced by state-controlled unions. The big industrialists kept their businesses, but were compelled to serve the requirements of the Nazi state.

A key part of this process, which included a huge program of public works, notably road-building and reforestation, was to make

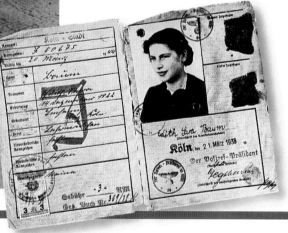

BROKEN GLASS, BROKEN LIVES After *Kristallnacht* came the task of clearing up the glass on the streets (left). A Jewish passport (below) is stamped with a "J" and shows "Sara" as its owner's middle name.

Germany economically self-sufficient. Hitler's brilliant economics minister, Hjalmar Schacht, provided the money by a policy of strict exchange control, high taxation, regulation of wages, prices and profits, and careful management of resources. As a result, Germany was the first country to emerge from the Great Depression. Living standards for ordinary working people did not rise much, but unemployment began to fall and by 1936 was virtually eliminated. From 1936 there was a Four Year Plan—to prepare the armed forces and the country's economy for war in four years' time. That meant the production of weapons and materials on which an embattled country would have to rely.

Toward a greater Reich

In 1936 Hitler, now openly rearming, decided that the time had come to test the Western democracies' resolve. In March that year he sent troops into the Rhineland, which had been declared a demilitarized zone, initially under French and British supervision, in the Versailles settlement. His officers had orders to retreat at once if the French showed any sign of resistance, but there was none. A moment in which a new world war might be averted had passed. Hitler had demonstrated an apparently infallible political instinct.

By 1938 Hitler was pressuring his native Austria with its own expanding Nazi Party. In February he summoned the Austrian chancellor, Kurt von Schuschnigg, to his villa at Berchtesgaden and compelled him to put Arthur Seyss-Inquart, a leading local Nazi, in charge of the Austrian police. Later, Schuschnigg tried to outmaneuver the Nazis by calling a plebiscite on the issue of Austrian independence. Nazi disturbances obliged him to cancel the referendum, however. He resigned and Seyss-Inquart took his place as chancellor, appealing to Germany for help in "restoring order."

In March 1938 Hitler fulfilled his own dream, and that of many Austrians, by bringing the country into the German Reich with no resistance. The *Anschluss* was again in breach of Versailles and particularly abhorrent to Mussolini's Italy. As Hitler had calculated, there was now no likelihood of the other European nations uniting to oppose it. The *Anschluss* became a fact in a mere 24 hours. On March 14 Hitler drove through Vienna along swastika-bedecked streets lined with cheering crowds. Meanwhile, the SS moved in with the help of local Nazis to seek out Austrian Jews, liberals, socialists and communists. Elderly university professors were made to clean the streets with their bare hands. Thousands of people—undesirables — were killed or sent to concentration camps.

Despite these brutalities, a plebiscite the next month confirmed support for the *Anschluss*. Hitler had again achieved a bloodless victory leading to his next move. Possession of Austria meant that German territory now beset western Czechoslovakia on three sides. On April 21, 1938, he ordered his generals to prepare an invasion plan.

THE RISING TIDE OF FASCISM

THE APPARENT SUCCESS OF ITALIAN FASCISM SPAWNED MANY IMITATIONS IN THE EUROPE OF THE 1920S AND 30S

In October 1935, in order to divert attention from discontent at home, and as the first stage of his project to enlarge the empire of his new imperial Rome, Mussolini invaded Abyssinia (Ethiopia). The ancient Christian kingdom, whose rulers claimed descent from the Old Testament's Queen of Sheba, was a poor, technologically backward country in which slavery still flourished. In invading it, Mussolini claimed for Italy the same civilizing mission that other European nations had invoked in their overseas expansion. By May 1936 Abyssinia was in Italian hands, and its emperor in exile.

Italy's invasion of Abyssinia had a crucial, even a tragic, effect on the international politics of Europe. Before it, Italy had been a potential ally of France and Britain against Hitler's Germany. Italy had been at war with Germany and Austria less than 20 years earlier in the First World War. It greatly feared an Austria united with Germany on its northern frontier and was therefore opposed to Nazi plans for *Anschluss*. Mussolini at this time had little respect for Hitler, whom he regarded as a brutal and fanatical upstart; in particular, he deplored Hitler's anti-Semitism.

Immediately after the invasion, the League of Nations denounced Mussolini as an aggressor and imposed sanctions on Italy. The sanctions operated by the French and British were mild and half-hearted, and thus ineffective, but they were enough to turn Mussolini into an enemy. The Nazis, seeing their opportunity, began to court him with flattery; Hitler called him "the leading statesman in the world." By the end of 1936 Mussolini was referring to a "Rome-Berlin Axis" and actively cooperating with the Germans in sending military aid to the right-wing nationalists in the Spanish Civil War. In 1937 he left the League of Nations. In April 1939, emboldened by German support, he continued his conquests by invading and annexing Albania. One month later he signed a "Pact of Steel" with Hitler.

Italian fascism and, later, German

FIGURES OF INFLUENCE Goering (in the white jacket) playing host to Mussolini during *Il Duce*'s visit to Germany in September 1937. Germany wooed Italy as a potential ally. The two countries formed a "Pact of Steel" in 1939.

1928 Zog I becomes King of Albania; Iron Guard founded in Romania

ALL SMILES Hitler supplied Franco with men and arms in the Spanish Civil War. Spain remained neutral in the Second World War, though Spanish troops took part in the German attack on Russia.

National Socialism helped to inspire similar parties or movements in most European countries during the 1920s and 30s. France had Action Française and Colonel François de La Rocque's Croix de Feu; Belgium had the Rexists. Britain had Oswald Mosley's British Union of Fascists; Spain had the Falange, Romania the Iron Guard. All tapped into ultranationalist forces in their countries, and some—for example, the Spanish Falange —were shaped as much by these forces as by the fascist example. There were also strong National Socialist parties, directly modelled on the German one, in Austria, Sweden and among ethnic Germans of Czechoslovakia.

The dictators

Even before these parties had started to sprout, many of the fragile new democracies created by the Versailles settlement had collapsed and been replaced by regimes that were authoritarian, if not strictly fascist. In Hungary, liberal democracy survived only five months. Following the suppression of Béla Kun's Soviet-style republic in August 1919, Admiral Horthy, who had formerly commanded the Austro-Hungarian navy, assumed

power and conducted a "white terror" against communism which also had the effect of undermining liberal institutions. Horthy was nominally regent for a Habsburg monarchy that parliament had voted to restore, but King Carl IV was never allowed to ascend his throne. Landlocked Hungary was a kingdom without a king, ruled by an admiral without a navy. Parliament and trade unions survived, but in the 1930s Horthy's regime turned increasingly into a right-wing military dictatorship. Strongly anti-Bolshevik and committed to the restoration of the territories Hungary had lost in the Versailles settlement, Horthy was ready to enter into an alliance with Hitler at the beginning of the Second World War.

Greece, which had joined in the war against Germany in 1917, should have gained from the Allied victory. But after a disastrous invasion of Turkey in 1919, it was forced to give up its claims to Asia Minor, and 1.5 million Greeks were obliged to flee across the Aegean in an early version of "ethnic cleansing." In 1922 General Ioannis Metaxas, the country's wartime chief of staff, who had opposed the invasion of Turkey, attempted a coup d'état. It did not succeed, but it was the first of several attempts to overthrow an increasingly unstable parliamentary democracy under Prime Minister Eleutherios Venizelos.

Much of Greece's instability came from a running conflict between royalists and republicans. In 1924 the republicans succeeded in ousting the king, George II, and established a presidential regime. In 1936, after a plebiscite, the king was recalled from exile. But the parliamentary deadlock between royalists and republicans continued, with a small number of communist deputies holding the balance of power. The

DICTATORSHIP AND FRAGILE DEMOCRACY
Admiral Horthy of Hungary (above) disliked Hitler, but disliked communism even more. A Greek in traditional costume (below) votes in an election in 1935.

1940

1934 King Alexander of Yugoslavia assassinated   1935 Mussolini invades Abyssinia   1936 Metaxas becomes dictator in Greece   1939 Mussolini annexes Albania

SEIZE THE ASSASSIN Confusion in Marseilles, where Alexander of Yugoslavia and the French foreign minister have just been shot by a Croat assassin, Petrus Kalerman (top). Above: Alexander with his son, Peter, in 1930.

king's response was to hand the government over to Metaxas, who at once abolished parliament and ruled as virtual dictator, calling himself "the First Peasant," the "First Worker" and the "National Father." Metaxas had strong sympathies with German notions of order and collective discipline, and his rule was semi-fascist. Later, however, in 1940, it was he who led the country's successful defense against an Italian invasion.

Crisis in the Balkans

The Balkans had been in a state of crisis ever since the Ottoman Empire started to break up in the 19th century. The postwar settlement, enshrined in the Treaties of St. Germain and Trianon, had merely drawn new frontiers on what was still a patchwork of nationalities with different traditions. In the past, Turkey, Austria and Russia had competed for possessions in the region; now France, Italy and Britain backed its different countries, while Russia backed the local communist parties.

Nowhere was the Balkan problem more acute than in the new state of Yugoslavia, with its uneasy coalition of Serbs, Croats, Slovenes Muslims and other groups, divided by culture, religion and political allegiances. The Slovenes resented what they saw as excessive Croatian influence in the national government; the Croats felt the same about the Serbs; the peasants were deeply suspicious of the mainly urban Muslims. A party of extreme Croat nationalists, the Ustachi, was formed in Rome with the support of Mussolini.

In 1928, Stjepan Radic, leader of the Croatian Peasant Party, was assassinated by a Serb. With Croats refusing to cooperate with Serbs and parliamentary government breaking down, King Alexander scrapped the constitution and assumed dictatorial powers. In 1934 he was assassinated in Marseilles by a Croatian nationalist and was succeeded by his 11-year-old son, who became Peter II, with Prince Paul, Alexander's brother, acting as regent.

Prince Paul continued his brother's autocratic rule, but recognized that the state could not hold together unless the Croats

AN ANCIENT ANGER

In 1937 the writer Rebecca West travelled through the Balkans with her husband, Henry Maxwell Andrews. Sitting with Serbian friends in a café in Sarajevo, she heard a man expressing rage at the forthcoming visit of the Turkish prime minister:

"'But how is it possible,' said my husband, 'that there should be so much feeling against the Turks when nobody who is not very old can possibly have had any personal experience of their oppressions?'

"The three men looked at my husband as if he were talking great nonsense . . .'Ah, no, no, no!' [they] exclaimed . . . 'You do not understand,' said Constantine; 'the Turkish Empire went from here in 1878, but the . . . Moslems remained, and when Austria took control it was still their holiday. For they were the favorites of the Austrians . . .' 'But why was that?' asked my husband. 'It was because of the principle, *Divide et impera* [divide and rule],' said the banker . . . 'Look, there were fifty or sixty thousand people in the town,' said the banker. 'There were us, the Jews, who are of two kinds, the Sephardim, from Spain and Portugal, and the others, the Ashkenazi, who are from central Europe and the East . . . Then there were the Christian Slavs, who are Croats and Serbs, and that is a division. But lest we should forget our differences, they raised up the Moslems, who were a third of the population, to be their allies . . . It is not that we do not like the Moslems. Since the war all things have changed, and we are on excellent terms. But it is not nice when they are picked out by the Government and allowed to receive a ceremonial visit from the representative of the power that crushed us and ground us down into the mud.'"

❞

were given greater autonomy in the part of the country in which they were the majority. In 1939, therefore, he set up a semi-independent Croatia as part of a Yugoslav federation. This was not enough to satisfy the Ustachi, but enough to be bitterly resented by the Serbs, who formed a large minority in Croatia. The country was still deeply divided when Germany invaded in 1941.

The complexity of Balkan politics was epitomized in the small, remote and backward state of Albania, a former Ottoman province that had become an independent nation as recently as 1912. The Austrians had occupied it during the First World War until ejected by Serbian, French and Italian forces in 1918. It still relied heavily on Italian protection. Its population was predominantly Muslim, and it was a member of a leading Muslim family, Ahmed Bey Zogu, who became its prime minister in 1920. Democracy was alien to its deeply traditional, mainly peasant, population, and in 1928 Zogu was able to have himself proclaimed king, taking the name Zog I. Zog brought internal stability to the country, but it remained dependent on Italy for defense

KING ZOG I In 1928 Ahmed Bey Zogu (right) created a new monarchy in Albania with himself as monarch. It was welcomed by the fiercely traditional peasant farmers of this mountainous country (below).

and financial support. In 1939 Mussolini marched his forces in and annexed it, deposing Zog in favor of Italy's Victor Emmanuel. Zog went into exile, never to return.

The Iron Guard

Romania was on the victors' side in 1918. It made large territorial gains from the breakup of the Austro-Hungarian Empire, leaving it with large minority populations of Hungarians, Germans, Jews and Bulgarians, as well as bringing many ethnic Romanians for the first time under Romanian rule. In particular, it acquired Transylvania from Hungary. To celebrate this, King Ferdinand and his English-born queen, Marie, were recrowned in 1922 as king and queen of all Romanians at the Transylvanian town of Alba Iulia.

Romania's postwar government was a coalition of peasant parties, but a revolutionary

BETWEEN TWO GIANTS

THE COUNTRIES OF CENTRAL EUROPE LIVED BETWEEN THE ANVIL AND THE HAMMER: IT WAS ONLY A MATTER OF TIME BEFORE THEY WOULD BE CRUSHED

Between Nazi Germany and Hitler's ultimate objective, Bolshevik Russia, lay Austria, Poland and Czechoslovakia. Austria, once the heartland of an empire, was reduced to a landlocked country of 7 million people, many of whom were desperate for *Anschluss,* or union, with their German kinsfolk. In the 1930s Hitler's theories found rich soil here in which to grow, and with public disorder increasing, Chancellor Dollfuss set up a conservative dictatorship, closer in spirit to Mussolini's fascism than National Socialism. In July 1934 Dollfuss was murdered by Austrian Nazis. The authorities responded with martial law and strong-arm methods that prevented a Nazi takeover—for the time being.

Since 1926 Poland had been under the near-dictatorship of Marshal Pilsudski. After his death in 1935, this was succeeded by the similarly autocratic "Government of the Colonels." Pilsudski's regime had brought a degree of stability and economic development to the country, but by the late 1930s there was increasing opposition from extremists of left and right. Poland also had Europe's largest Jewish population—which would suffer accordingly in the cataclysm ahead.

Thanks to the wise rule of Czechoslovakia's founding fathers, Tomas Masaryk and Eduard Benes, democracy had established itself there—despite divisions between the mainly rural east (Slovakia) and the industrial west (Bohemia) and the presence of some 3.5 million ethnic Germans in the

Sudetenland. Among the Sudeten Germans, however, a strong Nazi Party did emerge under Konrad Henlein and stirred up a sense of grievance with stories of injuries supposedly suffered at the hands of the Czechs. Czechoslovakia was one of the world's leading arms manufacturers with an army of nearly 40 divisions. But it was not strong enough to resist German invasion without help from Russia, France and Britain. The Sudeten Germans, now clamoring for independence, lived mostly in the area bordering Germany. A collision with the Nazis was all but inevitable.

DAYS OF CRISIS An armored car (top) patrols Vienna during the attempted Nazi *putsch* of 1934.
Right: Pilsudski at his desk. German-speaking children (below) welcome the German occupation of the Sudetenland.

fascist movement founded by Corneliu Codreanu in 1927 expanded quickly, drawing its strength from the country's traditional anti-Semitism—a year later, the movement took the name "Iron Guard." Also in 1927, King Ferdinand died, leaving the succession in some confusion. The old king had disapproved of his son Carol's lifestyle—notably Carol's liaison with his mistress, Madame Lupescu—and had forced him to renounce his right to the throne. This passed to Carol's son, the five-year-old Michael. In 1930, however, Carol returned from exile, ousted the regency council that had been ruling in his son's name and proclaimed himself king.

Instability continued. In the Depression years, the Iron Guard, like fascist parties everywhere, grew greatly in strength. In 1938, however, as the economy revived, Carol took the opportunity to have Codreanu killed and

ROMANIA'S ROYAL DICTATOR An admirer of Mussolini, King Carol suppressed Romania's Iron Guard, and then set up a dictatorship on Italian fascist lines with himself as dictator.

to put down the Iron Guard. From then on he ruled as effective dictator. In 1940, under pressure from Germany and the Soviet Union, Romania was obliged to hand over much of its territory to Russia, Hungary and Bulgaria. Humiliated, King Carol fled the country. General Ion Antonescu became dictator, and it was he who invited German troops to enter Romania in October 1940.

In October 1918 Bulgaria's king, another Ferdinand—who had sided with Germany in the war—abdicated in favor of his son Boris, who found himself at odds with a new government led by Alexander Stambolisky, which had come to power in 1919 on a policy of transferring land and political power to the country's predominant peasant class. Bulgarian politics were complicated by the presence of large numbers of Macedonians, displaced when their land was partitioned between Greece and Yugoslavia. Some of them formed a terrorist Internal Macedonian Revolutionary Organization (IMRO).

Stambolisky was overthrown in 1923 in a coup d'état engineered in part by IMRO, in part by King Boris; a short while afterwards Stambolisky was assassinated. A shaky parliamentary regime, with strong military and royalist influence, replaced him. Deprived almost entirely of foreign invesment capital,the country stagnated. In the Depression years, its high-cost peasant agriculture found it almost impossible to find markets abroad. After 1933 Nazi Germany won support by buying Bulgarian produce. King Boris moved closer and closer toward an alliance with Germany. In 1934 a coup d'état brought a military group to power that dispersed the gunmen of IMRO. By 1938 King Boris was dictator in all but name. In 1941 he joined the Axis pact, but strove to maintain Bulgaria's independence; he refused, for example, to send troops to take part in Germany's invasion of the Soviet Union. He died in 1943, shortly after an angry meeting with Adolf Hitler. His death almost certainly resulted from a heart attack—though there were rumors at the time that he had been poisoned.

HAILE SELASSIE, LION OF JUDAH

EVERY INCH AN EMPEROR Haile Selassie was the ruler of one of the world's most ancient monarchies when it was invaded in 1935.

The man who was to rule Abyssinia as the Emperor Haile Selassie ("Might of the Trinity") was born in 1892. His name at birth was Lij Tafari—*Lij* was a title given to all nobles. Later, as he rose in importance, he became *Ras* (Prince) Tafari.

The son of an influential courtier of royal blood, he grew up in the service of the monarchy. As a provincial governor he followed "modernizing" policies, which were closer in European terms to those of the 16th century than the 20th. His main concern was to curb the powers of the feudal nobility and to strengthen the authority of the central royal government. In 1916 he was appointed regent and co-ruler with the Empress Zauditu. After Zauditu's death in 1930 he succeeded as emperor.

Although the country's constitution provided for a parliament, it rarely met, and Abyssinia was in effect an absolute monarchy. Haile Selassie personally led the forces that resisted the Italian invasion in 1935 and went to the League of Nations to appeal, in vain, for military aid. Defeated, he went into exile in May 1936.

During the Second World War he raised an army of Abyssinian exiles which, fighting with British forces, invaded his own country and recaptured the capital, Addis Ababa, in 1941. Restored to his throne, he continued to reign until he was murdered in the course of a Communist-inspired coup d'état in 1974.

LIFE IN EUROPE'S DEMOCRACIES

IN BRITAIN AND FRANCE, THE DEPRESSION YEARS REVEALED BOTH THE STRENGTHS AND THE WEAKNESSES OF THE SOCIAL FABRIC

AT THE BARRICADES A crowd in London's East End clashes with police as it protests against a proposed fascist march in October 1936.

In Britain during the crisis years of the 1930s, the nation somehow held together. In France, on the other hand, much of the urban population, at least, was driven by class conflict or ideological conviction to the extremes of right or left; from time to time, violence erupted both in the streets and in parliament, and the country was further divided after 1940, when one side allied itself with the occupying Germans.

If Britain remained stable during those years, it was in part because ideology had small appeal for most people, while the sense of nationhood was robust enough to withstand great and manifest social inequalities. There was a sizable and influential British Communist Party, but both the Labor Party and the trade unions for the most part distanced themselves from it; there was a black-shirted British Union of Fascists, founded by the patrician socialist Sir Oswald Mosley on the Mussolini model, but it was despised and ridiculed by the majority of people of all classes and won no parliamentary seats. Both communists and fascists created a certain amount of public disorder by trying to break up each other's meetings, mainly

in London, but in 1936 the government passed a Public Order Act that banned provocative demonstrations and the wearing of political uniforms.

Ramsay MacDonald's coalition National Government (1931-5) and Stanley Baldwin's moderate Conservative government (1935-7) managed to maintain at least grudging public acceptance, and their policies achieved a steady economic recovery from 1934 onward. At the 1931 election the National Government had gained 554 seats against a total opposition of only 61; the Baldwin government of 1935 had a comfortable majority. Both therefore could govern with a secure popular mandate.

Most of all, perhaps, the shock of the Depression was cushioned by the fact that it was so unequal in its effects, especially in the distribution of unemployment and consequent deprivation. The

numbers employed in the new electrical and electronics industry actually increased by 25 percent between 1930 and 1936, and the aircraft manufacturing and chemical and petrochemical industries expanded similarly. There was a building boom that produced more than 3 million new houses, and the number of cars manufactured annually more than doubled in the same period.

On the other hand, the sufferings of the less fortunate were real enough, too. There were no television

TOOTHLESS LION Mosley's fascist newspaper had a roaring lion as its logo, but his party never won mainstream support. Right: Mosley reviewing some of his female followers in 1939. He would spend most of the war years interned, along with other leading British fascists.

MAKING ENDS MEET

Even with careful budgeting life on the dole meant mid-week hunger for the family of George Tomlinson, an unemployed miner from Nottinghamshire. He described his experiences in a book, *Coal-Miner* (1937):

"We can't be miserable on Friday, Saturday and Sunday because we are feeding fairly well . . . Sunday dinner is a thumping big meal of potatoes, bread, a small portion of roast beef and more potatoes and bread. That's the real secret of living on the dole—potatoes and bread. Monday and Tuesday are not too bad. There is usually a bit of meat left from the 'Sunday joint,' and with a few potatoes and greens it is possible to make a decent meal or two. It is on Wednesday and Thursday that the real pinch comes."

A child during the Depression, John Edwards remembered the ruses his mother resorted to:

"Mother was not above the practice of petty fraud . . . and would consider it a lucky day if a purchased egg proved to be bad. This provided an opportunity to halve the smelly contents into two teacups, add another half shell to each, and send the children with them to two different shops, thereby gaining two replacements for the price of one."

images to convey to the less affected areas the blighted misery of the industrial towns, and it was to make their plight visible that "hunger marches" were organized. The first had been from Glasgow in 1922 and 1929; in 1932 the National Unemployed Workers' Movement organized marches from all over the country, converging on London for a rally in Hyde Park. Then in 1936 Palmer's shipyard in Jarrow on Tyneside closed, leading to 68 percent unemployment in the town. On October 5, 200 unemployed local workers, led by the Labor MP Ellen Wilkinson, set out from Jarrow to march on London. They carried a petition with 11,572 signatures that they intended to hand in to Downing Street. Thousands turned out to see them off; the Bishop of Jarrow gave them his blessing in a packed church service before they left. The prime minister, Stanley Baldwin, refused to meet them, however, when they arrived in the capital a month later, but the marchers did win widespread sympathy.

Political extremism

In France the worst effects of the Wall Street Crash were not felt immediately. The blow that fell in 1929 had been softened by substantial gold reserves and by the fact that the French economy was comfortably balanced between industry and agriculture. From 1932 onward, however, unemployment rose sharply. Governments came and went with

great frequency; most of them sought to tackle the crisis by taking emergency powers and governing by decrees controlling such factors as wages, prices and rents. Pierre Laval's 1935 government, for example, issued no fewer than 500 decree-laws, and the ministry of Edouard Daladier (from April 1938 to March 1940) passed four Enabling Acts, which effectively transferred all powers from parliament to government.

Yet if French governments were increasingly discredited in the 1930s, it was not because they arrogated so much power to themselves. It was more that they seemed to many people to use it so incompetently or corruptly. In parliament, violent verbal abuse and even fistfights were relatively commonplace. The Press was scurrilous in its attacks on the political leaders. As elsewhere, the loss of faith in public institutions, and the apparent success of fascist governments in Italy and Germany, led to the creation or revival of fascist or semi-fascist organizations. These won support at all levels of society, not only from conservative army officers, churchmen, landowners and industrialists, but also from the petite bourgeoisie, and from ex-soldiers, unemployed workers and frustrated youths.

MARCHING TUNE Jarrow marchers playing their harmonicas (left) sum up the general good humor of their crusade. Below: Marchers enjoy a hot stew of corned beef and potatoes on a farm near Bedford.

Among such organizations were Action Française, founded during the Dreyfus affair at the turn of the century, and the Croix de Feu, founded as an ex-servicemen's organization in 1927 but now a rallying point of right-wing youth. Others were the Camelots du Roi, the Jeunesses Patriotes of Pierre Taittinger, Solidarité Française, founded by the perfume manufacturer François Coty, and such purely fascist groups as the Parti Populaire Française, Le Faisceau and the Phalanges Universitaires. All of them were to a greater or lesser extent anti-republican, anti-communist and anti-Semitic. All set out through propaganda and agitation and by stirring up disorder to bring democratic government into disrepute and to prepare the way for a fascist takeover.

The activities of the French extreme right culminated in the street riots of February 1934, triggered by the death of the financier Alexandre Stavisky and the scandal that followed it. These riots in turn provoked a general strike organized by the Left. But the convulsions of those days revealed that fascism in France was dispersed among too many organizations and lacked the will-to-power of a single leader, an equivalent of Mussolini or Hitler, to move it from riot to revolution.

In the mid 1930s, the Soviet Communist Party changed its policy regarding liberal and social democratic parties in other countries, whom it had hitherto dismissed as class enemies and lackeys of capitalism and imperialism. Faced with the threat of spreading fascism, the Comintern (Communist International) now instructed communist parties abroad to form Popular Front coalitions with

PILLARS OF THE LEFT   The communist Jacques Duclos (on the right) with the Nobel prize-winning writer and outspoken anti-fascist, Romain Rolland, during a Popular Front rally.

democratic parties of the left, while taking care that ultimate communist aims were not compromised. The British Communist Party proposed affiliation with the Labor Party in 1934, but this was rejected with the strong support of the trade unions. In France a Popular Front government was formed under Léon Blum in 1936. Once this had been elected with a large majority, however, the Communists withdrew their cooperation and reserved the right to attack the government from outside by means of industrial action.

The Popular Front government lasted just two years and carried out only a few of its aims. It disbanded the fascist organizations, but they merely reformed underground. It introduced some industrial reforms, but failed to cure the country's economic ills or to satisfy the political Left. Strikes were frequent and membership of the Communist Party grew. At the same time, however, the government's mild reforms enraged the political right, which now openly voiced the slogan "Better Hitler than Blum"; the cry was lent an extra virulence by the fact that Blum was Jewish.

In 1937 French police revealed the conspiracy of an underground fascist organization known as the Cagoulards or Hooded Men. The police had discovered in Paris and other cities a number of large caches of

SUTTON HOO SHIP

In 1939 a team of excavators led by C.W. Phillips on the Sutton Hoo estate, in Suffolk, England, found "the richest treasure ever dug from British soil." Under what appeared to be a burial mound they discovered the remains of a wooden longboat. Its form had been preserved by the impression left by its long-vanished timbers and by the iron bolts still in place. There were no human remains, but the boat contained the armor and other possessions of what had obviously been a man of considerable wealth and magnificence. They included a remarkable helmet of gilt bronze, a gold-mounted sword and shield, a purse-mount, and other personal ornaments, bejewelled and decorated with extraordinary sophistication. In all there were 41 items of solid gold. There was also a great silver dish of Byzantine manufacture and a bronze bowl of Near Eastern origin, indicating a wide range of either trade or robbery.

The purse contained 37 Frankish coins, and from these the burial has been dated to somewhere between 625 and 675 AD. The richness of the treasure suggests that it was almost certainly the cenotaph of a Saxon king whose physical remains had been buried elsewhere, possibly Redwald (who died in 625) or Aethelhere, who died in battle in Northumbria in 654. The contents of the Sutton Hoo ship are now in the British Museum.

UNKNOWN WARRIOR   As the world geared up for war in 1939, British archeologists unearthed the treasure of a chieftain from the 7th century.

THE STAVISKY AFFAIR

Alexandre Stavisky was a financier with a shady reputation, a Russian by birth, but operating mostly from France. In 1927 the French authorities indicted him for fraud, but his trial was constantly postponed and his bail renewed 19 times. Meanwhile, he continued his swindles, apparently with impunity. Then, in November 1933, the bonds of one of his credit companies were found to be worthless. Two months after that he was discovered dead with a bullet in his head. His death caused a major scandal and brought down two governments. It was reported as suicide, but many believed that he had been murdered by police in order to prevent awkward revelations about those who had protected him and benefited from his activities—including senior figures in the government, the police and the judiciary. Prime Minister Camille Chautemps was forced to resign when it was revealed that his brother-in-law was head of the prosecuting authority that had allowed Stavisky to enjoy immunity. He was replaced by the center-left Edouard Daladier. The scandal was seized upon by the Right as a symptom of government corruption. Demonstrations in Paris culminated in a major street battle on February 6, 1934, in which 15 people died. Before the month was out, Daladier too had resigned. An emergency government of the centrist parties was formed under Gaston Doumergue, and order gradually restored—but only after a general strike and several arrests and suicides.

RIOT DAMAGE   A crowd gathers in a Parisian café wrecked during the Stavisky riots of 1934.

ALL OUT Striking Parisian workers, some giving the clenched-fist salute, occupy a factory in April 1936. Industrial chaos accompanied the election that brought the Popular Front to power.

weapons and explosives supplied by Germany, Italy and the Spanish Falangists. The organization was found to be the link between several recent assassinations and explosions.

"The boy will ruin himself"

The relatively low temperature of politics in Britain was reflected in the unruffled character of its prime minister, Stanley Baldwin. In 1936 he found himself dealing with a crisis of a completely different kind, although its character was still intensely political.

Edward, the young and popular Prince of Wales, had visited areas distressed by industrial blight. In November 1936, as king, he made a similar visit to mining areas of South Wales that had been badly hit by unemployment and was heard to declare that "something must be done." His known admiration for Hitler stemmed partly from his strong sense of kinship with the German people, and partly from the belief, shared by many people at the time, that Hitler should receive credit for having done something about unemployment. He was almost certainly also influenced by his mistress, Mrs. Wallis Simpson, the wife of a wealthy Anglo-American businessman. She had developed an early enthusiasm for fascism.

Edward's concern for the plight of the unemployed may have been sin-

FROM KING TO DUKE Edward VIII meets coal miners in South Wales in 1936. Above right: By 1937, when he inspected this SS guard-of-honor in Germany, he was no longer king and his visit was unofficial.

cere, but while still Prince of Wales he had also shown signs of a character that was both weak and wilful. King George V, increasingly ill and desperately worried about his heir, said to the Archbishop of Canterbury: "After I am gone the boy will ruin himself in 12 months." In January 1936, the old king died and his son succeeded him as Edward VIII. Within a few months he was causing his ministers concern. He was neglectful of his official duties and careless in his handling of state secrets. He was outspoken in his view that relations with Hitler's Germany should be friendlier. And he made no attempt to conceal his close relationship with the previously divorced and currently married Mrs. Simpson.

The king's having a mistress was not in itself a major problem; there were ample precedents, and the press barons of the day could be relied on to handle such matters with discretion. In May, however, Edward began to confide his intention of making Wallis Simpson his wife. His relationship with Wallis, and the possibility that the two might marry, was now openly discussed in papers in the United States and elsewhere. The British press, although aware of the situation, exercised remarkable restraint, but by the autumn it was becoming increasingly difficult to keep the story from the British public.

On October 27, in Ipswich, the Simpsons were divorced on the grounds of Ernest's "adultery," and the matter became urgent. Stanley Baldwin told the king as forcefully as he could that the twice-divorced Wallis could

not be queen. On November 16, Edward told him that if he could not marry Wallis, he was prepared to give up the throne.

Some press barons and politicians, Winston Churchill included, took up the king's cause, but Baldwin's view was upheld by the rest of the British government, the Church of England, the parliamentary Labor Party, the Trades Union Congress and the heads of Dominion countries. On December 2, the story at last broke in the British papers. Elements of the popular press were at first sympathetic to the romantic couple, but over the next few days the mood changed to one of hostility toward the woman who was depriving the nation of a popular monarch.

On December 7, Edward informed his brother, the Duke of York, that he intended to abdicate. On December 8, he telephoned Wallis, now in France, and told her of his intention. Still desperate not to lose her relationship with a king, she begged him not to go through with it, but he was adamant. On December 9, he signed the Instrument of Abdication. The next day it was formally ratified by Parliament and his brother succeeded him as King George VI.

On June 3, 1937, Wallis and Edward, now Duke of Windsor, were married at the Chateau de Candé in France, lent to them by the U.S. industrialist and fascist sympathizer Charles Bedaux. No members of the British royal family were present. Furious that his wife was denied a royal title, Edward spent the rest of his life in self-imposed exile.

At one point, when the crisis was at its height, Edward raised with the prime minister the suggestion that his marriage might be morganatic; that is, that he would continue as king but his wife would not be queen, and any children of the marriage would not

inherit. Baldwin's reply was that such an arrangement would need an Act of Parliament, and Parliament would never pass it. Perhaps a compromise might have been found. But with hindsight, it may be that the true meaning of the Abdication Crisis was not as it appeared to be. The government may well have welcomed Edward's decision to marry Wallis Simpson as a pretext for ridding the country of a king who could not be relied on in the dangerous times ahead. As Ribbentrop, Hitler's ambassador to Britain, put it: "Edward VIII had to abdicate since it was not certain, because of his views, he would cooperate in anti-German policy."

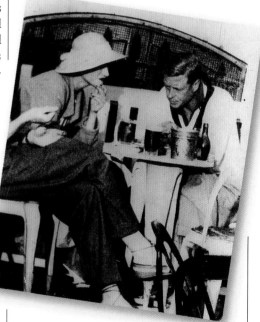

THE WOMAN I LOVE The Prince of Wales with Mrs. Wallis Simpson, on holiday at Biarritz in August 1934. This was the year in which they first became lovers.

WAKING NATIONS

THE EUROPEAN EMPIRES REACHED THEIR GREATEST EXTENT IN THE 1920S, BUT SUBJECT PEOPLES WERE QUESTIONING THE EUROPEAN PRESENCE

In the 1920s Britain's empire was the largest in the world, extending over a quarter of the land surface of the planet. Joining Britain as colonial powers were the French, Belgians, Dutch, Italians and Portuguese, all with overseas possessions in Africa and Southeast Asia. Also, the Soviet Union was still the vast multinational land empire assembled under the tsars. Germany had lost its colonies after defeat in the First World War, but the other European nations had mostly expanded theirs.

IMPERIAL GLORY A poster for the 1924 British Empire Exhibition at Wembley invokes images of the nation's seafaring heritage.

In the more temperate regions—in North Africa, for example, or South Africa—the colonies were colonies in the Roman sense, settled by numbers of people from Europe who regarded their adopted country as home, and raised their children there. In North Africa there were French families who had farmed and tended vineyards for generations. The tropical areas were not on the whole settled in this way, and the European communities—traders, managers, planters, administrators, magistrates, soldiers —were small, composed largely of people serving a tour of duty.

In none of their colonial possessions, however, were the Europeans ever more than a small minority. In the Dutch East Indies, for example, the European population was less than 1 percent; in French Indochina it was less than half a percent. In Algeria the French settler population was 15 percent, yet it owned one-third of all cultivated land; similarly, in South Africa, Kenya and Rhodesia, white settlers owned a hugely disproportionate share of the best land.

European rule was based on three main factors, which carried more or less weight according to circumstances: on religious, ethnic or social divisions among the people ruled; on consent, because of the benefits conveyed to the ruled as well as the rulers by what was perceived to be a superior civilization; and in the last resort, on fear. The fear had its basis in the Europeans' superior firepower and technical know-how, but also in something less tangible. If a handful of Europeans could win the obedience of thousands, and if, heavily outnumbered, they could order the beating or execution of an offender and see it carried out by the offender's compatriots, it was because they ruled by means of a magnificent bluff. In the years following the First World War, that bluff began to be called in some of the European colonies: by the 1930s it became clear to at least the more perceptive observers that the Age of Empire was passing away.

Awakening nationalism

Many of the colonial peoples had sent troops, voluntarily or involuntarily, to the First World War. In any case, the experience of that war had not escaped their notice. The spectacle of the European states slaughtering each other in such a dreadful debacle greatly diminished faith in the infallibility of white men. In the better-run colonies, a generation of young men had been given access to Western education and the professions. They had begun to question their obligation to be ruled, and the right of Europeans to rule them. Finally, the revolution in Russia, with its promise of a transfer of power to the masses, stimulated young followers of Marx in some colonial countries to turn revolutionary theory into practice.

The motive for possessing colonies was only partly economic; to a great extent, the powers had competed as a matter of prestige to paint the map of the world in their national colors. The colonies offered, in some cases, cultivable land on which the rulers' expanding populations could be settled; in others, important raw materials—oil, rubber, minerals, textiles, timber, tea, spices. But often they were barely profitable to the countries that owned them, which, with few exceptions, showed little enthusiasm for investing in their development. India was exceptional in having, by the 1930s, a large industrial and commercial sector in the hands of Indians.

In the case of French colonial rule in Africa and Indochina, there were inherent contradictions. The French recognized native rulers, but their aim was always assimilation to French civilization; the native elites were to be educated in French culture, so that in time the colonies would become part of France, and their inhabitants French. In 1930s France there was much talk of a population of "100 million Frenchmen." Yet by 1936 only 2,000 blacks under French rule

FUTURE REVOLUTIONARY The young Nguyen That Thanh—better known to history as Ho Chi Minh —at a conference in France in 1920. He was then a member of the French Communist Party. By the 1950s the French would have cause to remember his name.

had French citizenship and only 3 percent of Moroccans went to school.

This had the paradoxical result of making the French-educated native elites aware of the principles of the French Republic—Liberty, Equality, Fraternity—and prompting them to ask why these did not apply to them. The French imposed tariff policies that were clearly in the interest of France rather than of native businessmen. Natives were subject to forced labor and even to the salt tax, long abolished in France itself. And the imposition of French property laws disturbed traditional patterns of landholding and drove the native cultivators into the hands of landlords and moneylenders.

What provoked most resentment among Africans, in particular, was the assumption of the superiority of French civilization. This led to what became known as the *négritude* movement, associated with Léopold Senghor of Senegal (whose president he would one

HUMAN ORIGINS

In 1927 a Canadian anatomist, Davidson Black, found a tooth in a cave near Beijing (Peking). It evidently belonged to an ancestor of modern man; further digs unearthed most of a skull. "Peking man," along with remains found in Java, provided key evidence of an early human species now known as *Homo erectus*. He walked upright and stood over 5 feet tall. The remains found by Black dated from around 350,000 BC.

day become) and Aimé Césaire of Martinique in the French West Indies. Both lived in Paris and wrote in superb French. Rather than demanding political independence, they asserted the importance of African values in contrast to what they saw as the soulless materialism of Europe.

Marxist influence was much stronger in French Indochina. At the Versailles Conference in 1919, a young Vietnamese addressed a petition to the representatives of the victorious powers, demanding that the French in Indochina grant equal rights to their subjects. The powers did not respond, but the young man became a hero to Vietnamese nationalists. He would later adopt the name Ho Chi Minh.

In his youth, Ho had worked in several lowly jobs in France and become an active socialist. In 1920 he joined the French communists. He went to Moscow in 1923 and became an important figure in the Communist International, where he urged the need for armed struggle against colonialism and stressed the role of the peasants in any future revolution in his own country. Having founded the Indochinese Communist Party in 1930, he was in exile for most of the 1930s and condemned to death in absentia by the French authorities. His supporters, however, were at work in the cities of Hanoi, Hue and Saigon, organizing themselves for the coming revolution.

HOME EDUCATION Teaching housekeeping skills was a responsibility taken seriously by the authorities in French Cameroon. Around 1930, two teachers sit with their pupils in the courtyard of a school of domestic science.

Nationalist feelings had as yet scarcely awakened in Africa south of the Sahara. By the 1920s, the official British policy in its possessions there was one of trusteeship. One day, in a future that was probably distant, the possessions would be returned to their native peoples, once they had been educated and trained to run things properly themselves. Meanwhile, the British governors would look after them, aided by the young men of the colonial service, who were still being recruited in the thousands from the public schools.

Boyish masters

The Americans did not regard their own territorial expansion—into the Philippines, for example—as imperialist, and they deplored the imperialism of the European nations. Yet it was an American, the philosopher George Santayana, who said of the British Colonial Service: "Never since the heroic days of Greece has the world had such a sweet, just, boyish master."

The attitude of the Colonial Service at its best was summed up in a memorandum from the governor of the Gold Coast to his

1919

1919 Massacre at Amritsar | 1920 Treaty of Sèvres | 1922 Gandhi arrested and charged with sedition | 1923 Treaty of Lausanne recognizes Turkish sovereignty | 1924 British Empire Exhibition at Wembley | 1926 Ibn Saud completes conquest of Arabia

A VISIONARY IN AFRICA

Albert Schweitzer was born in Upper Alsace, then part of Germany, in 1875. By the age of 25 he had acquired doctorates in philosophy and theology, was a university lecturer and a Lutheran preacher, and was establishing himself as a gifted organist. In 1905 he published a major study of J.S. Bach; the next year, he produced a theological work on the life of Jesus that attracted worldwide attention. He seemed destined for a dazzling career as a musician or as an academic in any of several fields. In 1905, however, he announced his intention of becoming a medical missionary in Africa and began medical studies in preparation.

In 1913 Schweitzer set out for Africa with his wife, herself a distinguished scholar who had trained as a nurse in order to assist him. At Lambaréné in the forests of French Equatorial Africa, he built his hospital. During the First World War he was briefly interned by the French as a German citizen, and he spent the early 1920s in Europe working on philosophical writings. In 1924, however, he returned to Africa and rebuilt and expanded his hospital, which eventually encompassed a leper colony. Until his death at Lambaréné in 1965, he combined hospital work with musical and theological studies and a campaign for world peace and brotherhood, for which he won the Nobel Peace Prize in 1952.

In his later years, and after his death, Schweitzer attracted some criticism for his autocratic methods, his paternalistic attitude toward the Africans he worked among and his deliberately "low-tech" approach to medicine in Africa—though "high-tech" methods would have been impractical in the conditions he was operating in. By many, however, he was (and is) regarded as an example of benign European intervention in the developing world.

TROPICAL MEDICINE Albert Schweitzer at work in his simple operating theater at Lambaréné. He was already a theologian and musician before he turned to medicine.

staff: "We are in this country to help the African and to serve him. We derive our salaries from the Colony and it is our duty to give full value for what it pays us. I attach considerable importance to good manners . . . Those people who consider themselves so superior to Africans that they feel justified in despising them and insulting them are quite unfitted for responsible positions in the colony. They are, in my opinion, inferior to those whom they affect to despise, and often betray, by their arrogance and bad manners, the inferiority of which they are secretly ashamed."

On the whole, the young district officers who worked with local chiefs, sitting beside them in informal courts to settle disputes or to discuss irrigation systems or medical problems, followed these principles. Yet, as the memorandum implies, they were not shared by all whites.

Lord Delamere, a leader of the white settlers of the Kenya highlands, was a white supremacist. Much of the best country in Kenya was fenced off for whites-only ownership, and he wanted to see the Europeans control the country forever. Delamere dreamt of a white settler-ruled Africa that would include the whole of Rhodesia, plus Kenya, Tanganyika and Nyasaland. It would be an aristocratic land, like the old South in the days before the American Civil War. It was the dream men dreamt in Nairobi's green-lawned Muthaiga club, where non-whites were banned from membership and officials with pro-African views were not welcome. In the Africa of the 1930s, it still looked like a dream that could become reality.

The jewel in the crown

India was not a colony but an empire. The British monarch was its emperor, and its ruler was not a governor but a viceroy, who lived in magnificent style. Many of Britain's ablest young men were recruited into the Indian Civil Service. There were British families who had served in the country for generations; and Indian maharajahs who played cricket and were prominent members of London society.

British rule was not generally oppressive or overtly exploitative. Much of India's trade

HAPPY HOUR White customers relaxing at the cocktail bar of the Connemara Hotel in Madras in the 1930s. Indians were admitted to the bar only as servants.

and manufacturing was in Indian hands, as was most of the land. Indians were playing an increasing part in law and administration; the Indian middle and upper classes had access to first-rate Western education; and the superb Indian regiments were loyal to the Raj. Yet in the 1920s and 30s, there was a growing recognition that the days of imperial India, which had once seemed so permanent, were numbered.

It was among the Western-educated middle class that nationalist feelings first grew, in India as elsewhere. They could prosper; they could rise in their professions and become magistrates and judges. But as long as the British Raj lasted, they could be insulted or patronized as second-class citizens in their own country. They would be denied admission to the white man's clubs.

Such resentments scarcely affected the Indian masses, who had always been used to being subservient to rulers of one kind or another. It took considerable political skill to persuade them that their lives, too, would change for the better with independence. But there were men among the nationalists who had that kind of skill, and by 1919 they had massive public support.

In April 1919 a tragic event spelled the beginning of the end for the British in India. A wave of nationalist unrest had been sweeping through the subcontinent. In the city of Amritsar there had been violent riots, in which five Englishmen had been killed and a woman missionary assaulted. On April 13 several thousand Indians—unarmed men, women and children—defied orders forbidding riotous assembly and crowded into a garden-square in the center of the city to listen to a nationalist orator. Armored cars pulled up in the street outside the square. Fifty riflemen drew up in a line and began firing steadily at point-blank range into the defenseless crowd. After six minutes of firing, 379 people lay dead and 1,500 wounded.

The Amritsar Massacre was unprecedented; since the days of the Mutiny 60 years earlier, the British had never

INDIA ON THE MARCH The year 1930 saw Gandhi's Salt March (left) and a march by women of all castes and communities in Bombay (above). The women's march was triggered by the imprisonment of a Muslim woman, who had picketed a liquor shop.

dealt murderously with their Indian subjects. The officer responsible, Brigadier-General Reginald Dyer, was obliged to resign his commission, and henceforth the British would be reluctant to take firm action against the disturbances that were becoming increasingly common. Another result of the massacre was to exacerbate the discontents that were stimulating Indians to flock in the thousands toward the nationalist movement.

Behind that movement was the Indian National Congress and the slight figure of Mohandas Karamchand Gandhi, by now its undoubted leader. The son of a palace official in one of India's princely states, Gandhi had trained as a lawyer in London and worked in South Africa. Returning to India in 1914, he had plunged into nationalism and further developed a theory of passive resistance that was both a philosophy and a political tactic. He was a man of complex character, modest and saintly, but with great political astuteness and an iron determination. The Indian masses worshipped him as semi-divine. They did not always understand his pacifist teachings,

RACE EXTREMES IN THE UNITED STATES

**THE KU KLUX KLAN ON THE ONE SIDE, MARCUS GARVEY ON THE OTHER—
BOTH TOOK UP ENTRENCHED POSITIONS ON THE RACE ISSUE**

The Ku Klux Klan had been founded in the American South after the Civil War, to assert white supremacy and to terrify the newly enfranchised former slaves out of exercising their voting rights. Anti-communist and anti-foreign sentiment led to a revival in the 1920s when the Klan spread from the South to the Midwest. By 1924 it had more than 4 million members, prepared to don their pointed hoods and to attend its torchlit processions and ceremonies under the burning cross.

In the South blacks were effectively disenfranchised, and racial segregation—although contrary to the U.S. Constitution—was openly practiced, not only in housing but also in public places and on public transportation. Blacks had their own sections in eating places, if they were admitted at all, and their own cars on railroad trains. They had their own—mostly very inadequate—schools; and they were almost entirely excluded from any kind of public office. For most of them, the choices were limited to share-cropping, domestic service or migration to industrial jobs in the cities of the North.

In the North segregation was less blatant, but existed. Houseowners in white neighborhoods did not sell or rent to blacks; restaurants found they had no tables available when blacks tried to enter them; and black musicians had to use the tradesmen's entrance when they performed in hotels. They appeared in Hollywood movies—much less well paid than their white counterparts—but only as comic characters, entertainers or dim but lovable servants. There were black lawyers, doctors, professors and businessmen in the North, but Hollywood continued to stereotype blacks as a childish people whose talents were limited to music, dancing and domestic service.

Most American blacks wearily accepted their lot as second-class citizens. Many, however, did not. Some of those who had managed to obtain an education joined W.E.B. Du Bois's moderate National Association for the Advancement of Colored People. Thousands of others joined the Universal Negro Improvement Association, which in 1919 claimed a membership of 2 million. Based in New York's Harlem, its founder, the Jamaican Marcus Garvey, addressed himself mainly to the blacks of the industrial North. Garvey, the "Black Moses," preached black pride, the glories of African history and the need to build a strong black economy within the white capitalist structure. To this end, he set up the Negro Factories Corporation and the Black Star Line, and a number of other black-run enterprises, including a chain of restaurants and grocery stores, a hotel and a printing press. In 1920 he led a parade through Harlem, dressed in the style of a colonial governor. In 1921 he proclaimed an "empire of Africa," of which he was provisional president, and created the Universal African Legion, Universal Black Cross Nurses, the Black Eagle Flying Corps and Knights of the Nile.

Garvey's ideas were themselves separatist; he paradoxically approved of the Ku Klux Klan because it promoted racial separatism. His business methods were inefficient if not dishonest. In 1922 he and others in his movement were indicted for mail fraud in connection with questionable share dealings and he was sentenced to five years in jail. The sentence was commuted to two years, but in 1927 he was deported as an undesirable alien. His movement rapidly died out, although its central idea of black separatism would be revived by the Black Muslims in the 1960s.

BLACKS ONLY Even water fountains were segregated in Oklahoma City in 1939, where a young man drinks at a fountain for "colored" people (left). Like many whites, Marcus Garvey (right) believed in separation of the races.

however, and outbursts of mob violence followed in his wake.

Gandhi and his followers, who included the Harrow and Cambridge-educated lawyer Jawaharlal Nehru, knew how to exploit the essentially liberal attitudes of the British government. When Gandhi was arrested in the 1920s, the judge apologized to him and made sure that his sentence was short and comfortable. As George Orwell observed, Gandhi could not have survived, let alone succeeded, under any other regime.

In 1930, as part of his campaign of civil disobedience, Gandhi set off on a 250 mile march to the sea in protest against the British government monopoly on salt. Thousands flocked to join the Salt March, a classic example of passive resistance. Gandhi was briefly imprisoned afterwards, before being invited to talks with the Viceroy about the future of India. When these negotiations failed, the campaign was resumed.

Throughout the 1920s and 30s, the British government dithered about what degree of self-government the subcontinent should have. In 1935 it produced the Government of India Act, which proposed internal self-government in a federal system that would include Hindus, Muslims and the Princely

REVOLT IN THE RIF In 1921 Abd el-Krim (left) founded a Republic of the Rif in Morocco. He and his Berber army fought off French (below) and Spanish colonial forces until 1926.

OIL FOR SALE An Arab in 1926 loads his mule with containers of the Anglo-Persian Oil Company's refined petroleum for burning in lamps. Anglo-Persian marketed gas in Europe under the brand name BP—British Petroleum (left above).

States. This was no longer enough for Gandhi and Nehru who wanted total independence, and felt that it was important politically that this should be won by Congress after a struggle, not freely granted by the British. What would happen to India's vast Muslim population after independence was a question that remained unresolved. Already there had been outbreaks of violence among the Sikh, Hindu and Muslim communities. Nehru stated his belief that communal violence would disappear as soon the British had left. In this he was tragically mistaken, but the matter was suspended when India went to war as part of the British Empire in 1939.

The Middle East

The Ottoman Empire, which had reached the peak of its power and extent in the 16th century, steadily decayed and crumbled through the 19th. Then, in the First World War, it was defeated by the Allies, assisted by Arab guerrillas. The victorious British and French now partitioned the former Ottoman territories in the Arab world, drawing lines on the sands, often where none had been drawn before. In name, the new states passed to sheikhs and princes who had been friendly to the Allies; in effect, however, control passed to the European powers. France took Lebanon and, after two years as a nominally independent state, Syria as well. Britain took Iraq, Transjordan and Palestine, the last of these with the promise that it would become the Jewish national home. Britain already held protectorates over Egypt, the Sudan and the sultanates on the southern and eastern fringes of Arabia.

The main part of the Arabian peninsula, consisting largely of desert roamed by Bedouin and little regarded until its rich oil resources began to be valued, remained unclaimed by the great powers and mostly unmapped. Just as its vast potential as an oil producer was being discovered, Ibn Saud, the leader of one of its Bedouin families, set out from his capital at Riyadh with a mounted army of fundamentalist Arab warriors to take over the entire country. By 1926 he had succeeded. In 1932 Arabia became Saudi Arabia. Its territory included Mecca and Medina, the Holy Places of Islam.

In the 1920s, oil, now vital for transportation, industry and military use, dominated

A QUESTION OF HATS

One of Turkey's reforms in the 1920s was the abolition of the fez, the conical cap worn by males. Instead, men were obliged to wear Western hats or caps. The move provoked rebellions in rural districts. Yet, ironically, the fez had been introduced almost a century before by the modernizing Sultan Mahmud II. Originally it had been the cap around which men wound their turbans, but Mahmud had abolished these.

the politics of the Middle East. The other great oil-producing countries were Iraq and Persia (or Iran). Persia, although nominally ruled as an independent state by the Qajar dynasty of shahs, had been divided into Russian and British spheres of influence since 1907. In the postwar years, nationalist sentiment, resentful of foreign interference, appeared to threaten Western interests, in particular Western access to the country's oil. In 1924 the last Qajar shah was deposed in a coup d'état by Reza Khan Pahlavi. The Pahlavi dynasty, friendly to the West, would remain in power until 1979.

During the 1920s and 30s, there were stirrings of nationalist feeling throughout the Middle East and North Africa. Although the industrialized states of Europe were still dominant, they had been weakened by the war. The very idea of imperial rule as a permanent fact of life had been shaken; it was also being challenged by the League of Nations, the United States and the Soviet Union. In Morocco, Spanish and French rule was challenged by a revolt in the Rif mountains, led by the nationalist Abd el-Krim, and suppressed only after five years of fighting. There was a revolt against the French in Syria, which again was suppressed only with difficulty in 1927. In Iraq, a series of revolts persuaded the British to grant the country formal independence in 1932, although they retained a considerable measure of control. Egypt gained independence in 1922, although the British retained control over defense and foreign affairs. Thus, through a mixture of suppression and concessions, the Europeans managed to protect their interests—the Suez Canal, for example, remained firmly in Anglo-French hands. But resentments, and the desire for total national independence, continued to simmer.

New Turkey

The Arabs' former Ottoman masters, meanwhile, had been fighting their own nationalist struggle, led by the man who became known as Kemal Atatürk. At the end of the First

FIGHTING FOR A HOMELAND Atatürk, a believer in sexual equality, enlisted the aid of women fighters. Below: Greeks flee Izmir (Smyrna) after its recapture by the Turks in 1922.

World War the Turks had found themselves confined to the core Turkish territories of Asia Minor—and even these were under threat. According to secret treaties agreed among the Allies during the war, substantial parts of Asia Minor were due to be handed over to Russia and Italy—Russia, for example, was to have Istanbul (Constantinople) and the Dardanelles Straits.

Soviet Russia was no longer one of the Allies by the time the Treaty of Sèvres was signed in August 1920. According to this treaty, Istanbul and the Straits were to be put under international control. At the same time, the area around Izmir (Smyrna) was to be given to Greece, and two new independent states would be created, Armenia and Kurdistan. It took three years of Turkish resistance and war with Greece to reverse these proposals and to preserve the new state of Turkey for the Turks.

The Turks' position in their own homeland was somewhat ambiguous. When, in the 15th century, they completed their conquest of Asia Minor, Turkey itself was occupied by Greeks, Armenians and other peoples, all of whom had lived there for many centuries. After time, some of these merged with the Turkish population, but the Greeks and the Armenians remained distinct in language and culture, and in their sense of nationality.

In the days when the Ottomans ruled a vast multi-ethnic empire, including mainland Greece, this scarcely mattered. But as that empire decayed and shrank, nationalist feelings started to grow among the Turks themselves, and especially among the young men of the educated middle class and the army officers who at the end of the 19th century had formed the movement known as the Young Turks.

KEMAL ATATÜRK MODERNIZES TURKEY

The father of modern Turkey received the name Atatürk ("Father of Turks") in 1933. That was when, as part of his policy of modernization, it became compulsory for all Turks to have surnames. As a young army officer, Mustafa Kemal, as he was known then, had spent time in Western Europe and had been attracted by Western ways. Once he came to power in Turkey, he launched a program of "modernizing" reforms. He closed all institutions based on Islamic law, including the old religious schools, which he replaced with secular ones. He also replaced the Ottoman legal system with a modern one. He insisted on the equality of the sexes, including the right of women to vote and to stand for election; to this end he encouraged dances and other gatherings that brought the sexes together. He abolished the wearing of the veil. In 1928 he adopted the Roman alphabet in place of the Arabic script that had been used for centuries.

His methods were authoritarian. From time to time, he allowed political parties other than his own to emerge, but he quickly closed them down when they showed signs of serious opposition. His attempts to industrialize the country were less successful than his political, social and cultural reforms. Even these did not penetrate far beyond the cities and the educated middle classes; rural parts of Turkey remained largely unchanged. Even so, only Japan in modern times went through a transformation comparable to the one Turkey had undergone by the time of Atatürk's death in 1938.

UP TO DATE **Atatürk introduced the teaching of science in Turkish schools. The socialite Mademoiselle Sakhy (right) was his propaganda chief in the campaign to persuade Turkish women to wear European dress.**

In the course of the First World War, the Turks had attempted to eliminate the Armenian population, in the first genocide of the 20th century. In 1918, defeated, the Turks found themselves facing the dismemberment of their country. With the guns of the Allied fleets looming over Istanbul, the Sultan and his court tried to preserve what remained of their empire by putting it under Allied protection. Turkey's nationalists, however, were prepared to put up a stiffer resistance. Their leader was Mustafa Kemal, a young army officer who had played a key role in the successful defense against an attempted Allied invasion at Gallipoli in 1915. After the Armistice, when Turkey's German allies withdrew, Mustafa Kemal took command of a large part of his country's armed forces.

In May 1919, the Greeks occupied Izmir. In the same month, the sultan ordered Kemal to eastern Turkey to suppress a possible uprising there, giving him complete military and civil power in the area. On Kemal's journey eastward, he summoned a congress that met in the town of Erzurum in July and August; a second congress met in Sivas in September. Kemal called on all military and civil authorities to support him in the struggle for Turkish liberation. Faced with Allied demands for the demobilization of the Ottoman army, most of the military responded to Kemal's call and began seizing communications.

In December 1919 Kemal transferred the center of his national struggle to Ankara. By 1920 he was fighting a war on two fronts—against forces loyal to the sultan, who had turned against him, and against the Greeks who were advancing from Izmir into central Turkey. In August 1921 his forces defeated the Greeks at the Battle of Sakarya River; by September 1922 they had reoccupied Izmir, massacring a large part of its Greek population. In November 1922 the sultan fled his country on board a British warship. The next year, the Treaty of Lausanne gave international recognition to Turkish sovereignty. There followed a massive exchange of populations, as 350,000 Turks left Greek territory and more than a million Greeks moved from Anatolia to Greece. Turkey was proclaimed a republic, with Kemal as its president, who now embarked on a program of reforms designed to make his nation a modern secular state.

VOLATILE LATIN AMERICA

THE EXPORT-BASED ECONOMIES OF LATIN AMERICA SUFFERED GREATLY IN THE DEPRESSION, SPARKING OFF POLITICAL INSTABILITY

By the early 1920s most of the countries of Latin America were enjoying a degree of prosperity. None had manufacturing industries to any great extent, but all had rich natural resources, both agricultural and mineral. Brazil had coffee and rubber; Bolivia had silver and tin; Chile had nitrates, important both for fertilizer and for explosives; Venezuela and Mexico had oil; and Argentina, the richest of all, was a large-scale exporter of beef, wool and grain.

The wealth resulting from these resources was very unevenly distributed and there were massive inequalities between the Europeanized urban elite at the top of the social pyramid and the Indians, blacks and *mestizos* at its base. Although an organized industrial proletariat of the European kind scarcely existed in Latin America, there were simmering social resentments.

Most of the capital investment needed for infrastructure and development came from abroad—before the First World War mainly from Britain and other European countries, and by the 1920s mainly from the United States, which was providing more than 40 percent of it. The investing countries, concerned for the security of their investments, tended to favor regimes that could provide firm government and stability. This, too, provoked resentment, which was increasingly directed against the United States.

The United States had for long acted in accordance with the Monroe Doctrine: that is, it regarded Latin America as falling within its sphere of influence, and strongly discouraged European involvement in its affairs. On more than one occasion, it had shown that it

NATURAL RESOURCES Indian workers sort the ore from a Mexican silver mine. Throughout Latin America, the original inhabitants were at the very bottom of the social pyramid.

THE KILLING OF ZAPATA

On April 10, 1919, the Mexican revolutionary leader Emiliano Zapata was gunned down by soldiers of the Mexican government. Zapata had fought in the Mexican revolution from its beginning and then, with his army of peasant guerrillas, had gone on fighting the country's new rulers in the name of "Land and Liberty," robbing the rich and handing over land to the dispossessed. By 1919 he controlled a large part of the country.

Zapata was tricked to his death by General Pablo González, commander of the government forces opposed to him. In March 1919 one of González's regimental commanders, Colonel Jesus Maria Guajardo, conveyed a message to Zapata offering to desert with his regiment and join the Zapatistas. Zapata wrote back expressing interest in the proposal.

On April 9 the two men met, but Zapata was with his army and Guajardo was outnumbered. Guajardo proposed a further meeting the next day at his own base at the hacienda of Chinameca, where he would lay on a fiesta. Zapata took the bait. He entered the courtyard of Guajardo's headquarters with an escort of ten men to find himself surrounded on three sides by armed soldiers. Guajardo gave the order to fire, and Zapata fell dead, along with seven of his comrades. Guajardo was promoted to general and received a reward of 50,000 gold pesos. One of Zapata's oft-quoted sayings was: "It is better to die on your feet than live on your knees."

PEASANT LEADER Zapata, the son of a village horse-dealer, had wielded enormous power, but died as poor as he was born.

continuity of service to the nation and freedom from corruption. They had the power to make or break governments, and they were as likely to use it to support popular protest movements and to depose presidents who had become corrupt, incompetent or overweening, as to bring down radical regimes that threatened to move too far to the left. Regimes backed by the military became the norm in the 1930s and for long afterward.

Land and liberty

The Mexican revolution had begun in 1910. The overthrow of the dictatorship of Porfirio Diaz had been followed by years of chaos and bloodshed, but by the early 1930s revolutionaries like Emiliano Zapata and Pancho Villa were long since dead and the country had settled down to an uneasy peace. The rhetoric of the governing National Revolutionary Party (PNR) was still revolutionary and anti-clerical, but its reform program had slowed down as the leadership grew conservative and vested interests replaced the fervor of the early days.

Although there was effectively one-party government in Mexico, the constitution forbade the re-election of any president for a consecutive second term. All the same, when General Lázaro Cárdenas was elected president in 1934, much of the political apparatus remained effectively in the hands of the former president, Plutarco Elías Calles, and many people saw Cárdenas as little more than a stopgap president. On taking office, however, he surprised everyone by moving sharply to the left and reviving the revolutionary goals of taking land from the rich and giving it to landless peasants and village communities, strengthening trade unions

was prepared to take direct action if any regime became so unstable that European intervention was likely. U.S. troops were sent, for example, to Honduras in 1924 and to Nicaragua in 1926. While the politically conscious masses could sometimes be persuaded by left-wing agitators that their coun-

LISTENING EAR Anxious to maintain popular support for his regime, Mexico's President Cárdenas pauses to listen to a grievance. His carefully cultivated personal popularity was one of the secrets of his success.

tries were being run in the interests of U.S. capital, the middle classes resented the fact that they were denied their natural ties with the European homelands with which they still felt a strong cultural kinship.

The Great Depression which began in 1929 had a devastating effect on the region, as foreign capital investment was cut off and commodity prices fell sharply, hitting the already meager incomes of peasant producers and the workers in the mining and processing industries. In the course of the 1930s, many Latin American countries defaulted on their foreign debts and several resorted to the expropriation of foreign-owned assets, particularly those of the petroleum companies. The economic and social distress created by the Depression led, in turn, to disillusionment with the European oligarchies which had traditionally controlled the governments, whether liberal or conservative. From 1930 on, there were coups d'état in every country except Mexico.

In most if not all of these, the military played a leading role, sometimes a progressive one. Army officers throughout Latin America saw themselves as a body that upheld the liberal constitutions created during the 19th century. As far as they were concerned, it was a body that represented

1919

1919 Killing
of Emiliano
Zapata

1923
Assassination
of Pancho Villa

and nationalizing foreign-owned assets such as the country's railways.

In 1938 Cárdenas took over the foreign petroleum companies. The British, who had a major stake-holding in Mexico's oil, broke off diplomatic relations. In Washington, however, President Roosevelt had announced a new "Good Neighbor" policy toward Latin America, promising friendly cooperation instead of intervention in its affairs. He reacted sympathetically to the Mexican move, demanding only prompt compensation for the oil companies. As the United States and Europe moved to war production and manu-

BEEF ON THE HOOF Hereford cattle graze the Argentine pampas. President Agustín Justo (right) used beef and grain revenues to build Argentina's manufacturing economy.

factured goods became scarce, so Mexico's oil helped the country to fuel the development of its own manufacturing industries.

Military coups

In Bolivia the Depression had a disastrous effect on the tin-mining industry on which the country's economy depended. In 1932 the Republican government of President

Daniel Salamanca set out to provide a distraction from the country's problems by provoking a war with its neighbor Paraguay, over the disputed but largely uninhabited territory of Chaco Boreal. He entered the Chaco War of 1932-5 with an army that was better equipped and trained than Paraguay's. By the end, however, 100,000 Bolivian troops had been killed, wounded or captured, and Bolivia had lost more territory than it had claimed at the outset.

Angry veterans, feeling that their government had betrayed them, set up rival socialist and radical parties. The result of this threat was the overthrow of liberal democratic government and a return to military rule for the first time in decades. However, the army officers who ran the country until 1939 did so under a regime of what was termed

SANDALS AND GAS MASKS Bolivian machine-gunners take aim at their Paraguayan enemy in the "Green Hell" of the Gran Chaco. The German-trained Bolivians suffered horribly in the jungles and swamps of the Gran Chaco, where many of them died from snake bites and disease rather than enemy action.

1930 Getúlio Vargas comes to power in Brazil; General Uriburu becomes President of Argentina

1932 The Chaco War between Bolivia and Paraguay begins

1934 Cárdenas elected President of Mexico

1937 Vargas assumes dictatorial powers in Brazil

1938 Cárdenas nationalizes Mexico's petroleum industry

"military socialism." Before democratic government was restored they had expropriated Standard Oil, introduced labor legislation that enhanced the rights of workers, and written a new constitution with a strong social welfare component.

In 1930 a military coup d'état in Argentina brought to an end the democratically elected government of Hipólito Irigoyen's Radical Front, which had offended many of the

BRAZIL'S BENEVOLENT DICTATOR

Getúlio Vargas was born in 1883 into a landowning family. He trained as a lawyer, then entered politics, eventually becoming governor of his native province of Rio Grande do Sul. In 1930 he was narrowly defeated in presidential elections. A military coup overturned the verdict, however, and brought him to power. Promising another election within two years, he embarked on a raft of emergency reforms, designed to relieve the problems of the Depression, creating scarcities in order to push up commodity prices, setting up public works projects to increase employment, and establishing a 48-hour week and minimum wages.

When the elections at length took place in 1934, he was elected by a substantial majority—enlarged by the fact that he had given women the vote for the first time. In 1937, after suppressing an attempted communist rising, he made himself dictator. His regime, which he named the *Estado Novo* or "New State" after that of Salazar in Portugal, also had elements in common with Mussolini's. On the one hand, he suppressed free speech and political activity, while on the other he opposed the interests of big business and big landowners. He also encouraged rapid industrialization. Like Mussolini in his early years, he enjoyed considerable popularity, and was revered by his followers as "The Father of the Poor."

His dictatorship survived until 1945, when a group of army officers forced him to retire in order to restore democracy. In 1950, as leader of the Brazilian Labor Party, he was re-elected with a landslide majority but this time had to rule with the consent of Congress. In 1954, when the army once again demanded his resignation after political scandals, he committed suicide.

country's political and social elites, and brought to power General José Félix Uriburu, who was not only a conservative but a fascist sympathizer. Uriburu's time in power was brief. General Agustín Justo, elected president in 1932, made trade agreements with Britain, guaranteeing import quotas of Argentine beef and grain, essential for the country's economy. He also helped Argentina's development as a manufacturing country by imposing restrictions on the importation of manufactured goods.

Argentina remained neutral in the Second World War. In 1943 its pro-Axis government would be toppled by the most famous Latin American dictator of all, Juan Perón.

Vargas and Brazil

Brazil entered the 20th century with a democratic constitution based on that of the United States, in which much power was devolved to the individual states that made up the country. The country had followed the United States by declaring war on Germany in 1917, and had sent delegates to the Versailles Peace Conference.

By the 1920s, ambitious social programs and public works projects had taken Brazil deeply into debt. The consequent cut-backs in public spending resulted in considerable

UPRISING IN BRAZIL Crowds in São Paulo ransack the offices of the government-run newspaper *Gazeta*, following the overthrow of President Washington Luís in November 1930. This was the uprising that brought Getúlio Vargas (left) to power.

unrest and, when the Crash came in 1929, the country was near collapse. In 1930 an uprising supported by the military brought to power Getúlio Vargas, who set out on a radical program to raise Brazil out of depression. He ordered the large-scale burning of surpluses of coffee in order to raise its price, restarted public works programs, particularly the building of schools, and introduced a 48-hour week and a minimum wage. In 1934 Vargas brought in a new constitution, centralizing power and giving women the vote; in the elections that followed he won by a large margin. In 1937, following a communist revolt that he put down with great severity, he set up another constitution concentrating all power in his own hands.

In the late 1930s, Vargas encouraged friendly relations with Mussolini's Italy and Hitler's Germany, mainly as a ploy to win concessions from the United States, but he declared war on the Axis in 1942 and sent an armed force to fight on the Allied side in Italy.

THE STORM BREAKS

IN THE FAR EAST, TWO OF THE WORLD'S ANCIENT CIVILIZATIONS—CHINA AND JAPAN—CLASHED IN A WAR THAT WOULD EVENTUALLY ENGULF THE WHOLE OF THE PACIFIC. EUROPE'S DICTATORS USED A BLOODY CIVIL WAR IN SPAIN AS A MILITARY EXERCISE. THE DEMOCRACIES SOUGHT TO APPEASE HITLER'S NEWLY ARMED GERMANY BY SACRIFICING A FREE NATION—CZECHOSLOVAKIA—WHILE STALIN'S RUSSIA ENTERED INTO AN UNHOLY ALLIANCE WITH ITS BITTEREST ENEMY.

WAR IN THE EAST

FIRST CHINESE NATIONALISTS AND COMMUNISTS FOUGHT EACH OTHER, THEN UNITED IN A STRUGGLE AGAINST JAPANESE INVADERS

In 1911 revolution broke out in China, the world's oldest empire. By February the following year the last Chinese emperor had abdicated. A republic was established, but its leader Sun Yat-sen was quickly displaced by the powerful general Yuan Shikai, who set up what was in effect a military dictatorship.

The revolution that had ended more than 2,000 years of imperial rule in China had been fuelled by the discontents of Westernized intellectuals, army officers, capitalists, the mandarin class and the peasant masses. All had very different interests, and nothing positive was done to resolve them. China was totally unprepared for democracy. The vast country, lacking in modern communications, had been barely governable under

TAKE AIM . . . Nationalist troops, armed with Mauser pistols, in the suburbs of Shanghai. Chiang Kai-shek's Guomindang forces took control of the city in 1927.

the later Manchu emperors. Under the new government, which could not appeal to traditional assent, it simply fell apart.

Yuan died in 1916 after a failed attempt to make himself emperor. By then, regional military commanders—the warlords—had set up their own independent regimes across much of the country. On top of that were the areas in the major cities governed by foreign powers—a result of the "unequal treaties" forced on the Chinese over the previous 70 years. China's railways were owned by foreigners; there were foreign warships on its rivers. In the Versailles Settlement of 1919, Japan, which had sided with the Allies in the First World War, took over most of the concessions formerly belonging to Germany.

The fact that China was not master in its own house enraged nationalists. Sun Yat-sen had founded the Chinese Nationalist Party, the Guomindang, in 1914. In the years following the end of the First World War he

revived it, and set up a separate government in southern China. At this time the program of the Guomindang was one of social reform and anti-imperialism. The Soviet Comintern (Communist International) supported it with money and by sending military and political advisors. A Chinese Communist Party was also aided and advised by Moscow, but its membership in the early 1920s was small; in 1923 there were only 300 members, including Mao Zedong and Zhou Enlai.

Left and right in the Guomindang

At this time, communist policy was to co-operate with the nationalists, and many communists openly joined the Guomindang. The situation in the country was worsening, as warlords imposed their own taxes and even printed their own currency; local wars were constantly breaking out among them. At the Washington Conference, which began in November 1921, the Western powers and Japan had agreed to end their extraterritorial rights and to grant China full autonomy, but so chaotic was the country that they held on to their concessions in the major cities in order to protect their own citizens there.

The Guomindang by now had a considerable army, although it still also relied on alliances with the warlords. In March 1925 Sun Yat-sen died. Later that year, there were incidents at Shanghai and Huangpu in which

1922
Washington
Agreement

1925 Death of Sun Yat-sen;
Universal manhood
suffrage in Japan

1926 Hirohito
becomes Emperor
of Japan

1927 Communists
expelled from
Guomindang

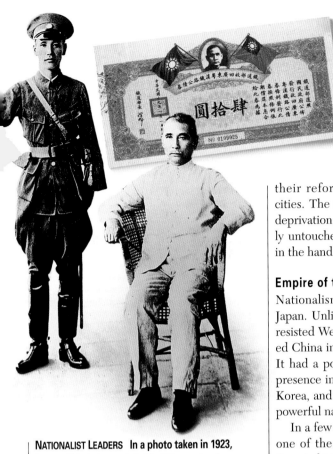

gram of modernization, encouraging the growth of industry, improving communications and establishing large-scale public education. But their reforms mainly affected life in the cities. The rural areas, with their profound deprivation and inequalities, remained largely untouched and the treaty ports were still in the hands of the foreign powers.

Empire of the Sun

Nationalism took a very different form in Japan. Unlike China, Japan had successfully resisted Western intervention. It had defeated China in war in 1894 and Russia in 1905. It had a powerful military and commercial presence in Manchuria and effectively ruled Korea, and it was without question the most powerful nation in Asia.

In a few decades, Japan had gone through one of the most extraordinary transformations in history. From being a feudal state, at a technological level equivalent to that of 17th-century Europe, it had become a modern industrial nation with a powerful army and navy. It had accomplished this largely for reasons of self-defense, in order to resist the sort of unequal trade terms the industrial nations of the West had imposed on China.

Japan had something like a Western constitution with a two-chamber Diet or parliament. Its urban citizens wore Western clothes and shopped in Western-style department stores, followed Western sports and increasingly listened to Western music. Its educated classes, and its new industrial proletariat, were influenced by Western liberal and, to some extent, socialist and communist ideas.

These changes were real and substantial, and yet at a deeper level Japanese society remained highly distinctive. Under the constitution, the person of the emperor was still regarded as divine—"sacred and inviolable." The inculcation of unquestioning, undying loyalty to the emperor was central to Japanese education—part of a deliberate policy to extend to the whole nation the ideals of the old feudal warriors or *samurai*. Democracy had not rooted very deeply, and the lower house of the parliament was often ineffective. Real power lay with the army and navy chiefs, with the emperor's aristocratic advisers, and with the *zaibatsu*—the handful of huge private firms that had been

NATIONALIST LEADERS In a photo taken in 1923, Chiang Kai-shek stands behind his mentor, Sun Yat-sen. Sun's image also appears on a Chinese government railway bond (top).

British and French troops and police fired on demonstrators, killing more than 60 Chinese. These incidents greatly increased support for both the Guomindang and the communists. Membership of the Guomindang rose to 200,000, and of the Communist Party to 10,000. By now, however, there was a deep division within the Guomindang between the radical left wing and the more conservative elements. The leader of the Guomindang army was Chiang Kai-shek. In June 1927, he expelled the communists from the party, killing many of them; at the same time he expelled the Russian advisers. In August that year, the Chinese Communist Party attempted uprisings in Guangzhou, Shanghai and Nanjing, all of which were put down with much bloodshed. The alliance between communists and nationalists was at an end, and the surviving communists withdrew to the remoter parts of central China.

In the last years of the 1920s, the nationalists steadily increased their control of the country, taking Beijing in 1928. They now set out on a pro-

ON GUARD British troops in Shanghai take up positions behind sandbags during the fighting in 1927. Shanghai was still a treaty port, with foreign troops stationed in the European settlements.

1931
Japanese seize
Manchuria

1934-5
The Long
March

1937
Japanese
invade China

created when the country began to industrialize at the end of the 19th century. Two of the greatest of the zaibatsu, the Houses of Mitsui and Mitsubishi, had been founded in the 1880s. They were regarded as owning many of the country's politicians, and certainly exercised enormous political as well as financial power.

In the early 1920s, there were attempts at moderate social legislation by Prime Minister Hara Takashi, the first non-aristocrat to hold the office, and his successor Kato Tataaki. But there was increasing resistance from the country's military and industrial elites. Takashi, who had tried to resist the power of the military, was assassinated in 1921. In 1925 the vote was given to all adult males, but fears of subversion among the industrial working classes stimulated a growing tide of reaction. Anti-trade union laws were passed, and in 1928 it became a capital crime to agitate against private property. At the same time, a special police force was set up to seek out those guilty of "dangerous thoughts," especially any that were disloyal to the emperor or sympathetic to Marxist ideas.

By the late 1920s, the population of Japan had grown to over 60 million, and the country was no longer self-sufficient in foodstuffs. Its industry, too, was heavily dependent on imports of raw materials. The Wall Street Crash of 1929 destroyed many of Japan's export markets, including the silk market on which many farmers and textile workers depended. The population could not be sustained by the country's own resources of land and raw materials, but emigration was restricted by the immigration laws of other countries, many of which had a racial bias against Chinese and Japanese.

Nationalism fed on these problems and on the apparent inability of the civilian government to deal with them. There was also some resistance to the supposedly growing influence in the country of Western immorality and decadence. A further grievance was the perceived selfishness of the zaibatsu. Increasingly, national expansion, and in particular the seizure of land and resources in China, was seen as the solution to Japan's economic problems. These aggressive nationalist ideas were particularly strong among young military officers. Officers of the Japanese navy were infuriated that the international Washington Agreement of 1922, signed by their own government, had restricted Japanese naval power; while Japan's army was angered by government cuts in its size.

These young

STATUS DIVINE Hirohito, Japan's emperor from 1926, was a marine biologist by training, but to the Japanese people he was the direct descendant of a goddess.

PANAY INCIDENT

On December 12, 1937, Japanese planes bombed and sank the U.S. gunboat *Panay*. The *Panay*, which had been escorting American oil tankers, had moved up the Yangtse to avoid the hostilities around Nanjing, carrying embassy staff and some foreign journalists as passengers. The Japanese planes dive-bombed the ship from 12:30 p.m. onward and then machine-gunned survivors attempting to get ashore. The *Panay* was seen to sink at 3:54 p.m. Of 80 people on board, three were killed and more than 50 injured. The captain of one of the escorted tankers was also killed.

The *Panay* incident caused international outrage. The American and British governments made strenuous protests to the Japanese authorities, which in due course apologized and paid over $2 million in compensation. The incident, however, showed that the U.S. government, while wholly sympathetic to the Chinese, was reluctant to become directly involved in the war with Japan.

nationalist officers had their allies among civilian nationalist extremists, who were opposed to all Western liberal ideas and committed to fanatical notions of national, that is racial, purity. Some of them had formed secret societies, of which the Ketsumeidan, or League of Blood, was the most extreme. Altogether, the revolutionary program of the Japanese nationalists, with its combination of authoritarian government, militarism, racism and a hostility to "Big Business," was very similar to that of German National Socialism. The Diet was not a forum in which such a program could be put into effect. The nationalists resorted to methods of terror, intimidation and assassination. This was partly to remove political opponents, many of whom were murdered, but also to bring about conditions of sheer disorder that might lead to the imposition of military rule.

In 1926 the Emperor Hirohito came to the throne. He was a young man of moderate views who had travelled in the West—he had been the first Japanese crown prince to travel abroad. He might have become a focus for resistance to nationalist extremism, but his advisers, anxious that any action might jeopardize the imperial monarchy, cautioned against any intervention.

Many of the most fanatical young army officers were stationed in Manchuria and urged further incursions into China. In 1928 some of them murdered Chang Tso-lin, the Chinese warlord ruler of that region, and yet the civilian government took no action. In 1930, Prime Minister Yuko Hamaguchi, a moderate, was murdered by extremists. The nationalists were firmly set on a course that would lead to war in Asia and the Pacific. It could be said that the true beginning of the Second World War was in 1937, when Japan invaded China. It was the resulting sanctions against Japan imposed by the United States that led eventually to the attack on Pearl Harbor and to U.S. entry into the war in 1941.

The Japanese had been in Manchuria since 1905 and had invested heavily in it. In 1931 Japanese forces seized total control of it, and in 1933 they established the puppet state of Manchukuo, with the last Manchu emperor as its nominal head. Thereafter, with an aggressively nationalist government now ruling Japan, they began to expand farther into northern China.

Civil war in China

As the threat from Japan grew more pressing, China was still in a state of civil war between Chiang Kai-shek's increasingly right-wing Guomindang government and the Chinese communists. By 1930 the communists had been driven underground in the cities, but Mao Zedong had established a Chinese Soviet Republic in the southeastern province of Jiangxi, ruling over some 50 million people, and in 1932 the party leadership moved there from Shanghai.

The Guomindang now directed its efforts to destroying Jiangxi's substantial communist army. In October 1934 it succeeded in dri-

WINNING THROUGH Survivors of the Long March (right) arrive in Shaanxi. Below: Communist students in Shaanxi listen to Mao Zedong, photographed (left) in 1937.

MAO'S LONG MARCH

In October 1934 some 100,000 men and 35 women set out from the communist stronghold in Jiangxi province. Their destination on what became known as the Long March was Shaanxi in northwestern China. This was close to their Russian allies, as well as to the front line of Japanese incursions into China. The group marching with Mao Zedong finally arrived in Shaanxi in October 1935 after a march of 6,000 miles; they had averaged more than 15 miles per day under almost continuous attack from Guomindang forces and had crossed 18 mountain ranges. Only about 8,000 reached Shaanxi, many thousands having perished along the way from military action, exhaustion, starvation and disease, among them Mao's two small children and his younger brother.

Party conferences were held during the march. In January 1935 the slogan "Go north to fight the Japanese" was adopted. In August 1935 it became official policy to bring about a united front of all parties against the Japanese. In the course of the march, Mao's position as leader, which in 1934 had been uncertain, was consolidated. In the longer term, this meant the triumph of his view that, contrary to orthodox Marxism, the Chinese revolution would be made among the peasant masses before it was taken to the industrial proletariat in the cities. This was precisely what happened when the Chinese civil war resumed after the Japanese surrender.

ving the communists out, forcing them into their now-legendary "Long March" to Shaanxi in the northwest.

By the end of the Long March, Mao Zedong was the undisputed leader of the Chinese Communist Party. For the moment, the Japanese threat had to be faced, and like the communists in Europe, Mao proposed to form a "Popular Front"—in this case with the Guomindang to fight the Japanese.

Chiang Kai-shek, however, was opposed to cooperation with the communists and ordered his generals in the north to attack them in Shaanxi. Several of his generals, including Chang, the commander of the Manchurian army, disagreed with this, and Chang went so far as to arrest the nationalist leader when he came to the Manchurian army's base at Xi'an in December 1936. Chang held Chiang until he had promised to

call off the civil war and unite the country. Secret negotiations between the parties were still being conducted when the Japanese invaded in July 1937.

The war between Japan and China was undeclared. It began with an incident at the Marco Polo (Lugou) Bridge over the Yonding river, near Beijing, when a Japanese soldier disappeared after a shot had been fired at Japanese troops on maneuvers in the area.

The soldier was subsequently found safe and well, and both the Japanese and the Chinese local commanders tried to calm the situation, but other interests—whether Japanese nationalist or Chinese Communist or both is uncertain—were at work, and the situation deteriorated rapidly as both sides sent in reinforcements.

AMID THE WRECKAGE Japanese troops enter Wuhan (Hankow) in 1937, left . Above: In November 1937, a father squats with his children in Shanghai railway station, smashed by a Japanese bombardment.

By the end of July 1937, the Japanese had taken control of Beijing and the two countries were in a state of general war.

The communists agreed to suspend their revolutionary program and place their forces under government command. The Chinese had an army of over 2 million, and Russia sent military advisers, munitions and aircraft with Soviet pilots. But the Japanese advance seemed unstoppable. In 1937 they captured Shanghai and the nationalist capital of Nanking, where they systematically slaughtered, raped, looted and burned. A postwar enquiry concluded that they had murdered over 350,000 of the city's inhabitants. By the end of 1938, they were in control of virtually the whole of the eastern part of the country.

The Chinese had lost most of the industrial areas of the country, and most of the railways and ports. Fighting desperately, they continued to hold out in the west, however, where the nationalists shifted their capital to Chongqing in the easily defended, mountain-rimmed province of Sichuan. Here, with virtually unlimited resources of manpower, with continuing military assistance from Russia and financial help from the United States, Britain and France, they were able to build new factories and train and equip new armies. The communists fought a continuous guerrilla war in the Japanese-occupied territories of northern China, gaining enormously in numbers, experience and popular support. By the time war broke out in Europe, the Chinese were still undefeated. In 1941, when Germany invaded Russia and military aid from the Soviet Union ceased, the United States began sending them aircraft and munitions.

THE RAPE OF NANKING

Rhodes Farmer, war correspondent for the *Melbourne Herald*, reported the first weeks of the Rape of Nanking in 1937:

"The execution squads worked around the clock.

"European observers estimated 20,000 soldiers and 30,000 civilians were mown down by machine-guns or else used as human dummies for bayonet practice. In the beginning the death mounds were allowed to rot unburied. Later, possibly influenced by fear of disease, the Japanese doused the dead with petrol but only succeeded in reducing them to revolting masses of scorched flesh . . .

"More than 20,000 women were raped during the two months. The refugee camps became holding pens from which the Japanese took women almost as they wanted them . . .

"At the time of Nanking's calvary, the *Japanese Advertiser*, a paper printed in English in Tokio [Tokyo] . . . published the following item: 'Sub-Lieutenant Mukai and Sub-Lieutenant Noda, in a friendly contest to see which of them will first fell a hundred Chinese in individual sword combat before the fall of Nanking, are well in the final phase of their race, running almost neck and neck. The score is: Mukai, 89; Noda, 78. Mukai's blade was slightly damaged in the competition. He explained that this was the result of cutting a Chinese in half, helmet and all. . . .'"

THE SPANISH CRUCIBLE

THE LONG-BREWING STRUGGLE BETWEEN LEFT AND RIGHT BECAME A BITTER FIGHT TO THE DEATH IN SPAIN'S BRUTAL CIVIL WAR

Democracy, in retreat almost everywhere in the 1920s, suffered severe setbacks in Spain and Portugal. In Portugal, General Carmona carried out a military coup d'état in 1926, and gradually handed over power to his finance minister, António Salazar, who became prime minister and effective dictator in 1932.

Salazar, who would prove to be the most enduring of the European dictators, had been a professor of economics, and academics played an important part in all his cabinets until his demise in 1970. He encouraged slow but steady economic growth, protected the currency against inflation, and while preserving the interests of the property-owning classes and the Church, also protected the rights of small farmers and the working class. He ruled with the help of a small but efficient and discreetly brutal secret police, the

THE MAIDEN AND THE LION A young woman representing the new Spanish Republic is surrounded by more traditional symbols of the Spanish regions in this poster of 1931.

PIDE (International Police for the Defense of the State), and kept leftist political activists in jail for long periods, but he refused to adopt the death penalty and his regime was benign in comparison with those of Mussolini, Hitler and Stalin.

Much the same could be said of General Miguel Primo de Rivera, who proclaimed himself dictator of Spain in 1923, with the support of King Alphonso XIII and the army. Determined to arouse Spain from its lethargy, he, too, set out to steer his country toward economic development, but his rule was more military than academic and his methods clumsy; he even tried, unsuccessfully, to abolish the siesta. In January 1930 Primo de Rivera resigned, having lost the support of the army. The following year, the king fled and a parliamentary republic was set up.

Popular front

The Spanish government of 1931-3 was a coalition of republicans and socialists, with the socialist trade union leader Francisco Largo Caballero as minister of labor. Largo Caballero introduced labor reforms that were favorable to the trade unions, but only succeeded in alarming employers without doing much to reduce unemployment. The socialists were moving steadily to the left, however, and when they lost the election of November 1933 to a conservative coalition, they turned to direct action in the form of strikes and workers' uprisings. In Asturias, the miners formed a Workers' Commune which was suppressed after two weeks by Spain's youngest general, Francisco Franco. There was also a Catalan nationalist uprising in Barcelona, which was quickly suppressed.

At the elections of February 1936, the country was almost equally divided between the center and the right on the one hand, and the left-wing parties of the Popular Front on the other. It was the Popular Front, however, that won the majority of seats. The

WORKERS AND FIGHTERS "Socialism Is Liberation," declares a POUM poster. For its cover, the anti-fascist German-language picture paper *AIZ*, published in Prague, has a heroic image of a worker-militiaman from Asturias in northern Spain.

> ## AT WAR IN SPAIN
>
> The English writer George Orwell joined a Spanish militia in December 1936 and a few weeks later was sent to the front:
>
> "I peered cautiously through a loophole, trying to find the Fascist trench.
>
> "'Where are the enemy?'
>
> "Benjamin waved his hand expansively. 'Over zere.' (Benjamin spoke English—terrible English) . . .
>
> "According to my idea of trench warfare the Fascists would be fifty or a hundred yards away. I could see nothing—seemingly their trenches were very well concealed. Then with a shock of dismay I saw where Benjamin was pointing; on the opposite hill-top, beyond the ravine . . . We were nowhere near them! . . .
>
> "The new sentries were no sooner in the trench than they began firing a terrific fusillade at nothing in particular. I could see the Fascists, tiny as ants, dodging to and fro behind their parapet, and sometimes a black dot which was a head would pause for a moment, impudently exposed . . . [Presently a] sentry . . . sidled up to me and began urging me to fire. I tried to explain that at that range and with these rifles you could not hit a man except by accident. But he was only a child, and he kept motioning with his rifle towards one of the dots, grinning as eagerly as a dog that expects a pebble to be thrown. Finally I put my sights up to seven hundred and let fly. The dot disappeared. I hope it went near enough to make him jump. It was the first time in my life that I had fired a gun at a human being."

1923 Dictatorship of
Primo de Rivera in Spain
begins (ends 1930)

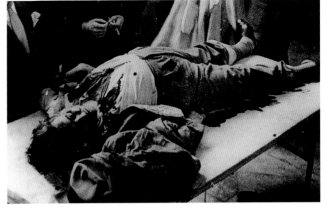

country was now polarized between left and right. Formerly moderate conservatives began to join the nationalist, anti-Marxist Falange, founded by José Antonio Primo de Rivera, son of the dictator, or the Monarchists; the small, Moscow-directed Spanish Communist Party began to take over the Socialist Party through its Youth Movement. The government itself was outflanked on the left by anarchist parties and by Spain's own revolutionary Marxist party, the POUM (Partido Obrero de Unificación Marxista).

The Popular Front government announced a radical socialist program. This was enough in itself to frighten the middle classes, the landowners, the army and the Church. More frightening still were the unauthorized activities of the extremists of left and right. The first churches and convents were burned on

MARCHING FOR MADRID Citizens take up arms to defend the Spanish capital against the advancing forces of General Franco in 1936. Madrid held out until March 1939.

the evening the election results were announced. In the countryside, the anarchists organized land seizures; in the towns, anarchists and the POUM seized factories and carried on a campaign of terror and murder. On the right, youth gangs of the Falange openly shot down their enemies. The government, divided between the moderates and extremists, looked on helplessly, as the country slid into chaos.

On June 16, the conservative leader José María Gil Robles read out to the Spanish parliament a list of outrages: 160 churches burned; 269 political murders; 1,287 cases of assault; 69 political offices; and 10 newspaper offices wrecked. The country, he declared, could live under a monarchy or a republic, under communism or fascism, but it could not live in anarchy.

On July 13, the leader of the monarchist faction in parliament, José Calvo Sotelo, was

ASSASSINATED In the early hours of July 13, 1936, police officers escorted the monarchist leader José Calvo Sotelo from his Madrid apartment to a waiting car, where shortly afterward they shot him. It was the spark that kindled war.

murdered by the newly formed republican riot police, the Assault Guards, in reprisal for the killing of two of their number by a right-wing gang. This was the trigger for a military uprising, first in Spanish Morocco, and then, on July 17, in garrisons of almost every city in Spain. On July 19, General Franco flew

1932 Salazar becomes dictator of Portugal

1936 Spanish Civil War begins

1937 Bombing of Guernica

1939 Franco takes Madrid

from the Canary Islands to the center of the uprising in Morocco.

The rebel nationalist forces rapidly seized control of the south and west of the country, but they were denied the speedy victory they had hoped for. The republican (government) side held on to Madrid and most of the north and east, and the civil war that began in July 1936 was fought along this dividing line.

Civil war

From the start, it was a war fought in a spirit of deep hatred, with terrible atrocities on both sides. In the towns and cities they controlled, the nationalists rounded up suspected leftists and executed them: the murders were carried out systematically by army firing squads or, less officially, by Falangist gangs. The poet García Lorca was only the most famous victim of these killings; the others included Popular Front politicians, military officers who opposed the uprising, and many professional people with leftist sympathies. Many of those killed were tortured first.

Among the main victims of republican atrocities were the clergy, although few of them were pro-nationalist at the start of the war. In all, 11 bishops were murdered, along with 12 percent of Spain's monks and 13 percent of the Spanish priesthood, several of whom were burned or buried alive. Over 250 nuns were also killed, some after being raped. Other republican executions were carried out on a class basis, the victims being either suspected members of the Falange or simply bourgeois "class enemies." In Ronda early in the war, 512 such people were flung to their deaths in the gorge that runs through the town, in an episode recollected in Ernest Hemingway's novel *For Whom the Bell Tolls*. Altogether, each side was responsible for the murder of over 50,000 noncombatants in addition to the casualties of fighting in the front line.

The war was prolonged by the fierce resistance of the republican militias and by foreign intervention. Franco arrived in Morocco to find that the sailors of the small Spanish navy had killed their officers and sided with the Republic; as a result, it would be impossible to bring the Army of Africa over to Spain by sea. He therefore asked fascist Italy and National Socialist Germany for bombers and transport planes. The Germans and Italians obliged immediately, and he started flying in ammunition and troops. Within less than two weeks, his Moroccan troops were able to link up with the mainland armies, and a month later he was appointed Chief of State and Generalissimo in charge of all nationalist resources. Meanwhile, aircraft and tanks supplied by Russia had greatly strengthened the defenses of the Republic.

ON THE FRONT LINE Republican militia go on the attack with the help of a captured artillery gun. The picture was taken by the American photojournalist "Chim" Seymour.

DEATH OF A POET

When Spain's civil war broke out, the 38-year-old Federico García Lorca, internationally renowned as a poet and playwright, was in Granada, staying with his family. Following Franco's *pronunciamento*, the city was taken over by its army garrison and the Falangists, and a reign of terror began. On August 9, 1936, a group of rightists called at the Lorca house, looking for a man they suspected of killing two of their number, and beat the Lorca caretaker. When Lorca protested, they made it clear that they knew him and detested him. Afraid for his life, Lorca went into hiding with the family of his friend, the poet Luis Rosales. On the afternoon of August 16, the Rosales house was surrounded by police and soldiers, and Lorca arrested. He was detained at the civil government building, accused, among other things, of communicating with the Russians using a clandestine radio. Lorca's fate was now in the hands of the civil governor, Jose Valdès, and it would have been Valdès who gave the order for his death. Early on August 18, Lorca was driven to the little village of Víznar, a nationalist stronghold. From there he was taken to a nearby olive grove along with three other men and shot. All four were buried in a rough trench near where they fell. The grave is unmarked.

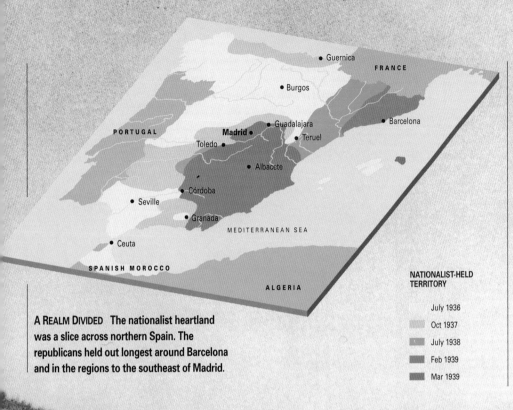

NATIONALIST-HELD
TERRITORY

July 1936

Oct 1937

July 1938

Feb 1939

Mar 1939

A REALM DIVIDED The nationalist heartland
was a slice across northern Spain. The
republicans held out longest around Barcelona
and in the regions to the southeast of Madrid.

In all, the Germans supplied the nationalists with some 600 aircraft, 200 tanks and
anti-aircraft guns. They also provided up to
10,000 men at any one time, including the
tank and aircraft units of the Condor Legion.
The Italians supplied 660 aircraft, 150 tanks,
800 artillery pieces and large quantities of
rifles and machine guns. They also sent
between 40,000 and 50,000 men at any given
time, of whom 4,000 were killed.

The Russians supplied the Republic with
1,000 aircraft, 900 tanks, 300 armored cars,
1,500 artillery pieces and vast quantities of
rifles, machine guns and ammunition. (The
republican government had to pay for these
in gold, exhausting the nation's gold reserves,
which before the war had been substantial.)
They also sent 1,000 pilots, several hundred
military advisers and other specialists, and,
more covertly, NKVD (secret police) officers. In addition, the republicans had the

CASUALTY OF WAR   A small boy lies dead on a Barcelona street in February 1938. He is a victim of bombing raids on the city by Italian planes based in Majorca.

help of some 40,000 volunteers from over 50 countries in the International Brigades organized by the Comintern, plus around 10,000 volunteer doctors, nurses and other civilian helpers.

Numbers and equipment on both sides were about equal. The nationalists eventually won because Franco fought with complete singleness of purpose. The republicans were divided by politics, as between socialists, liberals, anarchists, Moscow-directed communists and the independent Marxist

FRANCISCO FRANCO—SPAIN'S CAUDILLO

Francisco Franco Bahamonde, the man who led the nationalist forces to victory in the Spanish Civil War and ruled the country as *Caudillo* ("Leader") until his death in 1975, was born in 1892 and joined the army as a cadet in 1907. In 1912, as a young lieutenant, he volunteered for service in Spain's North African colony, and in 1923 he was given command of the Spanish Foreign Legion, which played a decisive role in the suppression of Abd el-Krim's rebellion in Morocco. At the age of 33, he became the youngest brigadier-general in the Spanish army and a national hero. Although not a military genius, he was noted for his administrative efficiency, dedication and concern for the welfare of the men under his command.

In 1934 he led the forces that put down a rising of the miners of Asturias, and the following year he was made chief of the general staff. In early 1936, as the country began to slide into chaos, he appealed to the Popular Front government to declare a state of emergency. The government refused, and Franco was dismissed and given a posting in the Canary Islands. In July 1936 he broadcast a manifesto declaring a military rebellion and flew to Morocco to take command of the Spanish forces there. Three months later, with his army halted outside Madrid, he was declared Generalissimo and head of the nationalist government.

Franco joined the rebellion because of his conviction that the country faced the kind of destructive chaos that the Bolsheviks had brought about in Russia. As a devout Catholic, he was also enraged at the murder of priests and burning of churches. In the years after the civil war, his rule was authoritarian, designed to preserve the status quo and to prevent any return of the social radicalism of the 1930s. In the 1960s his regime started to liberalize; in 1969 he designated Prince Juan Carlos as his official successor.

GENERALISSIMO   Franco became nationalist commander in chief in September 1936.

His relations with Hitler during the Second World War, in particular his meeting with the Führer at Hendaye on the French-Spanish frontier in October 1940, have been the subject of some controversy. After the war, pro-Franco propagandists suggested that the Caudillo had come under considerable pressure to enter the war on the Axis side but had stoutly insisted on maintaining Spanish neutrality. Most modern historians, however, believe that the opposite is closer to the truth. At Hendaye Franco was keen to come in on the German side in the hope of winning rich territorial pickings in North Africa. It was Hitler who had reservations about Spain, still devastated and crippled in the aftermath of the civil war, as an ally. He was certainly not impressed by Franco, whom he had once described as "not a hero but a little pipsqueak."

POUM. While fighting the war, the leftists were trying to create a revolution behind the lines. Communist units denied air or artillery support to non-communists fighting alongside them, or diverted supplies intended for them.

At end of 1936, the communists ousted the socialist prime minister Largo Caballero who was succeeded by another socialist, Juan Negrín. Effectively, however, the communists had taken over the republican government. In the spring of 1937, they turned on the POUM and the anarchists. In Madrid they used forged documents to implicate the POUM in a secret deal with Franco and began arresting the POUM leadership. Open fighting broke out in Barcelona between communist units on the one side, and POUM and anarchist forces on the other. In the course of 1937 and early 1938, many thousands of POUM members and other leftists were executed or tortured to death by the Spanish communists, working under the direction of the NKVD.

Guernica

George Orwell, the British writer who had fought with the POUM, managed to escape the Stalinist purge of the Left in Madrid and Barcelona. When he returned to England, however, the editor of the left-wing *New Statesman* refused to publish his account of the purge. Intellectuals in the democracies were almost entirely on the side of the republicans, and preferred to see the war in black-and-white terms.

In the spring of 1937, the attention of the democracies was drawn to another event. On April 26, 1937, 43 aircraft of the Condor Legion bombed the Basque town of Guernica. Roughly 1,000 people were killed and two-thirds of the town's buildings destroyed. The order for the assault came from Colonel Wolfgang von Richthofen, the Legion's commander (and a cousin of the First World War air ace, the "Red Baron," Manfred von Richthofen).

The object of the raid was terror, and to a world as yet unaccustomed to the aerial bombing of civilians it was deeply shocking. Pablo Picasso, already at work on a large

DISARMED Republican prisoners are marched away by nationalist troops after surrendering in the Somosierra Pass. The nationalists seized this key pass through the Guadarrama mountains north of Madrid in July 1936.

painting for the Paris World Fair, devoted it to the subject of Guernica, which became an icon of the war.

After POUM was destroyed, morale on the republican side declined. Franco kept up a war of attrition, ensuring that his odds were good before making an assault. In February 1938, after the winter battle of Teruel, he advanced to the Mediterranean and cut the republican forces in two. That autumn, Stalin, who took most of Spain's gold, abandoned the Republic's cause and cut off aid. Franco opened his last offensive in Catalonia and on January 28, 1939, he took Barcelona. On March 28, he took Madrid, and the Spanish Civil War ended.

During the war, 200,000 were killed in battle and a million crippled; more than

DEFEATED Citizens of Madrid contemplate the ruins of their homes after Franco's troops marched into the city on March 28, 1939.

100,000 had been executed; 10,000 had died in air raids, and 25,000 from malnutrition.

Having achieved victory, Franco set out to extirpate leftism. After Madrid had been captured, there were summary trials where almost 200,000 people were sentenced to death. Though many of these death sentences were commuted, tens of thousands were shot and others sentenced to long prison terms. Two years later, a quarter of a million political prisoners remained in Spanish jails; and while 500,000 Spaniards had gone into exile, nearly half of them would never return.

FROM APPEASEMENT TO WAR

THE EUROPEAN DEMOCRACIES DESIRED PEACE AT ANY PRICE; WHEN WAR WAS FORCED ON THEM, THEY WERE CAUGHT ILL-PREPARED

In April 1940, Joseph Goebbels gave a secret briefing to German journalists and talked about what had happened since Hitler came to power. He explained: "In 1933 a French premier ought to have said . . . : 'The new Reich Chancellor is the man who wrote *Mein Kampf*, which says this and that. This man cannot be tolerated in our vicinity. Either he disappears or we march!' But they didn't do it. They left us alone and let us slip through the risky zone, and we were able to sail around all dangerous reefs. And when we were done, and well armed, better than they, then they started the war!"

With hindsight, that is an accurate summary of what happened in the 1930s. Hitler had made his intentions plain in *Mein Kampf*. From 1934 onward, as Germany began to rearm and occupied the Rhineland in flagrant breach of the Versailles Treaty, it was becoming increasingly clear that Hitler posed a threat to the peace of Europe. In

CHRISTIAN PACIFIST George Lansbury resigned as Labor leader in 1935 when a party conference voted in favor of possible military action against the Italians in Abyssinia (Ethiopia).

1934 Hitler's Germany was still militarily weaker than France, and it was very much weaker than France and Britain combined.

That year was the "risky zone" to which Goebbels referred: with firm action in 1934, Hitler could have been

stopped. Yet the strategy of British and French politicians in the 1930s was for the most part one of appeasement. To be fair, any other policy would have been politically very difficult, for the mood of the time was deeply opposed to war. Soon after Hitler came to power, students at the Oxford Union voted 275-152 in favor of the motion "This House would in no circumstances fight for King and Country."

At about the same time, in a poll in the United States, 75 percent of Americans declared they were opposed to involvement in any European war. British and French socialists voted against rearmament right up until the outbreak of war. George Lansbury, leader of the British Labor Party in 1933, wrote: "I would close every recruiting station, disband the Army and disarm the Air Force." His successor, Clement Attlee, declared: "We are unalterably opposed to anything in the way of rearmament."

In the mid 1930s, memories of the terrible losses of the First World War were still fresh in the minds of most adults. Among many on the political left, there was a conviction that wars were created by bankers and armaments manufacturers in the interests of capitalism and imperialism. For their part, numbers of British churchmen and intellectuals collected signatures for the Peace Pledge Union.

In Britain and the United States particularly, feelings about Germany had moved from the vindictiveness of 1918 to the belief that the defeated country had been harshly treated in the Versailles settlement. Many people felt that in remilitarizing the Rhineland and in marching into Austria, Hitler was merely restoring a nation dismembered by

CHAMBERLAIN: MAN OF MUNICH

The British prime minister identified with the policy of appeasement toward Adolf Hitler was born in 1869, the son of the industrialist, social reformer and politician Joseph Chamberlain. Neville followed in his father's footsteps by working in industry in Birmingham before entering local and then national politics. In the Conservative governments of the 1920s and 1930s, he served as postmaster general, health minister and chancellor of the exchequer before succeeding Stanley Baldwin as prime minister in 1937.

DAPPER PREMIER Chamberlain's reputation was ruined when his appeasement policy failed.

Chamberlain was a gifted politician, of complete integrity, but his strengths lay in domestic rather than foreign affairs. As a moderate and civilized man, he could not enter the mind of someone like Hitler. History remembers him for his visits to Germany in September 1938 and his claim that he had produced "peace with honor" after leaving the Czechs defenseless. When Hitler seized the rest of Czechoslovakia, however, Chamberlain began to rearm Britain, published guarantees of military support for Poland and introduced conscription. When Hitler invaded Poland, he kept his word and declared war, but by then his reputation was fatally damaged. After the fiasco of the Allied expedition to Norway in April 1940, as much Churchill's fault as his, support for him fell away. On May 10, he resigned. He continued to serve in Churchill's government, but he was already seriously ill. He died in November 1940 as Britain was fighting for its very survival.

Versailles. Hitler had done good things for the German people, they believed, and however brutal it might be, German National Socialism was certainly better than Russian communism. Moderate, sensible people, Prime Minister Neville Chamberlain among them, simply could not grasp what Hitler was capable of, that *Mein Kampf* was not mere rhetoric but the expression of a program aimed at the "ethnic cleansing" of Germany and at German domination, first of Europe, then of the world.

Behind the antiwar mood of the time lay simple fear, and in particular fear of the results of aerial bombing. Even Winston Churchill, one of the few voices calling for opposition to Hitler, warned the British parliament in 1934 that as many as 40,000 Londoners would be killed or injured in the first weeks of war. It was believed that the Germans would drop gas bombs. A leading military expert, Major-General John Fuller, predicted that London would become "one vast raving Bedlam."

Crisis at Munich

Up until the beginning of 1939, Hitler was still striving to find some kind of legitimacy for his acts. Marching into the Rhineland reversed one of the injustices of Versailles; the *Anschluss* with Austria reunited the German people, and newsreels showing jubilant crowds suggested that it was welcome to the Austrians as well—which it was, by and large. In 1938, after the success of the *Anschluss*, Hitler turned his attention to Czechoslovakia, his next target, and found his claim to legitimacy in the alleged sufferings of the young republic's Sudeten Germans.

Czechoslovakia, formed after the First World War, was a developed industrial country, with a population of 15 million which included some 3 million Germans. Most of these lived in the area bordering on Germany known as the Sudetenland, which contained much of Czechoslovakia's industry as well as a crucial line of defensive fortifications.

In the early years of the Great Depression, the Sudeten Germans suffered like the rest of the Czechoslovaks, but the rapidly growing Sudeten Nazi Party tried to persuade them that they were, in fact, the victims of oppression by the Slav majority. When, in 1936, the moderate Czech government of Eduard Benes adopted emergency powers to suppress extremist parties, the Nazi leader Konrad Heinlein began to agitate for greater rights of local government for the Sudetenland. In April 1938, with the vociferous support of Germany, he demanded virtual autonomy for the province and stepped up the level of violence.

CRISIS SUMMIT Europe's "big four"— left to right: Chamberlain, Daladier, Hitler and Mussolini— pose for the camera during the conference of September 29, 1938. The Czechs were not represented at Munich.

Czechoslovakia in 1938 had a substantial and well-equipped army. It also had guarantees of military aid from both France and Soviet Russia in the event of its being attacked. Britain's prime minister, Neville Chamberlain, reluctant to provoke Hitler into war, declined to give such a guarantee. Hitler, however, knew that France would not act without British support, and that Russia

"PEACE IN OUR TIME" It's smiles all round as Chamberlain arrives back in England after Munich. Many genuinely believed that the prime minister had ensured peace.

| March 1938 Anschluss with Austria | September 1938 Munich Agreement | March 1939 Germany occupies Czechoslovakia | April 1939 Mussolini invades Albania | May 1939 "Pact of Steel" between Germany and Italy | August 1939 Molotov-Ribbentrop Pact | September 1939 Germany invades Poland; war is declared |

THE MUNICH AGREEMENT 1938

■ To Germany ▨ To Hungary ■ To Poland

CUTTING UP CZECHOSLOVAKIA The Munich Agreement handed over a million Czechoslovak citizens and much of the country's industry to Germany, and left its frontiers indefensible in the event of further aggression.

would not act without the French, and decided to embark on separate negotiations with Britain.

In August Britain sent a representative, Lord Runciman, to Prague. Under increasing pressure, the Czech government agreed to almost everything Heinlein had demanded in April, but Heinlein rejected the offer and broke off negotiations. In September Chamberlain himself flew to Berchtesgaden, Hitler's mountain retreat in the Bavarian Alps, for his first meeting with the Führer. Hitler now demanded outright cession of the Sudetenland to Germany, threatening war if the demand was not met. Chamberlain was ready, as the price of peace, to persuade Czechoslovakia to yield territory to a hostile neighbor. Of Hitler at this time he wrote: "In spite of the hardness and ruthlessness I thought I saw in his face, I got the impression that here was a man who could be relied upon when he had given his word." This was tragically naive.

Four days later, Britain and France confronted President Benes and insisted that he meet the German demands. Given no choice, the Czechoslovak government yielded, handing over not only territory but almost a million Czech-speaking citizens and the

country's vital defenses. Chamberlain now flew to a second meeting with Hitler, at Godesberg, at which Hitler demanded immediate occupation of the German-speaking areas by German troops. Chamberlain protested, but the only concession Hitler made was to delay occupation until October 1.

On September 24, the Czech and French armies mobilized. On September 27, the British navy was mobilized. In Berlin Hitler declared emphatically that this was positively the last of his territorial demands in Europe. Chamberlain broadcast to his nation: "How horrible, fantastic, incredible it is that we should be digging trenches and trying on gas masks here because of a quarrel in a faraway country between people of whom we know nothing."

WILKOMMEN! German troops enter Czechoslovakia in October 1938 and are welcomed by Sudeten Germans. But Czechoslovakia was the last country they would enter without armed resistance.

On September 29, Chamberlain flew to Munich for a four-power conference with Germany, France and Italy. The Italian leader Mussolini preened himself on the fact that he could speak all four languages, while the others had to rely on interpreters. The Czechoslovak representatives were not admitted. Just after midnight the powers reached an agreement. On September 30, the Czechoslovak government was informed that it must yield to Germany's demands.

Chamberlain flew back to London and waved a piece of paper, declaring that he had brought "peace in our time." He was fêted as a hero.

Toward Poland

Germany moved into the Sudetenland, thus acquiring all of Czechoslovakia's defenses and most of its industrial areas. Despite the belief that their betrayal had secured peace, Britain and France accelerated their

THE NAZI-SOVIET PACT

UNHOLY ALLIANCE Stalin and Ribbentrop shake hands after the pact was signed.

On August 23, 1939, Stalin's Russia and Hitler's Germany signed a non-aggression pact. Its signatories were Vyacheslav Molotov, Stalin's ruthless henchman, who had been wily enough to survive his master's purges, and Joachim von Ribbentrop, Hitler's foreign minister, a man so vain and stupid that even the other Nazi leaders despised him.

The pact between the two regimes was one of the most cynical in modern history. Hitler's coming to power had been largely based on his opposition to communism; his long-term aim was the invasion of Russia and its colonization by Germany. For the Russians, National Socialism represented everything that communism opposed. The pact's true nature lay in the secret protocols appended to it. Under these, Russia and Germany would divide Poland between them; Germany would have Lithuania; Russia would have Finland, Estonia, Latvia and part of Romania.

Hitler had no difficulty in making these concessions to his new and temporary ally, calculating that once he had conquered Russia he could take them back. Stalin, no less cynical but perhaps more naive, later claimed that the pact had been a tactical move, designed to give Russia time to prepare its defenses. Yet the evidence suggests that at the time he believed that the pact would endure. When Germany invaded Poland from the west, Russia soon afterward invaded it from the east. When Germany invaded Russia in June 1941, both Molotov and Stalin were profoundly and genuinely shocked.

FRANCE AND BRITAIN PREPARE FOR WAR

France faced the prospect of war with an army of 2.7 million men and a force of tanks equal in numbers and quality to the Germans'. The French generals, however, had ignored or rejected new ideas about the most effective use of armor—ideas that had been thoroughly absorbed by the German high command. The French nation was deeply and bitterly divided. Following the signing of the Molotov-Ribbentrop Pact, French communists were actively working to sabotage the war effort. Most of all, perhaps, French strategic thinking was based on the Maginot Line, the chain of massive fortifications built between the wars along France's eastern frontier. The problem with the Maginot Line, and with the "Maginot mentality" it induced, was that it did not stretch all the way—once outflanked, it was virtually useless. In May 1940 it would indeed be outflanked when the Germans sent their panzer divisions through the Ardennes.

The British approached the war in a spirit of remarkable national unity. They had a small regular army, the only fully mechanized one at this stage of the war, and a large conscript force which they were not yet able to arm and equip fully. They had barely enough tanks for one armored division. They had, however, a navy in which they had complete confidence and a recently strengthened air force equipped with Hurricane and Spitfire fighters. There were as yet only a few hundred of them, but they could be optimally deployed against attacking bombers because of the coastal radar stations linked to the air defense system: the stations of Chain Home, which could "look" out to sea a distance of 120 miles, and Chain Home Low, which could pick up low-flying aircraft at a range of about 50 miles.

Aerial bombing of civilian targets and possible gas attacks were expected from the outset. Air-raid sirens were put in place to warn people of an impending attack. Wires were suspended from barrage balloons to impede enemy planes. Plans were made for the mass evacuation of children from the cities to the relative safety of the countryside. People were advised to attach adhesive tape to their windows to reduce the shattering effects of blast; they were issued with gas masks and shown how to install Anderson air-raid shelters in their gardens. More secret arrangements were made to move many of the national treasures to secure hiding-places in Wales and elsewhere, and there were contingency plans to evacuate the royal family and the government to Canada. All over the country, underground government centers were built and equipped for radio communication in case London and other major cities fell to the enemy.

GETTING READY Trenches are being dug in London's St. James's Park, and national treasures are being prepared for storage in a secret location in the Welsh mountains.

rearmament program, but Hitler now knew that he had nothing to fear from them. On March 14, 1939, the Czech president was summoned to Berlin and told that he must surrender his country or see Prague bombed to rubble. The next morning, German troops marched into Bohemia and Moravia, taking over what remained of Czech industry, including the Skoda armaments works, plus large stocks of aircraft and weapons and the country's gold reserves.

Hitler had now gone beyond any kind of legitimacy. He had shown that his territorial ambitions lay beyond German-speaking territory. It was obvious to all that his next objective was Poland. Britain, followed by France, gave Poland a guarantee of support in the event of attack by Germany; they gave a similar guarantee to Greece, Romania and Turkey, which were also seen as being on Hitler's list. In April 1939 Mussolini, encouraged by Hitler's effortless conquests, invaded Albania. The following month, Germany and Italy signed a "Pact of Steel." It was evident that a European war was now inevitable. Britain introduced conscription for the first time in its peacetime history.

On August 23, Russia and Germany signed a non-aggression pact—the Molotov-Ribbentrop Pact, after the two countries' foreign ministers. Stalin had seen that Russia was vulnerable and needed allies: either Britain and France, or Germany. He chose Germany, calculating that Russia's share of Poland would place a buffer zone between the two countries, and that a destructive war between Germany and Western Europe could only bring benefits to Russia. Now that prospects for his conquest of Poland were eased and his Eastern flank was secured, Hitler could turn his attention to revenge on France for the humiliation of 1918. The conquest of the Soviet Union was his long-term aim, but it could wait until he had beaten the French into submission.

On September 1, 1939, eight days after the Molotov-Ribbentrop Pact was signed, Hitler attacked Poland without declaring war. On September 3, Britain and France declared war on Germany: the Second World War had begun.

TIMECHART

1919

JANUARY

3 Professor Ernest Rutherford of Manchester University transmutes **atoms** of nitrogen into atoms of oxygen by bombarding them with alpha particles.

5 The communist **Spartacus** League is in open revolt in Berlin. It is suppressed with considerable bloodshed.

The National Socialist German Workers', or **Nazi**, Party is formed in Germany. Adolf Hitler is not among the first members.

10 Winston Churchill becomes secretary of state for war in the British coalition government.

15 The German communist revolutionaries **Rosa Luxemburg** and **Karl Liebknecht** are murdered by the Freikorps in Berlin. The body of Rosa Luxemburg will later be found in a Berlin canal.

18 The Peace Conference opens in **Paris** to establish the terms of a postwar settlement.

TREATY PARTY The Paris peace talks effectively completed, President Wilson (center) and French premier Clemenceau (on his left) visit Versailles where the treaty will be signed.

21 In Dublin, the nationalist **Sinn Fein** Party establishes an Irish parliament and proclaims an Irish Republic. Two policemen are shot dead by nationalist gunmen, generally seen as the start of the postwar Irish rebellion.

FEBRUARY

1 Allied delegates to the Paris Conference agree to the basic principles of the **League of Nations**.

8 In Chicago, James B. Herrick publishes the first **electrocardiogram** of a diseased heart.

22 In **Bavaria** soldiers and workers' committees declare a Soviet Republic.

MARCH

3 Although Russia is still torn by civil war, Lenin forms the Communist International, or **Comintern**, to spread communism across Europe.

21 The communist **Béla Kun** declares Hungary a Soviet Republic.

23 Benito Mussolini, a journalist and former socialist, founds the **Fascist** movement in Italy.

APRIL

5 In Ireland, **Eamon de Valera** is elected president of Sinn Fein.

8 In the Russian **Civil War**, the Red Army invades the Crimea.

10 The Mexican revolutionary Emiliano **Zapata** is murdered by government troops.

13 After five Europeans had been killed in earlier rioting, Brigadier-General Dyer orders his men to fire on a crowd at **Amritsar**, killing 379 people and wounding 1,500.

17 Four of the highest paid figures in Hollywood, director D.W. Griffith and film stars Charlie Chaplin, Douglas Fairbanks and Mary Pickford, form their own film company, **United Artists**.

HEAVY HAND General Dyer, who ordered his men to fire at Amritsar. The massacre prompted Gandhi to form his Non-Cooperation Movement.

MAY

2 Troops loyal to the Berlin government arrive in **Munich** to suppress the Bavarian soviet.

6 At the Paris Peace Conference, Germany's former **colonies** in Africa are shared out among the victors.

27 Two U.S. Navy fliers cross the **Atlantic** (Newfoundland to Lisbon) in a seaplane, the NC-4, in 44 hours.

JUNE

3 As Allied intervention in the Russian Civil War continues, the British send troops to the port of **Archangel**.

6 Finland declares war on its former imperial master, Russia.

15 British flyers John **Alcock** and Arthur **Brown** make the first nonstop transatlantic flight, landing in Ireland in their Vickers Vimy biplane.

21 The German fleet, held by the British at **Scapa Flow** in the Orkney islands, scuttles itself in a final act of defiance. Seventy vessels are sunk.

28 The Paris Peace Conference ends with the signing of the **Treaty of Versailles**. Germany is forced to accept punitive terms. The treaty will determine the fate of Europe for decades to come.

JULY

4 Jack Dempsey takes the world heavyweight boxing championship when he defeats Jess Willard.

5 Twenty-year-old Frenchwoman **Suzanne Lenglen** wins the women's tennis final at Wimbledon.

31 Germany adopts the **Weimar** Constitution establishing it as a democratic republic.

AUGUST

4 The communist regime of Béla Kun in **Hungary** surrenders to Romanian troops.

31 General **Jan Smuts** becomes prime minister of South Africa.

SEPTEMBER

16 Hitler joins the **German Workers' Party**, later to become the National Socialist German Workers' (Nazi) Party.

23 Italian poet Gabriele **D'Annunzio** takes the city of Fiume with a force of 2,600 men and claims it for Italy.

OCTOBER

12 As the tide of civil war in Russia turns, British troops evacuate **Murmansk**.

NOVEMBER

13 The United States Senate formally rejects President **Wilson**'s peace proposals, including a proposal that the U.S. join the League of Nations.

28 American-born Nancy **Astor** is elected to British Parliament and becomes the first woman to take a seat in that body.

DECEMBER

J.M. Keynes publishes *The Economic Consequences of the Peace*, predicting that the Versailles settlement will have disastrous consequences for the world economy.

DOWN TO EARTH AGAIN (background) Alcock and Brown's flight came to an undignified end when their plane crash-landed at Clifton on the west coast of Ireland.

1920

JANUARY

3 The last American **troops** leave France.

5 Babe Ruth traded by the Boston Red Sox to the New York Yankees for a record sum of $125,000.

16 The **League of Nations**, set up by the Versailles Conference, meets for the first time. The United States and Soviet Russia are not members.

The **Volstead Act** comes into effect in the U.S. It enforces the Eighteenth Amendment to the Constitution, prohibiting the manufacture and sale of alcohol throughout the United States. The mayor of New York says he will need 250,000 police to enforce Prohibition.

23 The ex-**Kaiser Wilhelm II** is now living in exile in Holland. The Dutch government rejects a demand from the Allies for his extradition.

FEBRUARY

7 Admiral **Kolchak**, commander of White Russian forces on the eastern front in the civil war, is executed by the Bolsheviks.

8 The Bolsheviks capture **Odessa**.

MARCH

10 The Unionists of the six counties of Northern Ireland (**Ulster**) vote to accept the Irish Home Rule Bill, under which they remain part of Great Britain but have their own parliament. There is open war in Ireland between Irish nationalists and British soldiers and police.

13 In Berlin, Wolfgang Kapp attempts a right-wing coup d'état with the help of Freikorps troops, but the **Kapp Putsch** fails after a general strike by Berlin workers.

16 Constantinople, capital of the defeated Ottoman Empire, is occupied by the Allies.

26 As the death toll in Ireland mounts, 800 specially recruited police auxiliaries arrive to enforce law and order. They will become known as **Black and Tans**.

THE RED FIST STRIKES "Good-for-nothings! Is that what you wanted?" A communist poster from Hungary comments on proceedings at the conference of Trianon, which settled terms with the Allies.

29 Mary Pickford and Douglas Fairbanks marry and become Hollywood's most glamorous wedded couple.

APRIL

5 In Ireland **Sinn Fein** guerrillas burn 120 police stations and 22 tax offices.

25 The League of Nations gives Britain a **mandate** for Palestine and Mesopotamia, and France a mandate for Syria.

27 Tomas Masaryk, a philosopher turned independence fighter, becomes president of the new nation of **Czechoslovakia**, with Eduard Benes as his foreign minister.

28 War is declared between **Poland** and Russia.

JUNE

4 The **Treaty of Trianon** is signed in Paris, settling the peace terms between Hungary and the Allies. Hungary is reduced to a quarter of its size under the Austro-Hungarian Empire. A large part of its former territory is passed to Romania.

JULY

3 At Wimbledon, **William "Big Bill" Tilden** becomes the first American to win the men's singles.

8 The Mexican revolutionary **Pancho Villa** surrenders to the Mexican government. He is given a pension for life and retires to a country ranch.

31 Bolshevik forces open a major offensive against **Poland** and threaten Warsaw.

AUGUST

1 The newly founded **Communist Party** of Great Britain opens its first congress. It is part of the Moscow-run Communist International.

10 The **Treaty of Sèvres**, last of the postwar treaties, deprives the defeated Ottoman Empire of 80 percent of its former territories, ceding even parts of Anatolia to Greece. Mustafa Kemal leads a resistance movement sworn to retain all territory in which Turks form a majority.

14 The sixth modern **Olympic Games** open in Antwerp, Belgium. Gold medalists will include the Finnish runner Hannes Kolehmainen in the marathon and his compatriot Paavo Nurmi in the 10,000 meter and the cross-country. Britain's Albert Hill wins gold in the 800 and 1,500 meter races.

19 The Bolshevik army is defeated by the Poles at **Warsaw**.

28 American **women** get the vote for the first time. The 1920 presidential election is the first one open to them.

SEPTEMBER

5 The American film comedian Roscoe **"Fatty" Arbuckle** is charged with the rape and murder of a young actress.

OCTOBER

6 Russia and Poland sign an **armistice.**

18 Baseball is rocked by the **Black Sox Scandal** in which eight members of the Chicago White Sox were accused of conspiring to fix the 1919 World Series. Among those indicted were two stars of the early years of the game: left fielder "Shoeless" Joe Jackson and star pitchers Eddie Cicotte and Lefty Williams.

NOVEMBER

2 Republican **Warren G. Harding** is elected president in a landslide victory.

10-11 The bodies of two **unknown soldiers** are brought from France and interred in Westminster Abbey in London and under the Arc de Triomphe in Paris.

13 Representatives from 41 nations meet for the first full session of the **League of Nations** in Geneva.

14 The **Red Army** captures Sebastopol in the Crimea, cutting off retreat for White forces there. The Russian Civil War has effectively ended in victory for the Bolsheviks.

21 On a day that will become known as **Bloody Sunday** 14 British officers, mainly undercover police detectives, are killed in their homes. Later the same day, troops and Black and Tans fire into a crowd at a soccer match, killing 12.

DECEMBER

10 Woodrow Wilson is awarded the Nobel Peace Prize.

11 Martial law is declared in large parts of Ireland.

COMRADES IN ARMS Cavalrymen of the White Army cut dashing figures, but the anti-Bolsheviks were a motley band, dogged by disunity.

1921

JANUARY

28 German war **reparations** are fixed at the enormous figure of 200 billion gold marks, to be paid over 42 years. They will never be paid in full, but they cause profound resentment in Germany.

FEBRUARY

3 **Charlie Chaplin**'s first full-length film, *The Kid*, has its American premiere.

9 Poland and Soviet Russia sign a **peace treaty** at Riga, ending months of conflict.

HOLIDAYS AND THE AUTOMOBILE Ranks of cars line the beach on Independence Day in Massachusetts. Already the car was offerings thousands of people a new freedom to get away from it all.

17 Figures are published showing that there are now more than 9 million **automobiles** in the United States.

18 French aviator Etienne Oehmichen makes the first-ever **helicopter** flight.

CHAMPION The "Manassa Mauler," Jack Dempsey (background), born in Manassa, Colorado, was world heavyweight boxing champion for seven years from 1919 to 1926.

19 The United States Congress passes legislation limiting **immigration**. The new quotas favor immigrants from northern Europe and restrict immigration from Japan.

28 Sailors at the **Kronstadt** naval base outside Petrograd (St. Petersburg) revolt against the Bolshevik government, demanding more power to the soviets, less to the state.

MARCH

6 A police chief in Pennsylvania bans **skirts** shorter than 4 inches below the knee.

12 Lenin announces the **New Economic Plan**, which to an extent ends state control of the economy and allows private trade.

17 Russian government troops crush the **Kronstadt mutiny**.

Scottish-born Marie Stopes, famous for her manual *Married Love*, opens the first British **birth-control** clinic in a working-class district of London.

23 Germany announces that it must **default** on war reparations. The British are inclined to be lenient, but French prime minister Poincaré insists that pressure be put on the Germans.

APRIL

10 **Sun Yat-sen** is elected President of the Republic of China.

MAY

14 In Italy, Mussolini's **fascists** win seats in parliamentary elections.

25 In Dublin, republican **fighters** seize the Custom House as a symbol of British rule and burn it down.

JUNE

1 A race riot in **Tulsa**, Oklahoma, is caused by rumors that a Black shoeshine man accused of attacking a white woman in a downtown elevator is about to be lynched. Eighty-five are killed and 30 blocks in the Black neighborhood are burned to the ground.

30 A communist party is formed in China. Among the first members is the young **Mao Zedong**.

JULY

1 World heavyweight boxing champion **Jack Dempsey** retains his title by defeating **Georges Carpentier**.

14 In Massachusetts, Italian-born anarchists **Nicola Sacco** and **Bartolomeo Vanzetti** are found guilty of the murder of two men during an armed robbery. Many people worldwide feel that they have been scapegoated for their political beliefs.

18 In France, Albert Calmette and Camille Guérin give the first **BCG** vaccination against tuberculosis.

26 In Morocco, the Berber rebel **Abd el-Krim** wipes out a Spanish garrison of 2,000 men.

29 **Adolf Hitler** becomes the president of the National Socialist German Workers' Party.

AUGUST

3 The great tenor **Enrico Caruso** dies in Naples, aged 48. He was the world's first recording star, earning huge royalties on sales of his records.

9 Lenin asks the world for help with the **famine** which is devastating large parts of Russia.

OCTOBER

4 The **League of Nations** rejects Russia's application for membership.

21 **Peace talks** begin between Irish nationalists and the British government.

31 The new Hollywood sensation **Rudolf Valentino** stars in *The Sheik*.

NOVEMBER

4 With **inflation** out of control, the German currency begins to collapse.

7 Benito Mussolini names himself **Il Duce** ("leader") of the Italian Fascist Party.

12 A **disarmament** conference opens in Washington, intended to limit naval power in the Pacific.

DECEMBER

1 The French mass-murderer Henri Landru, known as **Bluebeard**, is found guilty by a jury at Versailles.

6 Britain signs a **peace treaty** with Ireland. This partitions the country into Northern Ireland, which remains part of the United Kingdom, and the Irish Free State, an independent dominion under the British Crown.

10 **Albert Einstein** wins the Nobel Prize for Physics.

11 America's **Unknown Soldier** buried at Arlington National Cemetery.

FREE STATERS The Irish leaders Michael Collins (left) and Arthur Griffiths are photographed in London after signing the Irish peace treaty.

1922

JANUARY

James Joyce's **Ulysses** and T.S. Eliot's **The Waste Land** are published. *Ulysses*, banned in Britain and the United States, is published in Paris in an edition of 1,000 copies.

15 Michael Collins, former IRA chief, forms an Irish government. Eamon de Valera has refused the presidency, predicting "internal strife." The stage is set for civil war.

FEBRUARY

5 The first **Reader's Digest** is published in the United States by DeWitt Wallace.

25 In France, Henri Landru, **Bluebeard**, is executed by guillotine.

MARCH

18 In India **Gandhi** is sentenced to six years' "simple imprisonment" for sedition, following his campaign of civil disobedience.

25 In Rome, the newly elected Pope Pius XI (formerly Cardinal Achille Ratti, Archbishop of Milan) calls for a campaign against **immodesty** in women's dress.

CIVIL WAR IN IRELAND An "irregular" of the IRA totes a Lewis machine gun. The irregulars were fighting the forces of the new Irish Free State.

APRIL

3 In Moscow **Stalin** becomes General-Secretary of the Communist Party, the relatively minor post from which he will make himself dictator.

12 In San Francisco **"Fatty" Arbuckle** is acquitted on charges of rape and murder but his career is in ruins. Most American movie houses stop showing his films.

PRESENT AND FUTURE LEADER Lenin and Stalin in 1922, the year that Lenin's health started to collapse.

MAY

20 Over objections of the Vatican, Britain and the United States agree on a **Mandate for Palestine** that will protect U.S.interests, but, the Vatican fears, will also promote Zionist aims of establishing a Jewish homeland.

26 The Russian communist leader **Lenin** suffers a stroke.

JUNE

22 Irish-born **Sir Henry Wilson**, formerly Chief of the Imperial General Staff, is shot dead by Irish republican gunmen near his home in London.

24 Germany's foreign minister, **Walter Rathenau**, a Jew, is murdered by nationalist gunmen.

28 The new Free State government of Ireland bombards the Four Courts building in Dublin, which Irish republicans have occupied. This is the beginning of a **civil war** between the new government and those Irish republicans who do not accept home rule and the partition of Ireland between north and south. The men occupying the Four Courts surrender on June 30.

JULY

9 The American swimmer **Johnny Weissmuller** breaks all records by swimming 100 meters in 58.6 seconds. Later in his career, he will star in *Tarzan* movies.

AUGUST

22 Michael Collins, now commander in chief of the Irish Free State army, is shot dead by Irish republican gunmen.

24 After a brief recovery, the German **mark** drops sharply compared to the British pound sterling and U.S. dollar.

SEPTEMBER

9 In the war between Turkey and Greece, the Turks occupy **Izmir** (Smyrna). In the following days, they will burn the city and kill many of its Greek citizens.

27 In Greece, following the defeat by Turkey, King **Constantine** abdicates and is succeeded by George II.

OCTOBER

7 The U.S. Senate swears in its **first woman member**— Rebecca Latimer Felton from Georgia.

15 The Greeks sign the **Mudania Treaty**, formally ending the war with Turkey.

28 Benito Mussolini's blackshirts seize Rome and set up a fascist state. Mussolini himself is not present at the **March on Rome**, but waits in Milan until the coup is successful and he is summoned by King Victor Emmanuel to take over the government of Italy.

NOVEMBER

1 Mustafa Kemal, later known as **Atatürk**, abolishes the Turkish monarchy and declares a Turkish Republic.

In Germany the **mark** has now fallen to around 4,000 to the U.S. dollar.

4 Howard Carter discovers the first signs of what proves to be the tomb of the boy-pharaoh **Tutankhamun**. Soon afterwards, he will open it to find some of the most astonishing treasures the modern world has ever seen, a time capsule of Egyptian life in the second millennium BC.

15 The BBC begins regular **news broadcasts** from London.

16 In Britain the Conservative Party returns to power under Prime Minister **Bonar Law**. But the Labor Party has now replaced the Liberals as the main opposition party.

18 French novelist **Marcel Proust** dies in Paris aged 51. His novel-sequence *A la Recherche du Temps Perdu* seems to epitomize the world swept away by the Great War.

21 The British Labor Party elects **Ramsay MacDonald** as its leader.

DECEMBER

10 The Nobel Prize for Physics is awarded to the Dane **Niels Bohr** for his work on the structure of the atom. His work will lead eventually to nuclear energy and the nuclear bomb.

11 At the Old Bailey in London, Edith Thompson and her lover,

MAN OF DESTINY Italy's new leader, Mussolini, poses with two bodyguards shortly after his arrival in Rome.

Frederick Bywaters, are sentenced to death for the murder of her husband, Percy Thompson. The **Thompson and Bywaters** trial is one of the most sensational of the 1920s.

30 Soviet Russia is renamed the **Union of Soviet Socialist Republics** or U.S.S.R.

1923

JANUARY

11 French troops occupy Germany's industrial heartland in the **Ruhr**, in an attempt to enforce payment of war reparations and to seize stocks of coal and steel. The mark plunges still further.

FEBRUARY

1 In Germany **inflation** is now out of control;$1 will buy 1 million marks.

MONOPOLY MONEY Three German children and their puppy play with building blocks of marks rendered next to worthless by hyperinflation.

16 In France, Gabrielle "**Coco**" **Chanel** launches the sweater look that characterizes the young fashions of the 1920s and her trademark scent, Chanel No. 5.

MARCH

9 In Russia, Lenin suffers another **stroke** and goes into retirement. He has expressed grave concern at the character and behavior of Joseph Stalin.

31 French troops fire on Germans rioting at the Krupp works at **Essen** in the Ruhr, killing nine.

APRIL

4 The **Earl of Carnarvon**, sponsor of Howard Carter's discovery of Tutankhamun's tomb, dies. The probable cause is an insect bite, but there are rumors of a Mummy's Curse.

16 Police in Baltimore break up a **dance marathon** contest after a couple dance continuously for 53 hours; both were rushed to a hospital.

26 Crowds turn out in London for the marriage of the Duke of York, the future King **George VI**, to Lady Elizabeth **Bowes-Lyon**.

MAY

3 U.S. Army Lts. Oakley Kelly and John Macready make the first non-stop **transcontinental flight** from Long Island to San Diego.

8 English cricketer **Jack Hobbs**, one of England's greatest athletes, scores his 100th century.

21 Stanley **Baldwin** becomes British prime minister, succeeding Bonar Law.

PLAYER'S CIGARETTES

J. B. HOBBS (SURREY)

MAN OF CENTURIES English cricketer Jack Hobbs scored his first century in first-class cricket in 1905, his last in 1934. During his career, he scored a grand total of 61,237 runs.

26 The first **Grand Prix** 24 hour motor race takes place in Le Mans. The winners are French drivers Lagache and Leonard.

JUNE

9 In Berlin, **coffee** now costs 30,000 marks per pound, tea over 40,000 marks.

30 In the United States, the **Ku Klux Klan** claims that it has a million members.

JULY

6 French tennis player **Suzanne Lenglen** wins at Wimbledon for the fifth time.

10 In Rome **Mussolini** dissolves all opposition parties.

20 In Mexico **Pancho Villa**, now living in retirement on his ranch, is murdered by six gunmen in what is probably a revenge killing. The former bandit-revolutionary had recently been learning to read.

AUGUST

2 Warren G. Harding dies suddenly (and suspiciously) and vice-president **Calvin Coolidge** succeeds him as president.

SEPTEMBER

1 Tokyo and Yokohama are devastated by a massive **earthquake**, leaving 2.5 million people homeless.

10 The **Irish Free State** is admitted to the League of Nations.

13 In Spain, in a military coup plotted by King Alphonso XIII, General **Primo de Rivera** becomes head of a military directorate that will rule the country.

OCTOBER

1 Britain agrees to make **Southern Rhodesia** a self-governing state within the Commonwealth.

12 The national capital of Turkey is moved from Istanbul to **Ankara**.

22 **Hyperinflation** rages in Germany as a mark—now worth barely a trillionth of a dollar—is nearly worthless.

29 **Mustafa Kemal**, who has defeated the Greeks and successfully negotiated agreement on Turkey's new frontiers with the Allies, becomes president of the new Republic of Turkey.

NOVEMBER

8 In Munich Adolf Hitler stages his abortive **Beer Hall Putsch**. Three days later, he is arrested and imprisoned. General Erich Ludendorff, who has supported the attempted coup, is held under house arrest but not prosecuted. Hermann Goering is badly wounded.

15 To end the inflation crisis, the German government introduces a new **currency unit** worth a trillion of the old marks. In recent days, the mark has fallen to 4 trillion to the U.S. dollar and the price of a loaf of bread has soared to 201 billion marks.

23 Gustav **Stresemann** resigns as German chancellor.

DECEMBER

7 In a British **general election**, the Conservatives lose their overall majority in Parliament.

10 The great Irish poet **W.B. Yeats** is awarded the Nobel Prize for Literature.

BURNING CITY Izmir (Smyrna) blazes after the Turks captured the port city from the Greeks (background).

1924

JANUARY

21 Vladimir Ilyich **Lenin**, creator of the Soviet Union, dies after a long illness. A triumvirate of Zinoviev, Kamenev and Stalin succeeds him.

1870-1924

A LIFE IN REVOLT Lenin had remodelled Marxism to fit the circumstances of Russia. In death, his body would be embalmed for permanent display in Red Square.

22 In Britain **Ramsay MacDonald** becomes the first-ever Labor prime minister. Labor has fewer seats than the Conservatives, and depends on the support of Liberals in Parliament.

26 The Russian city of Petrograd, formerly St Petersburg, is renamed **Leningrad** in memory of Lenin.

FEBRUARY

1 The British **Labor** government officially recognizes the U.S.S.R.

4 Mahatma **Gandhi** is released from prison and resumes his campaign of civil disobedience. Publication this year of E.M. Forster's novel *A Passage to India* draws the sympathy of British and American readers to his cause.

12 George **Gershwin**'s *Rhapsody in Blue* has its first performance.

In Egypt, Howard Carter opens the sarcophagus of **Tutankhamun** and reveals a beautiful gilded effigy of the young pharaoh.

16 In Britain a **dock strike** paralyzes the country and forces up the price of bread.

MARCH

3 In Turkey, Mustafa Kemal abolishes the **Caliphate**, the spiritual leadership of Islam. He also makes national education secular, and abolishes polygamy.

18 Douglas **Fairbanks** stars in a new film, *The Thief of Baghdad*.

25 The Greek parliament formally deposes King **George II**, already living in exile in Romania. The following month, a referendum will show the majority of Greeks in favor of abolishing the monarchy.

31 The former Conservative MP **Oswald Mosley** joins the Labor Party.

Britain forms its own national airline, **Imperial Airways**.

APRIL

6 Italian **fascists** win an overwhelming victory in elections.

9 The **Dawes Committee** produces its plan for solving the problem of Germany's inability to make reparation payments.

17 Metro-Goldwyn-Mayer formed–Hollywood's largest studio.

MAY

21 In Chicago, 19-year-old Nathan **Leopold** and Richard **Loeb** confess to the kidnap and murder of 14-year-old Bobby Franks. The wealthy young men state that they committed the crime as an intellectual exercise.

JUNE

10 The Italian socialist Giacomo **Matteotti** is murdered by fascists, after a speech condemning their political methods and claiming they rigged elections.

19 News reaches London that Leigh Mallory and Andrew Irvine have been lost on **Mount Everest**. It will never be known for certain whether they reached the summit.

JULY

5 The 8th Olympic Games open in Paris. The Scottish runner **Eric Liddell** refuses to compete in the 100 m because heats were to be run on a Sunday. The Finnish runner Paavo Nurmi wins five gold medals.

Jean Borotra wins the men's singles at Wimbledon, the first Frenchman to do so.

AUGUST

3 The Polish-born novelist **Joseph Conrad** dies.

17 Following acceptance of the **Dawes Plan**, the French begin to withdraw from German territory.

OCTOBER

2 Leon Trotsky is put in command of the Red Army suppressing a revolt in **Georgia.**

13 In Arabia the tribal army of **Ibn Saud** enters the holy city of Mecca. He is well on the way to conquering the country that will bear his family name.

14 Farewell U.S. Tour of Anna **Pavlova**, famed ballerina, begins .

24 The British Labor government is damaged by publication of the "**Zinoviev letter**" urging the British working class to revolution. Although Zinoviev, head of the Comintern, has

FUNCTION FIRST The lid of a Bauhaus-designed chess set displays the clean lines of the new style.

SERVING THE EMPIRE Airliners like this one (background) of Britain's Imperial Airways would crisscross the world with a growing network of air routes.

certainly written such letters to European communists, it is never established whether the British version is genuine.

31 In Britain the Conservatives win back their majority and **Stanley Baldwin** again becomes prime minister. He appoints Winston Churchill as his chancellor of the exchequer.

NOVEMBER

4 Republican **Calvin Coolidge** wins the presidential elections by a large margin.

5 Pu Yi, last emperor of China, is expelled from the Imperial palace in Beijing.

26 Outmaneuvered by Stalin, Leon **Trotsky** is denounced by the Russian Communist Party.

29 Giacomo **Puccini** dies aged 65, leaving unfinished his last opera, *Turandot*.

30 The last French and Belgian troops leave the **Ruhr**.

DECEMBER

20 Adolf Hitler is released from jail on parole, having dictated the first part of his autobiography *Mein Kampf* to his party colleague Rudolf Hess.

DIE SPIELSTEINE SIND IHREN FUNKTIONEN ENTSPRECHEND GESTALTET

LUXUS U.GEBRAUCHSSPIELE

BAUHAUS HARTWIG

GES. GESCH.

SCHACH ZU BEZIEHEN DURCH

STAATL. BAUHAUS WEIMAR

1925

Franz Kafka's **The Trial** is published posthumously. Scott Fitzgerald publishes **The Great Gatsby**. American writer Anita Loos creates the classic flapper in her novel **Gentlemen Prefer Blondes**.

JANUARY

1 The capital of Norway is given back its ancient name of **Oslo**. It had been renamed Christiana (after King Christian IV of Denmark and Norway) when it was rebuilt after a fire in 1624.

3 In Italy **Mussolini** assumes full dictatorial powers and moves to make the government wholly fascist.

8 Igor Stravinsky conducts the **New York Philharmonic** in the U.S. debut of "The Rite of Spring."

16 Leon Trotsky is dismissed as Soviet **war commissar**, and hundreds of his associates are arrested and exiled.

23 The government of **Chile** is overthrown in a coup d'état.

FEBRUARY

11 The government of **Portugal** is overthrown.

27 Although paroled on promises of not undertaking political agitation, **Adolf Hitler** addresses old comrades in the Munich beer-cellar where his abortive putsch began.

MARCH

4 Calvin Coolidge is inaugurated as 30th U.S. president.

8 The Chicago department of health announces that **crosswords** may be good for the brain. There has been a craze for them in Britain and the United States since 1924.

11 *No No Nanette*, one of the most successful shows of the 1920s, opens in London.

12 The founder of modern China, **Sun Yat-sen**, dies and is succeeded as leader of the Guomindang by Chiang Kai-shek.

23 Tennessee passes a law making it a crime to teach **evolution** in schools.

APRIL

1 Arabs demonstrate in protest of the opening of **Hebrew University** in Jerusalem.

14 King Boris of Bulgaria has a narrow escape when **Bolshevik revolutionaries** try to ambush his car and assassinate him.

25 The First World War veteran, Field Marshal **Paul von Hindenburg**, becomes German president. Although a monarchist, he swears to uphold the country's republican constitution.

28 In his budget, British chancellor Winston Churchill returns Britain to the **gold standard**. The pound returns to its prewar parity of $4.86.

30 A great Exhibition of Decorative Arts opens in Paris, giving birth to the **Art Deco** style in architecture, interior design and fashion.

MAY

1 Cyprus becomes a British colony.

8 As hemlines rise, bishops in Italy ban "**scantily dressed**" women from churches.

In South Africa a bill is passed making **Afrikaans** the country's official language.

28 The trial opens in Dayton, Tennessee, of John Scopes, charged with the crime of teaching Darwinism to children. The **Monkey Trial**, as it is known, is observed by the world's press. Scopes will be found guilty and fined $100, but the verdict will be overturned in a higher court.

JUNE

8 Nöel Coward's play *Hay Fever* opens in London.

25 In **Athens**, General Theodoris Pangalos seizes power in a military coup d'état.

JULY

6 Suzanne Lenglen wins her sixth Wimbledon singles title.

8 Adolf Hitler publishes his autobiography and manifesto ***Mein Kampf*** (*My Struggle*). Royalties from sales will bring him a comfortable income for the rest of his life.

AUGUST

8 The **Ku Klux Klan**, its membership growing rapidly, organizes a march in Washington.

16 Charlie Chaplin's film *The Gold Rush* opens in the United States.

26 Marshal **Pétain** takes command of French troops fighting Abd el-Krim's revolt in Morocco. Francisco Franco will command the Spanish troops in the same war.

SEPTEMBER

1 The high-kicking **Charleston** dance arrives in Britain from the United States and will go on to take the world by storm.

DANCE FEVER "These are some English and American dances that are all the rage across the entire world," proclaims a French album of dance music.

OCTOBER

8 Australian opera singer **Nellie Melba** announces her retirement.

27 Josephine Baker makes her Paris debut in the *Revue Nègre*. She will spend most of the rest of her life in France and become a French citizen.

31 In Iran, Reza Khan Pahlavi deposes the **Shah** and rules as dictator. In April 1926 he will have himself crowned as Shah and start a new dynasty.

NOVEMBER

6 In Britain, **P.G. Wodehouse** publishes *Carry On, Jeeves*.

9 In Germany, the *Schutzstaffel*, or **SS**, is formed as an elite bodyguard for Adolf Hitler.

13 Howard Carter and his team unwrap the mummy of **Tutankhamun**. They find a golden portrait mask covering his face and deduce that he was aged about 15 at the time of his death.

14 The first **Surrealist** exhibition opens in Paris, showing the work of such artists as Max Ernst, Paul Klee, Joan Miró and Pablo Picasso.

DECEMBER

1 Britain, France, Belgium, Germany and Italy attempt to solve Europe's problems peacefully by signing the **Locarno Treaty**. Among other things, the pact accepts the demilitarization of the Rhineland.

10 Anglo-Irish playwright **George Bernard Shaw** wins the Nobel Prize for Literature.

17 Army court martial finds **Billy Mitchell** guilty of insubordination for accusing superiors of weakening U.S. air defense.

21 Sergei **Eisenstein**'s film *Battleship Potemkin* opens in the U.S.S.R.

"BATTLESHIP POTEMKIN" Cossack troops mow down the crowds in the famous Odessa Steps sequence from Eisenstein's masterpiece.

1926

JANUARY

1 New York and London celebrate the **New Year** together via radio.

6 The German airline **Lufthansa** is founded.

8 The Arabian king, Abdul Aziz Ibn Saud, renames his kingdom **Saudi Arabia**.

HOLLYWOOD BOUND Austrian-born Fritz Lang fled Germany in 1933, after refusing the post of head of the German film industry under the Nazis.

8 Spectacular **Mayan ruins** of Muyid are uncovered in Yucatan, indicative of great, advanced civilization.

10 The German film director Fritz Lang's futuristic fantasy **Metropolis** is released.

27 The Scottish inventor M. John Baird gives the first demonstration of **television** in London.

FEBRUARY

4 The South African parliament gives a third reading to a **Color Bar** bill, which will bar non-whites from skilled occupations. It will, however, be rejected by the more liberal senate.

19 In Sicily Mussolini introduces mass arrests of **Mafia** leaders, as part of an attempt to eradicate the Mafia.

MARCH

13 Aviator **Alan Cobham** flies into Croydon airport after flying from London to Cape Town and back. It has taken nearly three months.

APRIL

21 The Duchess of York has her first child, **Elizabeth**, the future Queen Elizabeth II.

MAY

1 In Britain miners call a strike which, two days later, becomes a **General Strike**. The General Strike ends on May 6, although the miners stay out until November.

9 American naval aviator Commander **Richard Byrd** flies over the North Pole.

26 In Morocco **Abd el-Krim** surrenders to French and Spanish forces led by the elderly Marshal Pétain and the young General Franco.

JUNE

1 In Poland General **Pilsudski** becomes virtual dictator after a military coup. He is also appointed permanent commander of the Polish armed forces.

25 U.S. golfer **Bobby Jones** wins the British Open, having already won the British Amateur Championship.

23 In Paris a coalition government is formed under **Raymond Poincaré** as the franc collapses.

AUGUST

6 Gertrude **Ederle** becomes the first woman to swim the English Channel.

23 Rudolf **Valentino** dies aged 31.

SEPTEMBER

8 Germany is admitted to the **League of Nations**.

OCTOBER

7 **Mussolini** makes the Fascist Party the sole legal party of the Italian state.

23 In the Soviet Union **Stalin** ousts Zinoviev and Trotsky from the Politburo.

31 Harry **Houdini** dies, aged 52, from a ruptured appendix after a student responded to his invitation to punch him hard in the stomach.

NOVEMBER

1 Dr. Joseph **Goebbels** is sent to Berlin as Nazi Party Gauleiter.

2 After Mussolini escapes a fourth **assassination attempt**, Pope Pius XI announces that the *Duce* must have divine protection.

20 The **British Commonwealth** is born with the self-governing dominions of Canada, Australia, New Zealand and South Africa enjoying equal status with Britain. India is not yet independent, however, and King George V is still Emperor of India.

30 Sigmund Romberg's musical *The Desert Song* opens in New York.

DECEMBER

3 In a real-life mystery, the British crime writer **Agatha Christie** is reported missing. She is found in Harrogate on December 14 and claims loss of memory, but the mystery of her disappearance remains.

6 The Impressionist painter Claude **Monet** dies at his house at Giverny aged 86.

25 The 25-year-old **Hirohito** becomes Emperor of Japan following the death of his father. He takes the reign name Showa, "Great Peace."

POST DELIVERIES Women volunteers help to get the mail through during Britain's General Strike.

1927

JANUARY

1 The British Broadcasting Company becomes the **British Broadcasting Corporation**.

2 From Lisbon there are reports of an outbreak of **bubonic plague**.

5 In the United States the "**Movietone**" system for synchronizing sound with motion film is demonstrated. It will soon be used for newsreels.

13 First woman takes seat on **New York Stock Exchange** (NYSE), going against years of an all–male tradition.

OXFORD BAGS The fashion for wide-legged trousers was most popular with students.

26 An Oxford undergraduate magazine deplores the "**Oxford bags**" being worn by some British and American students.

31 As China is racked by **civil war**, Britain sends an army division to protect British nationals in Shanghai.

FEBRUARY

6 The violinist **Yehudi Menuhin** makes his Paris debut at age ten. He has been performing in public since the age of seven.

9 The British car company Morris Motors buys Wolseley Motors as part of a process of **amalgamation** that will continue in Europe and the United States throughout the 1930s.

MARCH

10 The government of **Bavaria** lifts the ban on Adolf Hitler from public speaking.

21 Kuomintang forces commanded by Chiang Kai-shek capture **Shanghai**, but make no serious attempt to occupy the international settlements defended by British troops.

23 In **Berlin**, Nazi and communist gangs clash in street battles deliberately engineered by Goebbels.

26 In Britain the **Gaumont-British Film Corporation** is set up in an attempt to break Hollywood's near-monopoly over film distribution. A bill is considered in Parliament to enforce a quota of British-made films on British movie theaters.

29 **Henry Seagrave** sets a new land-speed record of just over 200 mph in Daytona Beach, Florida.

APRIL

7 French film director **Abel Gance**'s epic *Napoleon* is premiered in Paris and is shown on three screens simultaneously.

16 **Cecil B. De Mille**'s epic *King of Kings* opens in U.S. movie theaters.

19 **Mae West** is fined and given a ten-day jail sentence for indecency in her Broadway show, *Sex*.

MAY

1 Adolf Hitler addresses his first Nazi Party meeting in the German capital, **Berlin**.

4 United States supervises elections in Nicaragua; **civil war** is temporarily halted.

20 Britain and France sign the **Treaty of Jeddah**, formally recognizing the independence of the kingdom of Saudi Arabia.

21 **Charles Lindbergh** arrives in Paris to a tumultuous welcome after the first solo flight across the Atlantic. When he returns to the United States, he is given a ticker-tape welcome in New York.

24 The British Government severs diplomatic relations with the U.S.S.R. and expels Soviet **diplomats** from London, accusing them of spying and subversive activities.

26 **Henry Ford** drives the 15 millionth Model T off the production line in Detroit. He will shortly introduce an even newer model, the Model A.

JUNE

4 Ahmed **Sukarno** founds the Indonesian Nationalist Party in the Dutch East Indies.

9 The Soviet government executes 20 Russians accused of **spying** or undertaking subversive activities for the British. Nine more will be executed in September.

30 American golfer **Walter Hagen** leads his team to victory over the British in the new Ryder Cup.

JULY

1 **Greta Garbo** stars with John Gilbert in *Flesh and the Devil*.

5 American **Helen Wills** takes the women's singles title at Wimbledon.

AUGUST

23 In Massachusetts, the anarchists **Sacco and Vanzetti** go to the electric chair after a six-year campaign to win a reprieve for them. Among other worldwide protests, thousands gather in London's Hyde Park to mourn their deaths. (Fifty years later, in 1977, the Governor of Massachusetts declares that they were improperly tried.)

SEPTEMBER

8 At its conference the British **Trades Union Congress** votes to sever ties with Russian trade unions.

14 The American exotic dancer **Isadora Duncan** dies at age 49; her neck is broken when her scarf is caught in the wheel of a Bugatti sports car.

22 **Gene Tunney** retains the world heavyweight championship against Jack Dempsey, despite a controversial "long count" after he went down in the seventh round.

30 **Babe Ruth** hits a record 60 home runs in one season for the New York Yankees.

OCTOBER

6 The **talkies** arrive with Al Jolson in the movie *The Jazz Singer*. Charlie Chaplin says they are a fad that will pass within three years.

NOVEMBER

15 **Trotsky and Zinoviev** are now expelled from the Soviet Communist Party after they head an opposition parade through the streets of Moscow.

18 In Paris, FIFA, the International Football Association, announces a new international soccer contest—the **World Cup**.

22 Addressing unemployed miners who marched to London from South Wales, labor leader A.J. Cook warns: "Unless the Government faces the situation, a **revolutionary situation** will be created in this country which no leader will be able to withstand."

George Gershwin's show *Funny Face* opens in New York.

DECEMBER

27 In New York Florenz Ziegfeld opens the hugely successful musical *Show Boat*, with music by Jerome Kern. It introduces a number of enduring hit songs, including "**Ol' Man River**," sung by Paul Robeson.

"SHOW BOAT" The wedding scene from Ziegfeld and Kern's fabulous musical.

1928

D.H. Lawrence publishes *Lady Chatterley's Lover*, which is immediately banned in Britain and the United States. The 25-year-old **Evelyn Waugh** publishes his first novel, *Decline and Fall*.

JANUARY

3 Pursuing the Monroe Doctrine, the United States sends troops into **Nicaragua** to suppress the Sandinista rebellion against the government.

6 In London **14 people drown** when a combination of a sudden thaw and a high tide leads to severe flooding as the Thames bursts its banks.

9 Trotsky is sent into internal exile along with many of his associates. Stalin is now supreme leader of the Soviet Union.

14 The English writer **Thomas Hardy** dies. He has published no novels since 1895 but has become a greatly loved poet. Despite his avowed atheism, his ashes will be buried in Westminster Abbey.

FEBRUARY

6 Austrian Nazis stage a protest when the black singer-dancer **Josephine Baker** performs in Vienna.

A woman arrives in the United States claiming to be "**Anastasia**," daughter of the last Russian tsar, who somehow survived the massacre of April 1918. Her claim will be long contested, and only finally refuted in the 1990s.

19 Malcolm Campbell sets a new land-speed record of 206 mph in

IN THE SADDLE Chiang Kai-shek, commander of China's nationalist forces.

his car *Bluebird*, beating Segrave's record of the previous year.

MARCH

26 Trading on **Wall Street** reaches an all-time high.

30 The Italian government bans **Boy Scouts** and all other non-fascist youth movements.

APRIL

9 Atatürk abolishes **Islam** as Turkey's state religion and introduces the Roman alphabet to replace the Arabic one.

MAY

1 English soccer player **Dixie Dean** scores a record 60 goals in one season.

7 In Britain the voting age for women is reduced from 30 to 21. This is called the **flapper vote**.

JUNE

8 Guomindang forces under Chiang Kai-shek take Beijing.

14 The women's rights campaigner **Emmeline Pankhurst** dies, age 69. She has lived to see British women get equal voting rights with men.

15 In a race from London to Edinburgh, the steam-driven **Flying Scotsman** narrowly wins over a competing airplane.

18 Amelia Earhart becomes the first woman to fly across the Atlantic.

JULY

7 Helen Wills again wins the women's singles at Wimbledon.

AUGUST

6 In Wyoming, a new **geyser** sprays 75 feet high in Yellowstone Park.

27 In Paris representatives of 15 nations sign the **Kellogg-Briand Pact** renouncing war. The pact is named after the United States secretary of state Frank Kellogg and the French foreign minister Aristide Briand.

31 Weill and Brecht's musical *The Threepenny Opera* is staged in Berlin.

SEPTEMBER

1 Ahmed Bey Zogu becomes monarch of the new kingdom of Albania under the name **Zog I**.

15 Alexander Fleming reports his discovery of the antibiotic **penicillin**, although little use will be made of it for years to come.

19 Mickey Mouse makes his debut appearance in the Disney sound cartoon *Steamboat Willie*.

ALL POWERFUL Stalin stands with Alexei Rykov (on the left), one of many former allies the increasingly megalomaniac dictator will eliminate in the years to come.

28 The United States officially recognizes the Chinese government of **Chiang Kai-shek**.

OCTOBER

1 In the Soviet Union Stalin launches the first **Five Year Plan** for the rapid industrialization of the country.

16 Chrysler Corporation announces plans for new building in New York.

NOVEMBER

1 The airship **Graf Zeppelin** arrives back in Germany after its return flight to the United States.

5 In Sicily **Mount Etna** erupts, causing widespread damage in Catania.

6 Republican candidate **Herbert Hoover** is elected United States president by a large majority, as the stock market continues to boom.

7 Democrat Franklin **Roosevelt** is elected governor of New York.

16 On **Wall Street** a record 6.6 million shares are traded.

DECEMBER

10 In London, **Piccadilly Circus** Underground station opens.

13 George Gershwin's *An American in Paris* is performed in New York.

24 Mussolini's government passes a law for the draining of the **Pontine Marshes**, which will make millions of acres available for cultivation.

1929

JANUARY

6 King Alexander becomes **dictator of Yugoslavia** in an attempt to end ethnic conflict within the country.

13 Wyatt Earp, the legendary former marshall of Dodge City, dies peacefully in his sleep, age 80.

16 Old Bolshevik **Nikolai Bukharin** resigns as head of the Communist International.

23 The Russian secret police or **OGPU** arrest 400 "Trotskyists" for plotting against the Soviet state.

24 Little, Brown & Co announce 150 unknown **Emily Dickinson** poems found.

30 Leon Trotsky is expelled from the Soviet Union. He will go first to Turkey and eventually to **Mexico**, where Stalin's agent will murder him in August 1940.

Edward, **Prince of Wales**, visits distressed areas in the North of England.

FEBRUARY

1 Leading Bolsheviks **Zinoviev and Kamenev** are put under house arrest in Moscow.

8 British troops open fire during **Hindu-Muslim riots** in Bombay, in which some 100 people are killed.

11 Mussolini signs the **Lateran Treaty** with the Pope, establishing relations between Italy and the Vatican State, and confirming Roman Catholicism as the state religion of Italy.

12 Lily Langtry, noted beauty and one-time mistress of the Prince of Wales, Edward VII, dies age 74. She had been known as "the Jersey Lily."

14 Al Capone's gunmen murder seven members of a rival gang in the **St. Valentine's Day massacre** in Chicago.

MARCH

4 The Republican **Herbert Hoover** is inaugurated as 31st president of the United States.

11 Henry Segrave wins back the land-speed record at 231 mph in his car *Golden Arrow*.

25 Mussolini's **Fascist Party** claims 99 percent of the vote in Italian elections. Opposition parties were forbidden to hold election meetings.

MAY

14 The first delivery of **airmail** from India arrives at Croydon airport.

16 The first "**Oscar**" Academy Awards are presented in Hollywood.

19 The fascist emblem, the **fasces**, a bundle of rods containing an axe, becomes Italy's official national emblem.

The **Barcelona Exhibition** opens. Miës van der Rohe's German pavilion

FIRST OSCARS The Academy of Motion Picture Arts and Sciences was founded to give dignity to the industry. One of the first winners of the "Oscar" for best actress was Norma Shearer (above).

is one of the most striking buildings at the exhibition.

31 The **Labor Party** under Ramsay MacDonald wins the general election in Britain with a small majority. The "flapper vote" is thought to have helped Labor. Thirteen women MPs are elected.

JUNE

7 Ramsay MacDonald's **Cabinet** has a woman member for the first time: Margaret Bondfield, minister of labor.

JULY

1 The American cartoon character **Popeye** appears for the first time.

5 Paintings by **D.H. Lawrence** are seized by police from a Mayfair gallery. They are deemed indecent.

29 The British government discusses the resumption of **diplomatic ties** with the U.S.S.R.

AUGUST

19 The Russian impresario Serge **Diaghilev** dies suddenly, age 56. His Ballets Russes have dominated ballet for the last two decades.

28 In London the **Flying Squad** of the Metropolitan Police starts operations with a new fleet of fast cars equipped with radio.

29 The German airship *Graf Zeppelin* arrives in Lakehurst, New Jersey, after an around-the-world flight which has taken just over 21 days.

SEPTEMBER

3 Share prices on **Wall Street** reach an all-time high.

7 Flying Officer Waghorn wins the **Schneider Trophy** for Britain, flying at over 300 mph in a Supermarine Rolls-Royce S.6B.

14 The U.S. joins the International Court of Justice at **The Hague**.

OCTOBER

14 The British airship *R101*, the world's biggest, makes its maiden flight.

19 Share prices begin to tumble on **Wall Street**. The day will become known as "Black Saturday."

R101 It's not the same as a liner, but passengers on the world's biggest airship can still relax in deckchairs.

24 It is **Black Thursday** on the New York Stock Exchange, as panic selling causes the market to collapse.

28 Shares fall sharply on the **London Stock Exchange** in reaction to the Wall Street Crash.

NOVEMBER

13 Shares on Wall Street reach their lowest level. The **Great Crash** has blown away share value amounting to $30 billion.

18 Japan begins the invasion of **Manchuria**.

DECEMBER

6 In **Turkey** women get the vote for the first time.

10 The Nobel Prize for Literature is awarded to the German novelist **Thomas Mann**.

22 Soviet troops called back from **Manchuria** as the result of truce.

Books and plays about the First World War are in demand again. The German writer Ernst Maria Remarque's novel, ***All Quiet on the Western Front***, is on the way to being an international bestseller. **T.E. Lawrence**'s *Revolt in the Desert* about his guerrilla war with Bedouin tribesmen against the Turks is also a bestseller. American novelist **Ernest Hemingway** has written about the war on the Italian front in *A Farewell to Arms*. R.C. Sherriff's antiwar play ***Journey's End*** is breaking box-office records.

1930

JANUARY

2 In India the National Congress votes in favor of **Gandhi**'s demand for total independence.

3 As famine threatens the Soviet Union, Stalin begins the forced **collectivization** of Russian agriculture. Reports will soon emerge of the execution of *kulaks*, the more prosperous peasants, in large numbers.

15 10th anniversary of **Prohibition**.

28 The Spanish dictator **Primo de Rivera** resigns.

31 Five Power **Naval Conference** meets in London. U.S., Britain, France, Italy and Japan will try to hammer out restrictions to avoid arms race.

FEBRUARY

12 Archbishop of Canterbury denounces **religious persecution** in the U.S.S.R., including the murder of priests, monks and nuns, and the turning of churches into "museums of atheism."

18 U.S. astronomer Clyde Tombaugh discovers a new planet in the solar system and names it **Pluto** after the

CIVIL DISOBEDIENCE Indian women defy the Salt Laws by evaporating their own salt from sea water.

Greek god of the underworld.

MARCH

2 The English novelist **D.H.**

Lawrence dies at Vence in the South of France.

8 President **William Howard Taft** dies at home in Washington at the age of 72, one month after resigning from his post as Supreme Court Justice.

16 Former Spanish dictator **Primo de Rivera** dies.

17 Al Capone leaves prison after serving ten months of a two-year sentence for being found in possession of a firearm.

APRIL

1 German actress **Marlene Dietrich** stars in Josef von Sternberg's film *The Blue Angel*.

7 In Britain the **Automobile Association** announces that it has issued its millionth badge to motoring members.

24 Englishwoman **Amy Johnson** becomes the first woman to fly solo from Britain to Australia.

28 The young actor **John Gielgud** stars in *Hamlet* at the Old Vic.

MAY

4 Gandhi is arrested after his symbolic 240 mile **Salt March**.

17 Jockey E. Sande Wins **Kentucky Derby** for 3rd time.

Young Plan for war reparations goes into effect.

19 A production of Shakespeare's *Othello* opens in London, starring

American **Paul Robeson** and British actors Sybil Thorndike, Peggy Ashcroft and Ralph Richardson.

JUNE

5 The British government rejects a plan for a **Channel Tunnel** between England and France.

6 Clarence Birdseye's **frozen peas** appear in stores in Massachusetts.

12 The German boxer **Max Schmeling** beats the American Jack Sharkey for the world heavyweight title.

13 Al Capone arrested on perjury charges in Miami.

20 Jazz musicians **Louis Armstrong** and **Fats Waller** open in New York in the revue *Hot Chocolate*.

30 American golfer **Bobby Jones** wins his third British Open.

JULY

7 At Wimbledon, Americans **Bill Tilden** and **Helen Wills Moody** win the men's and women's singles.

Sir Arthur Conan Doyle, creator of Sherlock Holmes, dies.

13 The first-ever **World Cup Soccer** competition begins in Montevideo, Uruguay. Uruguay wins, defeating Argentina 4-2 in the final. Europe was represented by France, Belgium, Yugoslavia and Romania.

AUGUST

7 Unemployment in Britain reaches over 2 million.

24 Nöel Coward's comedy *Private Lives* opens in London. Coward plays the lead male role opposite Gertrude Lawrence.

27 American golfer **Bobby Jones** completes the "Grand Slam" by winning the British and American Open and Amateur tournaments, the first golfer ever to do so.

SEPTEMBER

14 In Germany the **Nazis** win 107 seats in the Reichstag but Hitler himself is denied a seat because he is Austrian. A month later, the Nazi

deputies will come to the Reichstag in uniform, against German law.

OCTOBER

4 After a relatively bloodless revolution in Brazil, **Getulio Vargas** becomes president.

5 The British airship **R101** explodes in France. Forty-four out of 52 people on board perish.

10 Three American airlines merge to form Transcontinental and Western Airlines, or **TWA**.

14 George Gershwin's musical *Girl Crazy* opens on Broadway.

16 France announces plans for the construction of the **Maginot Line** along her frontier with Germany.

24 In China **Chiang Kai-shek** announces his conversion to Christianity.

30 After years of conflict, Turkey and Greece sign a **Treaty of Friendship**.

NOVEMBER

2 Ras Tafari becomes Emperor of Abyssinia (Ethiopia) as **Haile Selassie**.

14 Japan's premier **Hamagushi** is assassinated by a right-wing extremist.

DECEMBER

2 United States President Hoover asks Congress for $150 million to create jobs for the **unemployed**.

31 This year the American chemical company Du Pont has announced development of the synthetic material it has named **nylon**.

Greta Garbo has spoken on screen for the first time in the film *Anna Christie*. French cabaret singer **Maurice Chevalier** goes to Hollywood and will soon be followed by the new German star **Marlene Dietrich**. Hollywood also imports the German film directors **Josef von Sternberg** and **Ernst Lubitsch**, and the bestselling German novel *All Quiet on the Western Front* which it converts into an Oscar-winning film.

LINES OF MISERY Unemployed Americans stand in line in the desperate hope of a job vacancy (background).

1931

JANUARY

6 British archaeologist **Leonard Woolley** discovers the remains of a royal palace during his excavations at the ancient Sumerian city of **Ur**.

26 Gandhi is released from prison and enters talks with the Indian viceroy.

FEBRUARY

2 Nazi members of the Reichstag demand German **withdrawal** from the League of Nations.

5 Malcolm Campbell makes a new world land-speed record of 245 mph in *Bluebird*.

6 TWA begins first **air freight** service shipping livestock from St. Louis to Newark.

23 A Chicago judge orders the arrest of **Al Capone**.

24 Unemployment in Germany reaches 5 million.

28 Former Labor MP Sir **Oswald Mosley** forms a "New Party;" it later becomes the British Union of Fascists.

MARCH

3 "**The Star-Spangled Banner**" becomes the official anthem of the U.S.

13 London Transport created to coordinate city's public transport.

28 Hundreds die in fighting between **Hindus and Muslims** in Cawnpore.

APRIL

14 King **Alfonso XIII** of Spain abdicates. Spain is declared a republic.

MAY

1 In New York the **Empire State Building**, the world's tallest, is opened by President Hoover.

14 At a concert in Bologna, conductor **Toscanini** refuses to play the fascist anthem *Giovanezza*. After a month of house arrest, he will leave the country.

19 Stalin announces the second **Five Year Plan**.

27 Professor Auguste **Piccard** becomes the first man to reach the stratosphere, ascending in a balloon to a height of 9¾ miles.

31 In an encyclical letter, **Pope Pius XI** condemns the brutality of fascism.

JUNE

17 In Shanghai the British arrest Nguyen Ai Quoc—who has taken the name **Ho Chi Minh**—founder of the Indochinese Communist Party.

22 In Italy the fascist regime jails 124 **Mafia** members for life.

President Hoover proposes the suspension of **war debt** payments as a measure to stimulate the world economy.

28 In **Spain** the socialists win the general election and form a government.

13 Banks in Germany close as confidence in the mark collapses.

JULY

31 The British government embarks on a program of **public spending cuts**, including reduced unemployment benefits and salary cuts for teachers, police and other public sector workers.

AUGUST

2 The New York Federal Reserve and the Banque de France rescue the Bank of England with a **loan** of £50 million.

25 In Britain, as the country faces an economic crisis and unemployment soars, Ramsay MacDonald agrees to head an all-party coalition **National Government**. Three days later, he is ousted as leader of the Labor Party.

SEPTEMBER

15 In London, at a **Round Table Conference** on India, Gandhi politely but firmly demands independence.

20 The Japanese army in Manchuria captures the city of **Mukden**.

21 Britain comes off the **Gold Standard**, effectively devaluing the pound by about one-third against the dollar.

29 British flyer George Stainforth sets

a new **air-speed record** of 409 mph.

OCTOBER

13 Nöel Coward's *Cavalcade* opens in London.

NATIONAL GOVERNMENT Ramsay MacDonald (front row, center) sits with his cabinet at Downing Street. A genial-looking Stanley Baldwin is on his right.

20 The Irish government bans the **Irish Republican Army**.

22 In Chicago **Al Capone** is jailed for 11 years for tax evasion.

28 In the British general election Ramsay MacDonald's **National Government** is returned by 554 seats to 56. There are 473 Tory MPs in the new House of Commons, 52 Labor.

NOVEMBER

4 Gandhi meets King George V at Buckingham Palace, wearing only his dhoti and woollen shawl.

Neville Chamberlain becomes chancellor of the exchequer in the new British government.

30 Record companies His Master's Voice and Columbia merge to form Electrical and Musical Industries, **EMI**.

DECEMBER

4 Major **James Doolittle** sets record for coast to coast flight.

15 It is reported that **traffic lights**, tried out experimentally in London, will be installed in all British towns.

18 Gangster Jack **"Legs" Diamond** is shot dead in Albany.

31 At year's end, more than 8 million Americans, nearly 3 million Britons and nearly 6 million Germans are **unemployed**.

MAHATMA IN LONDON Gandhi leaves 10 Downing Street after a meeting with Prime Minister Ramsay MacDonald.

1932

JANUARY

2 The Japanese set up **Manchukuo** in Manchuria. Its puppet leader will be the former Chinese emperor Pu Yi.

Representatives of 60 nations meet in Geneva to discuss **disarmament**.

4 Gandhi and other **Congress** leaders are arrested after they resume their campaign of civil disobedience, including a boycott of British imported textiles.

14 Unemployment in the United States now stands at 8.2 million.

FEBRUARY

10 Britain's most prolific author, **Edgar Wallace**, dies aged 56, having written 170 books and plays.

25 Adolf Hitler is granted German **citizenship**. He has declared that he will run for the German presidency.

MARCH

1 The baby son of Colonel and Mrs. Charles **Lindbergh** is kidnapped from their home. As 100,000 police and volunteers join in a search, President Hoover promises to "move Heaven and Earth," and Al Capone offers a $10,000 dollar reward for the child's safe recovery.

15 The **BBC** makes the first broadcast from its new building in Portland Place, London.

18 The **Sydney Harbor bridge** opens.

29 Eamon **de Valera** wins elections to head the new government of the Republic of Ireland.

APRIL

10 In the German presidential elections, **Paul von Hindenburg** wins against Hitler with 19 million votes. Hitler receives over 13 million.

13 The Nazi paramilitaries of the **SA** and **SS** are banned in Germany.

23 The new **Shakespeare Memorial Theatre** opens at Stratford-on-Avon.

23 Shirley Temple celebrates her fourth birthday. She is already appearing in movies. By 1934 she will be one of Hollywood's biggest stars.

27 Imperial Airways opens a regular service between London and Cape Town.

MAY

10 French president **Paul Doumer** is assassinated by a White Russian emigré, Paul Gorguloff, believed to be insane.

12 Lindbergh baby found dead.

15 Japanese prime minister Ki Inukai is **assassinated** by militant nationalists.

20 Engelbert Dollfuss becomes chancellor of Austria.

22 Socialist **Norman Thomas** is nominated candidate for president at the socialist party's convention in Milwaukee.

29 Over 11,000 World War I Veterans— the **"Bonus Expeditionary Force"**—march on Washington demanding payment of bonus promised them by Congress.

30 Heinrich Brüning resigns as German chancellor. Hindenburg invites Franz von Papen to form a government.

JUNE

16 The new German chancellor **von Papen** lifts the ban on the Nazi paramilitaries.

21 American **Jack Sharkey** defeats German **Max Schmeling** for the world heavyweight title.

JULY

2 Helen Wills Moody has her fifth women's singles victory at Wimbledon.

Franklin Roosevelt is selected as the Democratic candidate in the forthcoming presidential election.

5 António **Salazar** becomes dictator of Portugal.

9 Meeting in **Lausanne**, the Allies agree to ease Germany's economic problems by suspending reparations payments.

17 In Berlin, 15 die in street battles between **Nazis** and **communists**.

31 In German elections, the Nazis win 230 seats in the **Reichstag**. They are now the biggest party but do not have an overall majority. The communists still have 89 seats.

AUGUST

5 Unemployment in the United States now stands at 11.6 million.

14 In the Olympic Games in Los Angeles, 18-year-old American **Mildred Didrikson** sets a world record for the 80 meter hurdles, wins the javelin contest, and takes silver in the high jump.

30 Leading Nazi Hermann **Goering** is elected president of the Reichstag.

OCTOBER

2 The New York **Yankees**, behind the slugging of Babe Ruth and Lou Gehrig, defeat the Chicago Cubs 13-6 to win the World Series in 4 straight games.

3 Iraq becomes officially independent as the British mandate ends.

9 In the U.S.S.R. Stalin exiles **Zinoviev** and **Kamenev** to Siberia.

25 George Lansbury is the new leader of the British Labor Party.

30 In London **"hunger marches"** organized by the British Communist Party lead to violent riots.

NOVEMBER

8 With the Depression at its worst, U.S. Democratic candidate Franklin Delano Roosevelt has a landslide victory in the presidential election. In his campaign he has pledged a **"New Deal"** for the American people.

9 Stalin's wife **Nadya Aliluyeva** commits suicide after denouncing him for his treatment of Russia's peasants.

16 The Prince of Wales opens **Stormont**, the Northern Ireland parliament's new building in Belfast.

Sing Along Women hunger marchers from Lancashire pose cheerfully on their way to London, where they will gather in Hyde Park with marchers from other parts of the country.

17 Von Papen resigns as German chancellor after failing to form a government, despite the fact that his Nationalist Party has been gaining seats from the Nazis. Hitler refuses the chancellorship if it means forming a coalition with non-Nazi parties.

DECEMBER

2 Kurt von Schleicher is appointed German chancellor.

7 Fighting breaks out between Nazi and communist deputies in the German Reichstag.

10 British writer **John Galsworthy** wins the Nobel Prize for Literature. He is best known for the *Forsyte Saga*, the first three volumes of which were published in 1922.

The Nobel Prize for Physics goes to **Werner Heisenberg**, whose "Uncertainty Principle" will still dominate particle physics 60 years later. In the same year, at Cambridge, British physicist **James Chadwick** discovers a new subatomic particle, the neutron, while **John Cockroft** and **Ernest Walton** use their particle accelerator to transmute lithium atoms into helium atoms.

15 The British Government pays the United States £27 million in **gold** in settlement of war debts.

Inauguration Franklin Roosevelt is sworn in as 32nd president of the United States at the start of his first term in March 1933 (background).

1933

JANUARY

22 The palaces of Persian monarchs **Xerxes and Darius** is uncovered in Persepolis, ancient capital of the Persian Empire.

THE NEW BOWLING Australian batsman W.M. Woodfull ducks Harold Larwood's bowling during the controversial bodyline tour.

23 During England's cricket tour of Australia, there is controversy over the **bodyline** bowling of Harold Larwood and Bill Voce.

28 Von Schleicher resigns as German chancellor.

29 Edouard Daladier becomes French prime minister.

ARSONIST OR SCAPEGOAT? Dutch communist Marinus van der Lubbe stands trial for causing the Reichstag fire. He was guillotined in January 1934.

30 Hindenburg appoints **Hitler** German chancellor. Goering is put in charge of Prussia's police, while Wilhelm Frick is minister of the interior.

FEBRUARY

25 Condemned for its actions in Manchuria, **Japan** leaves the League of Nations.

27 The **Reichstag** building in Berlin is set ablaze, and a young Dutchman, Marinus van der Lubbe, is accused of the crime. Hitler uses this as a pretext to begin eliminating all political opposition.

MARCH

3 The movie *King Kong* opens in New York.

4 Roosevelt is inaugurated as president and begins his "Hundred Days" of measures aimed at economic recovery.

7 Austrian chancellor **Dollfuss** suspends parliament as the Austrian Nazi Party grows in strength.

12 The flag of the German Republic is banned. Henceforth the **swastika** banner will fly alongside the old imperial flag.

15 Hitler proclaims the **Third Reich**.

20 The Nazis open the first concentration camp at **Dachau**, near Munich, for political dissidents.

22 Sir Malcolm Campbell sets a new land-speed record of 272 mph at Daytona Beach, Florida, in *Bluebird*.

23 An Enabling Act makes Hitler **dictator** and formally ends democracy and civil rights in Germany.

28 The Nazis order a **boycott** of Jewish businesses in Germany.

APRIL

4 Dirigible Akron, pride of the Navy air fleet, crashes off of the New Jersey coast after being struck by lightning.

30 The United States comes off the **gold standard**.

MAY

10 Joseph **Goebbels** organizes a ceremonial public burning of thousands of books in Berlin. There are similar book-burnings in other German cities.

13 Mexican painter **Diego Rivera** is told to cease work on his mural at Rockefeller Center because of its Marxist-Leninist message.

18 The Roosevelt administration sets up the **Tennessee Valley Authority**.

JUNE

19 In Austria, Chancellor **Dollfuss** bans the Nazi Party and arrests hundreds of its members.

27 Golfer **Henry Cotton** leads the British team to victory in the Ryder Cup.

29 Primo Carnera defeats Jack Sharkey for the world heavyweight boxing championship.

JULY

7 British doctors identify the **influenza** virus.

8 Helen Wills Moody wins the women's singles at Wimbledon for the sixth time.

15 The **Bauhaus** is closed and its building taken over by the Gestapo. Its director, Miës van der Rohe, and its founder, Walter Gropius, are in exile.

27 The Nazis announce plans for the compulsory **sterilization** of persons suffering from hereditary mental or physical deficiencies.

AUGUST

30 France sets up its national airline **Air France**.

SEPTEMBER

1 H.G. Wells publishes *The Shape of Things to Come*. Among other things, he predicts war between Poland and Germany in 1940.

George Orwell writes about his personal experience of poverty in *Down and Out in Paris and London*.

2 Hitler addresses a Nazi Party rally at **Nuremberg**.

10 British tennis player **Fred Perry** wins the U.S. Open, the first Briton to do so since 1903.

20 Chancellor **Dollfuss** assumes dictatorial powers in Austria.

OCTOBER

3 Dollfuss is shot by an Austrian Nazi but survives.

14 Germany leaves the **League of Nations**.

27 A state of emergency is declared in several towns in Palestine, as Arabs riot in protest at Jewish **immigration**.

NOVEMBER

3 Right-wing parties make large gains in elections in **Spain**. Bitter fighting breaks out as Spanish communists attempt to seize power.

10 Martial law is declared in Austria.

12 The Nazis win a vote of confidence in a **plebiscite**. Ninety-two percent of voters said Yes to the one-party state, including most of the inmates of Dachau concentration camp.

14 When the new **Reichstag** opens, all the members are Nazis; none are women.

16 In Brazil President **Vargas** becomes dictator.

DECEMBER

5 In the United States **Prohibition** is repealed amid great rejoicing.

22 In Leipzig Marinus **van der Lubbe** is sentenced to death for the Reichstag fire.

31 Fiorella **LaGuardia** is sworn in as mayor of New York.

1934

Clark Gable stars with French-born Claudette Colbert in *It Happened One Night*. American sales of male underwear plummet when Gable is seen as wearing no undershirt.

JANUARY

7 In Germany, 6,000 **pastors** preach denunciations of the Nazi takeover of the German Protestant Church.

8 The notorious swindler Alexandre **Stavisky** dies in Chamonix, officially as a suicide, but many believe he was shot by the police to preserve his silence.

FEBRUARY

7 French prime minister **Daladier** resigns after violent riots sparked by the **Stavisky Scandal**.

16 Britain and the U.S.S.R. sign a **trade treaty**.

17 The Austrian army brutally crushes a socialist **uprising**.

22 Rebel leader Augusto Sandino of **Nicaragua** is shot dead by National Guardsmen, whose leader is General Anastasio Somoza.

23 British composer **Sir Edward Elgar** dies aged 76. Two other British composers, Frederick Delius and Gustav Holst, will also die this year.

MARCH

3 American bank robber **John Dillinger** escapes from prison in Indiana using a pistol modelled from wood.

23 Bank robbers **Bonnie Parker and Clyde Barrow** are gunned down by police. Clyde is 25, while Bonnie is 23.

APRIL

18 Washeteria opens in Fort Worth, Texas—one of the first of the new laundromats.

BLUEBIRD The British "speedster" Sir Malcolm Campbell breaks another land-speed record at Daytona Beach in Florida (background).

MAY

19 In **Bulgaria**, fascists supported by King Boris seize power in a coup.

JUNE

6 Joseph P. Kennedy appointed head of the Wall Street watchdog, the Securities and Exchange Commission.

9 There is fierce fighting between British fascists and their opponents during a **fascist rally** at Olympia in London.

10 Italy wins the first **World Cup** Soccer tournament to be played in Europe, defeating Czechoslovakia 2-1. Before the match, the Italian team gave the fascist salute.

14 Hitler and Mussolini have an historic **meeting** in Venice. The two are mutual admirers but not yet allies.

The American **Max Baer** beats Italian Primo Carnera for the world heavyweight boxing championship.

30 Hitler orders the SS to murder the leadership of the SA and many others in what becomes known as the **Night of the Long Knives**.

JULY

7 Fred Perry wins the men's singles at Wimbledon, the first Briton to do so for 25 years.

13 Himmler's SS take charge of Germany's **concentration camps**, including ones previously run by the SA.

22 John Dillinger, dubbed **Public Enemy No. 1** by the FBI, is shot by G-men as he comes out of a movie theater in Chicago, where he was watching a gangster film.

25 In Austria, Chancellor **Dollfuss** is assassinated by SS gunmen, but an attempted Nazi coup fails after a gun battle with police. Hundreds of Austrian Nazis are rounded up. The new Austrian chancellor is Kurt von Schuschnigg.

27 Reacting to the assassination of Dollfuss, **Mussolini** moves 40,000 troops to Italy's frontier with Austria.

AUGUST

2 German president Paul von

ASSASSINATED   Engelbert Dollfuss had been Austrian chancellor since 1932. His methods were authoritarian, but had more in common with Mussolini's fascism than German Nazism.

Hindenburg dies. Hitler now combines the offices of president and chancellor, and styles himself *Führer* of the Third Reich.

19 In a **referendum** 90 percent of Germans approve of Hitler's becoming supreme head of state. In the armed forces, all officers and men must now swear an oath to the Führer personally.

Al Capone becomes an inmate of Alcatraz prison.

SEPTEMBER

9 There are violent clashes between British **fascists** and communists in the streets of London.

26 The liner **Queen Mary**, the biggest ship in the world, is launched.

28 Bruno Hauptmann, an illegal German immigrant, is arrested for the kidnapping and murder of the Lindbergh baby.

OCTOBER

1 Spanish miners in **Asturias** rebel and set up a workers' commune. It is suppressed after two weeks by troops led by the young General Francisco Franco.

5 Catalan separatists and anarchists attempt to set up an independent Catalan Republic in **Barcelona**. The rising is put down by soldiers and

police. There is also fierce fighting in Madrid and other Spanish cities.

9 King Alexander of Yugoslavia is **assassinated** by a Croatian nationalist during a state visit to Paris.

16 In China, the **Long March** of Mao Zedong and his communist followers begins. Only 10 percent of those who set out will reach their destination in remote northwest China.

NOVEMBER

13 Italian teachers are ordered to wear the fascist uniform during school hours.

21 Cole Porter's musical *Anything Goes* opens in New York.

25 Mustafa Kemal orders all Turks to adopt a surname. His own will be **Atatürk**.

DECEMBER

1 The assassination of **Kirov**, the communist leader in Leningrad, gives Stalin the pretext to begin the purges of his political enemies. An estimated 10 million people are already held in Soviet labor camps.

2 American swimming champion Johnny Weissmuller plays **Tarzan**

LONG LONG MARCH Men and women of the Red Army face the great trek to remote northwestern China.

for the first time in the film *Tarzan of the Apes*.

20 Stalin orders the arrest of **Zinoviev and Kamenev**. They will lose their lives in his Great Purge.

27 Persia changes its name to **Iran**, the name always used for their country by native Iranians.

1935

Fred Astaire consolidates his screen reputation dancing with **Ginger Rogers** in *Top Hat*.

TOP HAT The incomparable Fred Astaire and his long-term dance partner Ginger Rogers adorn the sheet music for one of their greatest hits.

Greta Garbo stars in the title role in the film *Anna Karenina*.

In Britain, Allen Lane launches the cheap paperback imprint he has named **Penguin Books**.

Benny Goodman, now known as the "King of Swing," forms the Benny Goodman Orchestra.

JANUARY

7 As Italian troops mass on its borders, **Abyssinia** (Ethiopia) appeals to the League of Nations for protection.

10 Hollywood stars Mary Pickford and Douglas Fairbanks are **divorced**.

FEBRUARY

13 In New Jersey **Bruno Hauptmann** is sentenced to death for the murder of the Lindbergh baby.

MARCH

1 The coal-rich **Saarland** returns to Germany after a plebiscite. Up till now it has been under League of Nations administration and France has been allowed to mine its coal.

11 As part of Germany's rearmament program, the **Luftwaffe** is set up by Hermann Goering.

16 The German government announces **conscription** and demands an army of 500,000 men, five times the number permitted by the Versailles Treaty.

APRIL

11 The first dust storm sweeps across the prairie states of the Midwest, already devastated by drought. The storms will create a huge **Dust Bowl**.

16 Pan American Airlines inaugurates the Pan Am Clipper seaplane service from San Francisco to the Far East.

23 Stalin opens the new **Moscow Underground**.

29 Night-time reflectors known as "Cat's-eyes" are used for the first time on roads.

MAY

6 In the United States the Roosevelt administration sets up the **Works Progress Administration**, aimed at creating jobs for millions of the unemployed in public works projects.

19 T.E. Lawrence, **Lawrence of Arabia**, dies in a motorcycle crash two months after leaving the Royal Air Force, in which he has been serving as "Aircraftsman Shaw."

JUNE

1 Gas masks are tried out as part of a major civil defense exercise in Britain.

7 Stanley Baldwin becomes British prime minister, following the retirement of Ramsay MacDonald on health grounds.

DUSTY TIMES Women battle through the great April dust storm in the Midwest town of Alva, Oklahoma.

12 Bolivia and Paraguay sign an armistice ending the three-year **Chaco War**.

28 President Roosevelt orders the building of a federal gold vault at **Fort Knox** in Kentucky.

JULY

6 At **Wimbledon** Fred Perry wins the men's singles and Helen Wills Moody wins the women's for the seventh time.

29 T.E. Lawrence's *Seven Pillars of Wisdom* is published posthumously in accordance with his wishes.

AUGUST

14 President **Roosevelt** signs a Social Security Act, setting up a federal program of unemployment insurance, pensions and public health care for the needy.

16 Beloved humanist **Will Rogers** and famed aviator **Wiley Post** die in an air crash during a tour of Alaska.

SEPTEMBER

3 Malcolm Campbell is first to break the 300 mph land-speed barrier.

8 In Louisiana the populist politician **Huey Long** is fatally shot by a political opponent.

15 Hitler announces the **Nuremberg Laws**, under which Jews are deprived of citizenship, barred from most forms of employment, and forbidden sexual relations with Aryans.

American millionaire **Howard Hughes** makes a new air-speed record of 347.5 mph.

30 George Gershwin's opera *Porgy and Bess* is performed for the first time in Boston.

OCTOBER

2 Italy invades **Abyssinia**, using all the resources of modern warfare against poorly equipped tribal armies. The League of Nations denounces the invasion, but imposes only limited economic sanctions against the invaders.

8 Clement Attlee becomes leader of the British Labor Party.

12 Black American jazz music is **banned** from German radio.

20 Some 8,000 survivors of Mao Zedong's communist army reach Shaanxi in northwest China after the 6,000 mile **Long March.**

UNEQUAL CONFLICT Lightly armed Ethiopian infantry come under fire from Italian war planes in the Ogaden region.

NOVEMBER

6 In Britain a prototype **Hawker Hurricane** fighter has a test flight.

16 A **general election** in Britain sweeps Stanley Baldwin back to power as prime minister.

30 Under a new German law, "non-belief in Nazism" becomes grounds for **divorce**.

DECEMBER

14 In Czechoslovakia 86-year-old President Tomas **Masaryk** retires and hands over the reins to his chosen successor Eduard **Benes**.

21 In Germany Jewish **doctors**, no longer permitted to treat Aryans, are also obliged to cease working in private hospitals.

22 Anthony Eden becomes British foreign secretary after the resignation of Sir Samuel Hoare. Hoare aroused anger because of the Hoare-Laval Pact under which Britain and France allowed Mussolini to keep the most fertile parts of Abyssinia.

31 J.M. Keynes publishes *The General Theory of Employment, Interest and Money*, arguing that governments can end depressions by increasing money supply through public works and deficit spending.

1936

Margaret Mitchell's **Gone with the Wind** is published.

Joe DiMaggio takes the New York Yankees to victory in the World Series.

JANUARY

18 Rudyard Kipling, the poet and short-story writer, dies aged 70.

20 King George V dies and is succeeded by his son, Edward VIII.

FEBRUARY

5 Charlie Chaplin opens his film *Modern Times*.

8 In India **Nehru** becomes president of the Indian National Congress.

16 In elections in Spain, a left-wing **Popular Front** coalition wins by a narrow majority.

26 Hitler opens a factory for the production of the

DEFIANCE A sandalled foot steps on a swastika in a Spanish anti-fascist poster from the civil war.

"people's car," the **Volkswagen**, designed by Dr. Ferdinand Porsche.

MARCH

5 In Britain the Vickers company puts on show the **Spitfire** fighter.

7 German troops march into the demilitarized **Rhineland** in defiance of the Versailles and Locarno Treaties.

APRIL

27 Germany announces an **Economic Plan** on Soviet lines, with Hermann Goering in charge.

28 Following the death of his father King Fuad, 16-year-old Prince **Farouk** becomes king of Egypt.

MAY

5 The Italians complete their conquest of **Abyssinia** by occupying the capital, Addis Ababa. Emperor Haile Selassie has fled the country.

22 The **Marx Brothers**' film *A Night at the Opera* opens.

JUNE

4 In France a Popular Front government under the socialist **Léon Blum** is elected.

12 Republicans nominate governor **Alf Landon** of Kansas for president; he will run with Colonel Frank Knox.

17 In Germany **Heinrich Himmler** is put in charge of all German police forces, including the Gestapo.

26 Haile Selassie addresses the League of Nations to protest at the invasion of his country.

JULY

3 Fred Perry wins the men's singles title at Wimbledon for the third consecutive year.

6 The German **airship** *Hindenburg* crosses the Atlantic in 46 hours.

11 In Spain a leading conservative politician, **Calvo Sotelo**, is murdered. This is the spark that will set off a military rebellion.

POPULAR FRONT Léon Blum, premier in France's new left-wing coalition government, holds up a miner's lamp as a sign of solidarity with the workers.

14 Britain begins mass production of **gas masks**.

17 A large part of the Spanish army under generals Mola, Queipo de Llano and Franco rises against the Popular Front government. This is the start of the **civil war**.

30 Boardgame **Monopoly** craze sweeps the U.S.

AUGUST

1 Adolf Hitler opens the 11th **Olympic Games** in Berlin. He will be infuriated by the triumph of the black American athlete Jesse Owens, who wins gold in the 100 meter, the 200 meter, the long jump and the 400 meter.

18 Spanish poet Federico García **Lorca** is executed by nationalists.

21 The BBC puts out its first **television broadcast** from Alexandra Palace.

25 Stalin executes 16 leading communists, including Zinoviev and Kamenev, as part of his **Great Purge**.

SEPTEMBER

21 British inventor Frank **Hornby** dies aged 73. He devised Meccano construction kits, Hornby model trains, and Dinky toys.

30 General Franco, now commander in chief of the Spanish nationalist forces, raises the siege of the **Alcázar** fortress at Toledo. He now moves on Madrid, but meets stiffening resistance from the republicans.

OCTOBER

6 The British **Labor Party** refuses to affiliate with the Communist Party.

11 Violence breaks out in London when 7,000 of Sir Oswald Mosley's **blackshirts** attempt to march through the East End.

27 Wallis Simpson divorces her husband Ernest and is now free to marry Edward VIII.

OLYMPIC RECORD German director Leni Riefensthal clutches the shoulder of her cameraman as they film the Berlin Olympics.

NOVEMBER

1 Mussolini announces a Rome-Berlin **Axis**.

3 Franklin **Roosevelt** wins a second term as president by a landslide.

11 The 200 **Jarrow Marchers** arrive in London after walking nearly 300 miles from the Tyneside town of Jarrow, disastrously hit by unemployment.

18 Germany and Italy formally recognize **Franco**'s nationalist government as the true government of Spain. Franco has occupied much of the country but not Madrid.

20 Antonio Primo de Rivera, leader of the Spanish **Falange**, is executed by republicans at Alicante.

24 Germany and Japan sign an **Anti-Comintern Pact**.

30 In London the **Crystal Palace**, built for the Great Exhibition of 1851, is destroyed by fire.

DECEMBER

3 British newspapers break the news of the crisis surrounding Edward VIII's wish to marry Wallis Simpson.

10 Prolific American playwright **Eugene O'Neill** wins Nobel Prize in Literature leading American charge in Stockholm of four Nobel Lauriates.

11 King Edward VIII announces his **abdication**. He is succeeded by his brother Albert, Duke of York, who becomes king as George VI.

1937

JANUARY

1 In Britain the Public Order Act bans political uniforms. It will particularly affect the British Union of **Fascists**.

9 Trotsky arrives in Mexico after being denied sanctuary in Europe.

19 English ballerina **Margot Fonteyn** has her debut at Sadler's Wells.

20 Franklin Roosevelt is sworn in for a second term as U.S. president.

FEBRUARY

4 German ambassador to London **Ribbentrop** greets King George VI with a Nazi salute.

MARCH

9 George Orwell publishes his study of unemployment and working-class poverty, *The Road to Wigan Pier*.

APRIL

5 The French liner *Normandie* beats the *Queen Mary* across the Atlantic to win the **Blue Riband**.

16 Boeing's **Flying Fortress** bomber is shown for the first time.

26 German aircraft of the Condor Legion bomb and strafe the ancient Basque town of **Guernica**, killing some 1,000 people. Pablo Picasso's great painting inspired by the event will become a memorial to the martyred town.

MAY

6 The German airship *Hindenburg* bursts into flames as it is about to land at Lakehurst, New Jersey. Thirty-three people die and many others are injured in the disaster.

12 King George VI and Queen Elizabeth are crowned at Westminster Abbey. The BBC covers the event with its first-ever live **television** broadcast.

DISPLAY OF POWER Nazi stormtroopers make an impressive showing as they wave swastika banners at the party's annual Nuremberg rally (background).

27 The **Golden Gate Bridge** opens in San Francisco—at 4,200 feet, it is the world's longest suspension bridge.

28 Neville Chamberlain succeeds Stanley Baldwin as British premier.

JUNE

3 The former Edward VIII, now **Duke of Windsor**, marries Wallis Simpson in France. No other member of the British royal family is present.

In Spain the nationalist General **Mola** is killed in a plane crash.

7 Jean Harlow, the Hollywood "sex goddess" of the 1930s, dies at age 26.

12 As part of his **Great Purge**, Stalin orders the execution of 12 generals including the great Marshal Tukhachevsky. Some 30,000 Russian military officers will have been executed by the time Russia is invaded by Germany.

19 Sir James Barrie, creator of **Peter Pan**, dies age 77.

22 Black American fighter **Joe Louis** is the new world heavyweight champion.

JULY

8 Following the **Marco Polo Bridge** incident, the Japanese invade China without declaring war.

11 George Gershwin dies from a brain tumor, at the age of 38.

18 The American aviator **Amelia Earhart** disappears on a flight somewhere over the Pacific.

19 The Nazis open an exhibition of **"Degenerate Art"** in Munich, showing the work of some of Germany's most important modernist artists.

28 Japanese troops take **Beijing**.

AUGUST

1 The Nazis open a new concentration camp at **Buchenwald**.

14 The Japanese bomb **Shanghai** killing hundreds of Chinese civilians.

30 Joe Louis successfully defends his world heavyweight title against British boxer **Tommy Farr** at Madison Square Garden.

GRAND ILLUSION A poster advertises the Dutch version of Jean Renoir's subtle antiwar film masterpiece.

SEPTEMBER

2 Sir Malcolm Campbell sets a new world **water-speed record** of 129 mph on Lake Maggiore in Switzerland.

28 The **League of Nations** condemns Japan's invasion of China.

29 Chiang Kai-shek and Mao Zedong unite to resist the **Japanese invasion**.

OCTOBER

10 British fascist leader, Sir **Oswald Mosley**, is stoned and knocked unconscious by a rock-throwing mob protesting his speech in Liverpool.

17 Local Nazis stir up violent riots among the **Sudeten** Germans of Czechoslovakia.

19 New Zealand-born **Ernest Rutherford**, the first scientist to split the atom, dies aged 66.

20 The British limit Jewish immigration into **Palestine**, because of increasing Arab violence.

22 The **Duke and Duchess of Windsor** make a controversial visit to Germany, where they are welcomed by leading Nazis.

NOVEMBER

4 Mexican president **Lazaro Cardenas** nationalizes 350,000 acres of oil lands of Standard Oil of California.

8 As war rages across China, the Japanese take **Shanghai**.

12 Danish writer **Karen Blixen** publishes *Out of Africa*, an account of her life in Africa running a coffee plantation.

17 British politician **Lord Halifax** arrives in Berlin for talks about issues including the Sudeten crisis.

DECEMBER

8 Joseph Kennedy becomes U.S. ambassador to Britain.

10 Palaeontologists on Java discover the remains of a **human ancestor**, later named *Homo erectus*.

11 Italy quits the **League of Nations**.

12 The Japanese take **Nanjing** and go on a rampage of rape and murder, in which many thousands of men, women and children are killed.

22 Tokyo apologizes for the sinking of the U.S. navy gunboat **Panay** and two American tankers.

27 French composer **Maurice Ravel** dies, aged 62.

29 In Ireland Eamon de Valera cuts the last ties with the British Crown and the Irish Free State becomes **Eire**.

BOMBING SHANGHAI Japanese planes bomb the Chinese city before its occupation by Japanese troops.

1938

JANUARY

14 Walt Disney releases his first full-length cartoon film, *Snow White and the Seven Dwarfs.*

19 Hundreds are killed in nationalist air raids on **Barcelona**.

FEBRUARY

1 The BBC now has regular evening **television broadcasts**.

4 Ribbentrop becomes Germany's foreign minister.

14 Hitler orders Austria's Chancellor **Schuschnigg** to free all Nazis.

15 After bitter fighting, Franco's forces capture **Teruel** and advance toward the east coast.

17 John Logie Baird demonstrates a prototype color TV.

21 Anthony Eden, who opposes the appeasement of Mussolini and Hitler, resigns as British foreign secretary. His successor is Lord Halifax.

MARCH

4 German religious leader **Pastor Niemoller**, an opponent of National Socialism, is sent to Sachsenhausen concentration camp.

9 Schuschnigg resigns and is succeeded as Austrian chancellor by the pro-Nazi Arthur **Seyss-Inquart**, who invites the Germans to invade.

12 German troops march into Austria to create the **Anschluss**, or union of Austria and Germany, expressly prohibited by the Versailles Treaty. Austrian-born Hitler is greeted by cheering crowds in Vienna. The Nazis begin immediately to treat Jews and political opponents with great brutality, forcing elderly Jews to scrub the streets with their bare hands.

15 After another **show trial** in Moscow, 18 high-ranking communists are executed, including the leading Bolshevik Nikolai Bukharin and Yagoda, former head of the Soviet secret police, himself responsible for the deaths of thousands of Russians.

APRIL

1 Actress **Bette Davis**, fresh off her Oscar winning performance in *Jezebel*, refuses to appear in a picture she calls "atrocious," thus challenging the studio system.

8 Edouard Daladier becomes French prime minister.

PRIME MINISTER IN PARIS Edouard Daladier broadcasting to the French nation. He was still prime minister when war broke out.

10 In a **plebiscite** held in Germany and Austria, 99.75 percent of votes cast in Austria are claimed to have gone in favor of *Anschluss* with Germany.

19 In Spain, **Franco's forces** reach the Mediterranean coast, splitting the republican forces in two.

21 Douglas Hyde is elected as the first president of Eire.

MAY

3 Hitler goes to **Rome** to reassure Mussolini, who had previously opposed *Anschluss*, seeing it as a threat to Italy. The dictators promise lasting friendship.

20 The Czech government orders 400,000 troops to the country's border with Austria-Germany.

29 Police force used to quell labor troubles at the **Goodyear Rubber** plant in Akron, Ohio.

JUNE

1 The British army begins using the **Bren gun**, originally made in the Czech town of Brno and now manufactured in Enfield.

8 Thousands die as the Japanese attempt to bomb **Guangzhou** (Canton) into submission.

22 Joe Louis defeats his old rival, the German boxer Max Schmeling, in the first round.

30 Superman appears for the first time in an American comic strip.

JULY

2 Helen Wills Moody wins the women's singles at Wimbledon for the eighth time.

3 The British steam locomotive *Mallard* sets a new speed record of 125 mph.

11 An exhibition opens in Munich showing the kind of **art** now favored by the Nazis.

14 As a consequence of its new friendship with Hitler's Germany, Italy officially adopts **anti-Semitic** policies.

15 The British government orders 1,000 **Spitfire** fighters for the Royal Air Force.

18 Douglas **"Wrong-Way" Carrigan** flies from New York to Ireland—"by mistake," he claims, after being denied permission to make the flight by aviation officials.

22 German Jews must carry special **identity cards** marked with a "J."

AUGUST

12 Germany mobilizes her armed forces as the Nazis foment a crisis situation in **Czechoslovakia**.

15 The *Queen Mary* sets a new record for the two-way crossing of the Atlantic, westward in just under four days, eastward in three days and 20 hours.

As part of his policy of **appeasement**, British prime minister Neville Chamberlain flies to Germany for talks with Hitler over the Czechoslovakia crisis.

SEPTEMBER

5 As the crisis deepens, French troops are sent to the **Maginot Line**.

27 The liner *Queen Elizabeth* is launched in England.

29 Chamberlain flies again to Germany and, at **Munich**, Britain and France agree to appease Hitler by giving the Sudetenland to Germany. The Czech government is not consulted. Chamberlain returns to England declaring that he has brought "peace in our time" and is given a hero's welcome, but Britain and France accelerate their preparations for war.

OCTOBER

1 Germany formally annexes the **Sudetenland**, which is now occupied by German troops.

21 The Japanese take **Guangzhou** (Canton).

30 Orson Welles's radio adaptation of H.G. Wells' *The War of the Worlds* causes a panic, and thousands of Americans flee their homes believing Martians have invaded New Jersey.

NOVEMBER

9 Anti-Jewish pogroms organized by the Nazis break out in Germany and Austria. Synagogues are destroyed, and Jewish-owned shops ransacked in what becomes known as *Kristallnacht*, "the Night of Broken Glass," from the broken glass on the streets.

10 Kemal Atatürk, father of modern Turkey, dies at the age of 57 after a long illness.

DECEMBER

31 The Germans announce that they are doubling their **U-boat** fleet.

GANGSTER HERO James Cagney specialized in gangster roles. *Angels with Dirty Faces* also starred a still relatively unknown Humphrey Bogart.

1939

The film version of **Gone with the Wind** is released, starring Clark Gable and Vivien Leigh in the lead roles. It will win nine Oscars and be one of the most successful films ever made.

SOUTHERN BELLE After a mammoth search for the right actress, British star Vivien Leigh was chosen to play Scarlett O'Hara in the great epic.

JANUARY

17 British police round up hundreds of suspected **IRA** members after a series of bombings in London, Birmingham and other mainland cities.

26 In the Spanish Civil War, Franco's forces take the republican stronghold of **Barcelona.**

28 The Irish poet **W.B. Yeats** dies.

FEBRUARY

10 Pope **Pius XI** dies. He will be succeeded by Cardinal Eugenio Pacelli as Pius XII.

20 In the United States **nylon stockings** go on sale for the first time.

27 Britain and France formally recognize Generalissimo **Franco** as the ruler of Spain. The United States follows suit on March 1.

MARCH

3 John Ford's film *Stagecoach* opens, starring **John Wayne**.

15 German troops march into what remains of **Czechoslovakia**, making it clear that Hitler's aggressive

FLYING FIGHTER When war broke out Britain had several hundred Spitfires ready for action (background).

ambitions go beyond the unification of the German people.

28 Madrid surrenders to Franco, and the Spanish Civil War is over.

31 Britain and France pledge support for **Poland**, now clearly threatened by Hitler.

APRIL

7 Italy invades **Albania**, which has long been a client state.

26 German pilot Fritz Wendel sets a new air-speed record of 484 mph in a **Messerschmitt**.

27 The British government introduces **conscription** for the first time in the country's peacetime history.

30 Futuristic exhibits are the highlight of **New York World's Fair**, opened by President Roosevelt.

MAY

4 Molotov replaces the moderate Litvinov as the Soviet foreign minister.

INTO EXILE Albanian soldiers and peasants enter Yugoslavia in flight from the invading Italians.

7 Spain leaves the League of Nations.

22 Hitler's Germany and Mussolini's Italy sign a **"Pact of Steel,"** pledging to aid one another in any war.

JUNE

7 King George VI and Queen Elizabeth visit the United States, the first reigning British monarchs ever to do so.

24 In Brazil, President **Vargas** gives sanctuary to 3,000 German Jews.

JULY

20 It is reported from Tibet that the new **Dalai Lama** has been found. He is a five-year-old boy.

AUGUST

18 Premier of film adaptation of Frank L. Baum's children's classic, *The Wizard of Oz*, with **Judy Garland** as Kansas girl, Dorothy.

23 Germany's Ribbentrop and Russia's Molotov sign a **non-aggression pact**. Secret protocols divide Poland between Germany and Russia, and give Russia a free hand in Estonia and Latvia.

British driver **John Cobb** makes a new land-speed record of 369 mph at the Salt Flats, Utah, driving a dramatically streamlined new car, the *Railton Special*.

25 Britain and France reaffirm guarantees that they will assist **Poland** in the event of German invasion.

Portable **national treasures** from museums and galleries in London are removed to secure hiding places.

30 Some 16,000 children are evacuated from Paris. The **evacuation** of 1.5 million British children to homes in the country begins.

SEPTEMBER

1 Germany invades Poland, using *Blitzkrieg* techniques to smash courageous Polish resistance.

3 Britain and France **declare** war on Germany. The Second World War has begun.

Churchill joins the British war cabinet as first lord of the admiralty.

17 The U.S.S.R. invades **Poland** from the east.

The British **aircraft carrier** *Courageous* is sunk in the Atlantic with the loss of 500 men.

23 The Austrian Jewish psychoanalyst **Sigmund Freud** dies in exile in London age 83. Most of his students have already emmigrated to the U.S

27 Warsaw falls to the Germans.

30 A **British Expeditionary Force** sails to France to hold the Allied left flank, just as it had done in 1914.

OCTOBER

10 The Nazis begin the **deportation** of Polish Jews.

14 The British battleship **Royal Oak** is sunk by a torpedo.

TAKING ALL PRECAUTIONS Neville Mooney, the first baby born in London after the declaration of war, arrives home in a special baby's gas mask.

NOVEMBER

4 President **Roosevelt** continues to oppose intervention in Europe, but the Americans lift an embargo on the sale of arms to Britain and France.

26 IRA bombs go off at Victoria and King's Cross stations killing one person and injuring 22.

30 The U.S.S.R. invades **Finland**.

DECEMBER

14 The U.S.S.R. is expelled from the **League of Nations**.

17 The German pocket battleship *Graf Spee* scuttles herself outside Montevideo harbor.

31 The Finns push back the **Red Army** along a 150 mile front.

INDEX

ACKNOWLEDGMENTS

Abbreviations:
T=top; M=middle; B=bottom; L=left; R=right

CB=Corbis/Bettmann Archives
MEPL = Mary Evans Picture Library
IWM = Imperial War Museum

3 AKG, L; CB/Lake County Museum, LM; Robert Opie Collection, RM; IWM,R. 6 Popperfoto, TR, ML; Hulton Getty, BL. 7 Roy Williams. 8 Jean-Loup Charmet, TL. 8-9 Arthur Lockwood. 9 MEPL, TR; David King Collection, BR. 10 *Aidez l'Espagne*, 1937, poster by Joan Miró/IWM, Department of Art, TR; Corbis-Bettmann, BL. 11 Corbis-Bettmann. 12 Jean-Loup Charmet, TR; Corbis-Bettmann, B. 13 Popperfoto, TM; MEPL, TR; AKG, BM. 14 Corbis-Bettmann, TL; *Metropolis*, 1927-8, by Otto Dix, triptych, middle section, Galerie der Stadt, Stuttgart/AKG, BL. 15 Hulton-Getty, background; Jean-Loup Charmet, L; Corbis-Bettmann, LM; Brown Brothers, R; AKG, RM. 16 David King Collection, BL, BM; AKG, BR. 17 David King Collection, TL, BR. 18 David King Collection, TR, BL; Jean-Loup Charmet, M. 19 AKG, ML, BL. 20 Thomas D. McAvoy/Katz Pictures, TR; Fratelli Alinari, BL. 21 Jean-Loup Charmet, TL; IWM, R. 22 Bilderdienst Süddeutscher Verlag, TR; AKG, TL. 23 German Youth Festival, 1934, German World War Two poster/IWM, Department of Art, TL; Hulton-Getty, MM; Culver Pictures Inc, BR. 24 Culver Pictures Inc, TL; Brown Brothers, BR. 25 Corbis-Bettmann, TL; Popperfoto, TR, BR. 26 Brown Brothers, TL; Hulton-Getty, BR. 27 Jean-Loup Charmet, TL; Corbis-Bettmann, BR. 28 Popperfoto, BL; Hulton-Getty, BR. 29 Hulton-Getty, TL, BR. 30 CB, T;B. 31 Culver Pictures Inc, TR; Corbis-Bettmann, BR. 32 John Frost Historical News Archives, background, TL; Roy Williams, TL; Hulton-Getty, BR. 33 Kobal Collection, background; *Indestructible Object* (or *Object To Be Destroyed*), 1964, by Man Ray, Replica of 1923 original, The Museum of Modern Art, New York, James Thrall Soby Fund, Photograph © 1998 The Museum of Modern Art, New York, L; Culver Pictures Inc, LM; Jean-Loup Charmet, RM; AKG, R. 34 Popperfoto, TR, BL; Jean-Loup Charmet, MR. 35 Hulton-Getty, BL; *Pillars of Society*, 1926, by George Grosz, SMPK, Nationalgalerie, Berlin/AKG, TR. 36 AKG, TL, TR; Bilderdienst Süddeutscher Verlag, BL. 37 Popperfoto, MR; Bilderdienst Süddeutscher Verlag, B. 38 Bilderdienst Süddeutscher Verlag, foreground/Roy Williams, TR; Jean-Loup Charmet, BL. 39 *Indestructible Object* (or *Object To Be Destroyed*), 1964, by Man Ray, Replica of 1923 original, The Museum of Modern Art, James Thrall Soby Fund, Photograph © 1998 The Museum of Modern Art, New York, TR; *Dialogue of Insects*, 1924-5, by Joan Miró, Galerie Daniel Malingue, Paris, BL. 40 *My Egypt*, 1927, by Charles Demuth, Collection of Whitney Museum of American Art, New York, purchase, with

funds from Gertrude Vanderbilt Whitney, TR; *Automat, 1927*, by Edward Hopper, Des Moines Art Centre Permanent Collection, 1958.2, BL. 41 Adolf Loos/*Chicago Tribune*, TL; SuperStock, TM; *Guernica*, 1937, by Pablo Picasso, Museo Nacional Reina Sofia, Madrid, B. 42 Treppenhaus, 1921-2, architect, Walter Gropius/AKG, TL; Staatliches Bauhaus in Weimar, 1919-23, by Herbet Bayer/AKG, BM; Bauhaus Archive, BR. 43 Corbis-Bettmann, TL; *Making Tortillas, 1926*, by Diego Rivera, University of California, San Francisco, MR. 44 Akademie der Künste der DDR, Berlin, TL; Andromeda Oxford Ltd, TM; David King Collection, BR. 45 University of Nottingham, TL; Corbis-Bettmann, BR. 46 AKG, TM; Corbis-Bettmann, BR. 47 CB, T; B. 48 CB, TL; Jean Loup Charmet, TR; CB/Hulton Deautsch Collecton, BL; CB/Lake County Museum, BR; CB/Schenectady Museum-Hall of Electical History Foundation, TM. 49 CB, TL; Culver Pictures, Inc. BR; Bilderdienst Süddeutscher Verlag, BL. 50 Corbis-Bettmann, TL; AKG, BR. 51 Jean-Loup Charmet, TL; AKG, TR; Bilderdienst Süddeutscher Verlag, B. 52 Library of Congress, TL; Culver Pictures Inc, TR; *Dick Tracy*, by Chester Gould © Chicago Tribune, New York, Sunday, October 21, 1934, BL. 53 Kobal Collection, TR; The Ronald Grant Archive, BL. 54 The Ronald Grant Archive, TL; Kobal Collection, TR, BL. 55 *The Jazz Singer*, poster, 1927/Warner Bros/Christie's Images, TL; Kobal Collection, BR. 56 *CB rom*, TL, Kobal Collection, MM, B. 57 The Ronald Grant Archive, MR, B. 58 MEPL, TR; The Ronald Grant Archive, MR; Kobal Collection, BL. 59 Anonymous Poster, 1934/ Christie's Images, TR; Lapi/Roger-Viollet, ML; Bilderdienst Süddeutscher Verlag, B. 60 Popperfoto, TL; CB/Hulton Deutsch Collection, BL; BM; Culver Pictures Inc, BR. 61 Corbis-Bettmann, BM, BR. 62 Popperfoto, TL; Brown Brothers, TR; CB/Lake County Museum, BL. 63 CB, TL;M; B. 64 Culver Pictures Inc, TR; Jean-Loup Charmet, BL; Topham Picturepoint, BL. 65 Science & Society Picture Library, TR; CB, BL; Robert Opie Collection, MR. 66 Jean-Loup Charmet. 67 Hulton-Getty, TL, TR. 68 Brown Brothers, TR; Corbis-Bettmann, TL; Jean-Loup Charmet, BL. 68-69 CB; CB TR 70 Bilderdienst Süddeutscher Verlag, TL; Robert Opie Collection, TR; CB, B. 71 URLA, Paris, TR; AKG, BL; Corbis-Bettmann, BR. 72 Topham Picturepoint, T, B. 73 Popperfoto, background; Bridgeman Art Library, L; AKG, LM; David King Collection, RM; Popperfoto, R. 74 CB, T, B. 75 Corbis-Bettmann, BL; Brown Brothers, BR. 76 Popperfoto, TR; Ullstein Bilderdienst, BL. 76-7 Ullstein Bilderdienst. 77 MEPL, TM. 78 MEPL, TR; Corbis-Bettmann, BL. 79 Brown Brothers, TL; Culver Pictures Inc, BL; Culver Pictures Inc/Roy Williams, MR. 80 *Soil Erosion,*

Alabama, 1937, Arthur Rothstein, from *The Depression Years, As Photographed by Arthur Rothstein*, Dover Publications Inc, 1978, TL. 80-81 Brown Brothers. 81 *Tenant Farmer Moving, Hamilton County, Tennessee*, 1936, Arthur Rothstein, from *The Depression Years, As Photographed by Arthur Rothstein*, Dover Publications Inc, 1978, TR. 82 Brown Brothers, TL; Ullstein Bilderdienst, TR; MEPL, BR. 83 MEPL, TL; Culver Pictures Inc, MR; *Steel Workers, Pennsylvania*, 1938, Arthur Rothstein from *The Depression Years, As Photographed by Arthur Rothstein*, Dover Publications Inc, 1978, BL. 84-86 David King Collection. 87 AKG, TR; Hulton-Getty, BL; Roger-Viollet, BM. 88 AKG. 89 Roy Williams, TL; Ullstein Bilderdienst, TR, BL; AKG, BM; Bilderdienst Süddeutscher Verlag, BR. 90-91 IWM, T; Arthur Lockwood, B. 91 Ullstein Bilderdienst, TR. 92 Wide World/AP, TR; Topham Picturepoint, BL; AKG, BM. 93 Popperfoto, TL; Ullstein Bilderdienst, TR; IWM, MR. 94 Arthur Lockwood. 95 Hulton-Getty, TL; Popperfoto, TR; Ullstein Bilderdienst, BR. 96 Hulton-Getty, T; Popperfoto, B. 97 Popperfoto, BR. 98 AKG, TM, MR, B. 99 AKG; Popperfoto, BL. 100 Hulton-Getty, TR; John Frost Historical News Archives, BL; AP, BR. 101 Hulton-Getty, TL, BR. 102 David Seymour/Magnum Photos, TR; British Museum/Michael Holford, BL. 103 Hulton-Getty, ML; AKG, B. 104 Hulton-Getty, TL, TR, B. 105 Victoria & Albert Museum, London/Bridgeman Art Library, TL; Roger-Viollet, BR. 106 Harlingue-Viollet. 107 Popperfoto, TR; AKG, BL. 108 AKG, BL; Popperfoto, TR. 109 Corbis-Bettmann, BL; Popperfoto, BR. 110 Topham Picturepoint, TM; AKG, TR; The British Petroleum Company, ML, BL. 111 Hulton-Getty, BL; AKG, BR. 112 Popperfoto, MM, BL, BM. 113 Brown Brothers. 114 Hulton-Getty, TL; Culver Pictures Inc, BL. 114-15 Popperfoto, T. 115 Topham Picturepoint, MR, BL. 116 Hulton-Getty, TL; UPI/Corbis, TR. 117 AKG, background; Hulton-Getty, L, RM; Topham Picturepoint, LM; Corbis-Bettmann, R. 118 Hulton-Getty. 119 AKG, TL, TM; Hulton-Getty, BR. 120 Corbis-Bettmann. 121 Hulton-Getty, BL, BM, BR. 122-3 Walter Bosshard/Magnum Photos. 123 Hulton-Getty, TR. 124 AKG, TM; Topham Picturepoint, TR, BL. 125 AKG, TR, B. 126 Topham Picturepoint, ML. 126-7 David Seymour/Magnum Photos. 127 Roy Williams. 128 Corbis-Bettmann, TL; Topham Picturepoint, MR; Hulton-Getty, B. 129 Hulton-Getty. 130 Hulton-Getty, BL, MR. 131 AKG, TR; Hulton-Getty, B. 132 Roy Williams, TL. 132-3 Hulton-Getty. 133 Hulton-Getty, TR. 134 Hulton-Getty, BL, BM. 135 Popperfoto, ML, background, B; Topham Picturepoint, BM. 136 Jean-Loup Charmet, TR; David King Collection, BR. 137 Culver Picture Inc, ML, background; Corbis-Bettmann/UPI, BR. 138 David King

Collection, TM; Corbis-Bettmann/UPI, BL; Hulton-Getty, BR. 138-9 Topham Picturepoint, background. 139 MEPL, TR; AKG, ML. 140 David King Collection, TL; AKG, BR. 140-1 Science & Society Picture Library, background. 141 Jean-Loup Charmet, MM; Kobal Collection, BR. 142 Roger-Viollet, TL; Popperfoto, BR. 143 Private Collection, Flammarion, from *A History of Men's Fashion*, by Farid Chenoune, 1995, TL; Culver Pictures Inc, BR. 144 Topham Picturepoint, BL; David King Collection, TR. 144-5 Corbis-Bettmann, background. 145 Corbis-Bettmann, MM; Hulton-Getty, BR. 146 Popperfoto, BL. 146-7 Brown Brothers, background. 147 Hulton-Getty, TR; Popperfoto, BR. 148 Hulton-Getty, TR. 148-9 Popperfoto, background. 149 Hulton-Getty, TL; Ullstein Bilderdienst, BL. 150 AKG, T, B. 150-1 Brown Brothers, background. 151 Culver Pictures Inc, TL; Popperfoto, TR; Brown Brothers, BM. 152 Kobal Collection, TR; David King Collection, ML; Robert Capa/Magnum Photos, BM. 152-3 AKG, background. 153 The Ronald Grant Archive, T; AKG, B. 154 AKG, T; The Ronald Grant Archive, B. 154-5 Hulton-Getty, background. 155 The Ronald Grant Collection, TL; Hulton-Getty, MM; Hulton-Getty, MR.

Front cover: Archive Photos, T; URLA, Paris, M; Culver, B;

Back cover: Kobal Collection, T; German Youth Festival, 1934, German World War Two poster/IWM, Department of Art, M; Topham Picturepoint, B;

The editors are grateful to the following individuals and publishers for their kind permission to quote passages from the publications listed below:

HarperCollins Publishers Ltd, from *The Invisible Writing*, by Arthur Koestler, 1954.
Daily Mail, November 27, 1922.
Milena Jesenská from *A Stroll through Everyday Life*, translated by Mary Hockaday.
Allison & Busby, from *A Small Yes and a Big No*, by George Grosz, translated by Arnold J. Pomerans, 1982.
The Saturday Evening Post, R.D. Lusk, 1933.
Random House, from *The Secret History of Stalin's Crimes*, by Alexander Orlov, 1953.
Chatto & Windus, from *The Past is Myself*, by Christabel Bielenberg, 1968.
Macmillan, from *Black Lamb and Grey Falcon*, by Rebecca West, 1941.
Routledge, from *Idle Hands: The Experience of Unemployment, 1790-1990*, by John Burnett, 1994.
Hutchinson, from *Coal-miner*, by G.A.W. Tomlinson, 1937.
Brunel University Archive, from *The Lean Years*, by John Edmonds.
Melbourne Herald, Rhodes Farmer, 1937.
Estate of the late Sonia Brownell Orwell and Secker & Warburg Ltd, from *Homage to Catalonia*, 1938.

078-006-01